KANSAS POLITICS AND GOVERNMENT

Politics and Governments
of the American States

Founding Editor
Daniel J. Elazar

Published by the University of
Nebraska Press in association
with the Center for the Study
of Federalism at the Robert B.
and Helen S. Meyner Center
for the Study of State and Local
Government, Lafayette College

H. EDWARD FLENTJE AND JOSEPH A. AISTRUP

Kansas Politics and Government

THE CLASH OF POLITICAL CULTURES

UNIVERSITY OF NEBRASKA PRESS
LINCOLN AND LONDON

© 2010 by the Board of Regents
of the University of Nebraska
All rights reserved
Manufactured in the United States
of America
∞
Library of Congress Cataloging-in-
Publication Data
Flentje, H. Edward.
Kansas politics and government: the clash of
political cultures / H. Edward Flentje and
Joseph A. Aistrup.
p. cm. — (Politics and governments of the
American states)
"Published by the University of Nebraska Press
in association with the Center for the Study
of Federalism at the Robert B. and Helen S.
Meyner Center for the Study of State and Local
Government, Lafayette College."
Includes bibliographical references and index.
ISBN 978-0-8032-2028-7 (cloth: alk. paper) —
ISBN 978-0-8032-6919-4 (pbk.: alk. paper)
1. Kansas—Politics and government.
2. Political culture—Kansas. I. Aistrup,
Joseph A., 1960– II. Title.
JK6816.F57 2010
320.4781—dc22
2009026565

CONTENTS

TABLES

Acknowledgments

The rich history of Kansas politics continues to spawn an abundant literature on the subject. Our state's beginning as Bleeding Kansas followed by
prohibition, populism, the progressive era, a national depression, and the
Dust Bowl has given local and national scribes, as well as scholars, an intriguing topic for conversation and serious study. More recent developments
in state affairs involving national intervention, evangelical movements, and
taxpayer discontent, among others, have drawn similar attention. Historians
and biographers have shed light on pieces of this history, just as journalists
help in understanding various slices of current political affairs in the state.
Rarely, however, are past and present connected in order to fully illuminate
our understanding of Kansas politics and government.

This volume uses the prism of political cultures in order to interpret Kansas politics and to show the intimate connections of the state's past with its
current politics. The framework of political cultures evolves from underlying political preferences for liberty, order, and equality, and these preferences
form the basis for the active political cultures of individualism, hierarchy, and
egalitarianism. This volume makes the case that Kansas politics, historically
and currently, may best be understood as the clash of these political cultures.

The chapters that follow bring together for the first time in one volume
a comprehensive examination of Kansas politics. This volume addresses
the state's primary political institutions—the constitution and courts, the
legislature, and the governorship. It also explores the vehicles of political
process—party politics, elections, and interest groups, in addition to the influence of political cultures on institutions and process. Further, it examines
within the framework of political cultures the impact of federalism on state
politics and government, and finally, it covers the politics of state finance—
taxing, spending, and borrowing.

This volume is addressed to anyone, both casual observers and serious scholars, with an interest in Kansas state politics or in state politics in general. This audience would include any citizen of the state, elected and appointed officials in Kansas governments, students and teachers of Kansas politics and government, journalists, and academics.

The authors wish to acknowledge the support received in preparation of this volume from their respective universities, Wichita State University and Kansas State University, and thank university officers for their encouragement on the project. In addition, a special thanks goes to staff members of the Hugo Wall School of Urban and Public Affairs at Wichita State, specifically to Graduate Assistants Michelle Ponce and Deanna Carrithers for research and editorial assistance and to Associate Director Jo Turner for bringing the manuscript into final form. Further, David Warren provided editing assistance on various versions of several chapters.

Special thanks goes to Jeremy Stohs, who at Kansas State University wrote a fine senior thesis on the growth of professional lobbyists in Kansas. He is a coauthor of chapter 6 that focuses on interest groups. We also wish to thank Mark Bannister at Fort Hays State University, who conducted a large number of interviews with party operatives in Kansas. His interviews were used in chapter 3 to analyze the historical development of state party organizations in Kansas.

Through personal interviews and through access to numerous official documents, many current and former state officials assisted in this endeavor. The authors particularly wish to thank the staff of the Kansas Legislative Research Department and the Kansas Division of the Budget for assistance in this regard.

Introduction

Few news stories in recent memory have come to symbolize Kansas politics in the twenty-first century more than the controversy over the inclusion of Darwin's theory of evolution in the science standards for Kansas public schools. This saga was not Kansas' first brush with the issue, but it is the state's most memorable one.[1] In 1999 six Republicans on the Kansas State Board of Education voted to eliminate references to "macroevolution" and the "big bang" theory from the state's science standards. Their decision set off a firestorm of criticism both inside and outside Kansas. National science groups refused to grant the board its copyrighted materials. Republican Governor William Graves ridiculed the decision as "terrible and tragic." Late night TV comedians quipped that Kansas had become "Y1K compliant."[2] For its part the board's majority noted that its decision did not preclude any local school board in Kansas from allowing its science teachers to teach macroevolution or the big bang theory but that state assessment tests for science would not include questions on these topics.

The board's vote mobilized a slate of self-proclaimed moderate Republican candidates to challenge four of the six antievolution Republicans who stood for reelection in the 2000 GOP primaries. Three moderate Republicans won both the primary and the general election.[3] Upon taking office in 2001, the new board's first order of business was to reinstate the old science standards that included discussion of evolution and the big bang theory. This story would have ended in most states but not in Kansas.

In the wake of the 2000 Republican primary Kris Van Meteren, the executive director of the Kansas Republican Assembly, which is a voice for the evangelical wing of the Kansas GOP, stated, "Next time, when all the liberals are up, you can rest assured we'll be going after them."[4] Van Meteren made good on his promise. In the 2002 GOP primary two Republicans endorsed by the Kansas Republican Assembly defeated proevolution Republican incumbents; the result was a board evenly split on the evolution issue.[5] The tie would be broken after the 2004 Republican primary when Kathy Martin, endorsed by the Kansas Republican Assembly, defeated incumbent Republican Bruce Wyatt.

In 2005, with antievolution Republicans restored to majority status, the board again initiated a review of the state's science standards. The hearings to adopt the new standards approached a circus atmosphere as attorney Pedro Irigonegaray targeted the majority's expert witnesses with heavy sarcasm. Political theatrics aside, the board majority approached the issue with more subtlety in 2005 than in 1999. The definition of science was revised to allow for natural and "unnatural" explanations of natural phenomena and to permit criticisms of evolutionary theory. Although never mentioned in the new standards, the subtext of the new tactic was to give local school boards and science instructors the option of teaching intelligent design in addition to evolutionary theory.[6] After 2000 intelligent design had gained widespread popularity among religious groups opposed to the teaching of evolution. These groups felt intelligent design provided a more scientific justification for their belief that life is too complex to be explained by random chance and that consequently a God is responsible for tailoring the universe and creating life in his image.

History has a way of repeating itself in Kansas, sometimes again and again. In shades of the 2000 GOP primary a slate of four moderate Republican candidates challenged three incumbent board members, all of whom had voted to revise the science standards, and contested an open seat vacated by another member who had voted for the revisions. Proevolution candidates won two of these seats, thus regaining the majority. In January 2007 the first order of business was repealing the handiwork of the old board and reinstating the prior science standards.

Some may argue that this ongoing political conflict represents a side show that is not reflective of Kansas politics. This view, however, fails to recognize that political conflicts like the scrap over evolution reveal the cleavages among the dominant political cultures that have shaped state politics and government from the moment the Kansas Territory opened for settlement in the 1850s. These competing cultures have fundamentally different visions of the role of government in enforcing moral order, encouraging individual liberty, and pursuing equality. Thus these competing visions provide both the spark and the fuel for political flames that often burn brightly for years and are visible throughout the country. One does not need to look far into Kansas history to find other political fires that exceed both the intensity and national significance of the evolution debate.

The first of these political infernos started raging with the birth of Kansas, which is synonymous with one of the darkest segments of U.S. history, the Civil War. The earliest battles of the Civil War were fought in the Kansas Territory between supporters of slavery, most of whom migrated from neighboring Missouri, and free-soil immigrants from a variety of midwestern and northeastern states. Unlike any other state, the settlement and formation of Kansas was a battleground over competing visions of moral order regarding the issue of slavery. Not long after abolitionists had won this battle, they started to promote the use of government power to enforce their vision of a good society on other issues unrelated to slavery.

Even though abolitionists dominate the early history of the state, most who settled Kansas also brought values associated with Jacksonian democracy. Of the Jacksonian mix of individualism and equality, the former found fertile soil and set deep roots in Kansas politics. Kansans embraced individual liberty with a constitution that placed strict restraints on state government and accordingly encouraged grassroots democracy and economic freedom to blossom outside the confines of state government. Kansans' passion for liberty made Kansas the boom state of the post–Civil War period. Within the first thirty years of statehood nearly two million people immigrated into Kansas; entrepreneurial towns sprung up across the state; nine thousand miles of railroads were built; and fifty million acres of Kansas soil moved from public domain into private hands.

Jacksonian democracy produced lively and often chaotic politics in Kansas. Diverse streams of immigration also brought contrasting political views into the state.[7] Even so, in the aftermath of the Civil War most immigrants embraced the party of Lincoln, which quickly rose to dominance. Though often fragmented, Republican Party politics, along with predominant economic interests—primarily railroads—ruled state politics into the twentieth century. Politics and business intermixed, and political deal making permeated Kansas politics for most of the state's early history.

Jacksonian Democrats and Gilded Age Republicans could heartily agree upon the ideal of limited government and a diffusion of political power. Strict limits on the taxing, spending, and borrowing authority of state government were written into the state constitution. Restraints on the legislative institution assured that citizen volunteers rather than career politicians would be in charge of legislating. Executive power was restrained and diffused among the governor and six additional executives elected statewide. Local control thrived. Kansans would spend most of the twentieth century working to loosen the legal shackles cuffed on state government in the last half of the nineteenth century.

Another strain in Kansas political life emerged from the battle to make Kansas a free state in the 1850s. Amid the disorder of rampant individualism, the abolitionists' message of a good and orderly society found a willing audience among the flood of immigrants aligned with evangelical Protestant denominations. These societal reformers coalesced into a countervailing force in the politics of the day and eventually resorted to the coercive powers of state government to achieve their vision of a good society. They embraced, for example, the prohibitory movement—writing a prohibition on the sale of intoxicating liquors into the state constitution as early as 1880—and moved with vengeance to enforce the ban, thus embroiling Kansans in a century-long struggle over regulating intoxicating liquors. Republican partisans embraced this evangelical movement and established themselves as the party of prohibition. So early in the political life of the state, the Kansas Republican Party placed itself on seemingly contradictory footings as it championed on the one hand economic liberty—free markets and restraints on government—and on the other moral order—prohibition and various other measures designed to establish standards of community conduct through the force of law.

Kansas also experienced a unique egalitarian moment in the 1890s. Hammered by national policies protecting creditors and the railroads as well as by drought, farmers rebelled and demanded an end to the inequities brought on by the politics of individualism. These populists championed a national agenda of graduated taxation, public ownership of railroads, government loans, and confiscatory land reform. Over four election cycles, 1890 through 1896, they undermined Republican hegemony, electing two governors and a U.S. senator and winning a majority of contested seats in the U.S. House and the Kansas legislature. After winning control of most state offices in 1892, the populists became embroiled in internecine warfare, and their surge stalled. Their inherent distrust of authority, even that exercised by their own officeholders, subverted their ability to govern. The Populist Party departed from the scene shortly thereafter but sowed a passion for equality into Kansas political soil that lives to the present day.

In part motivated by the rise of the populists, after the turn of the twentieth century the Republican Party dislodged itself from the railroad interests that had dominated state politics for decades and moved toward an emerging business and professional constituency, becoming progressives dedicated to both political and moral reform. Progressive era Republicans remained devoted to a moral agenda of enforcing prohibition, outlawing abortion, banning cigarettes, and forbidding evil in various other forms.

More important, the progressives unleashed an array of political and economic reforms aimed at reforming state politics, regulating the economy, and broadening the authority and scope of state government. Political reforms—primary elections, recall procedures, suffrage for women, and direct election of U.S. senators, among other measures designed to make state politics more accessible to ordinary citizens—were authorized. Economic regulation of workplace conditions, fraudulent securities, public utilities, food and drugs, and child labor laws were instituted. Newly created state offices, expansions in higher education, and broader state authority in environmental protection and public health, among many other enactments, augmented the scope of state government.

All of the reform movements—abolition, prohibition, populism, and progressivism—did give Kansas a distinct political heritage and placed the state in the forefront of national political change. Early in the twentieth century William Allen White, the worldly editor of the *Emporia Gazette*, opined that "when anything is going to happen in this country, it happens first in Kansas."[8] The upcoming decades, however, would temper these passions and reshape state politics and government in fundamental ways.

For starters the 1930s were not kind to Kansas. On top of a national depression, a good part of the state was smothered by the Dust Bowl—an extended period of drought, withering heat, terrible winds, and air thick with blowing dust. Grain prices plummeted. Rural Kansas lost one hundred thousand people, one-seventh of its population, between 1930 and 1940. Kansas' infamous goat-gland doctor, John Brinkley, appealed to those in distress and nearly won the governorship—by write-in ballot no less. Unable to escape their political past, Kansans reverted to belt tightening on state government as a solution, and in desperation both fiercely independent farmers and state leaders turned to the national government for help. National assistance was forthcoming, and at least for a time many joined FDR's New Deal and cast their votes in the Democratic column.

Grudging acceptance of agricultural assistance was followed quickly by Kansans' overwhelming endorsement of national income security. Kansas voters willingly adjusted their constitution to allow state government and its local jurisdictions to abandon past restraints and participate in income support and welfare assistance administered nationally through the Social Security Act of 1935. Shortly thereafter World War II deepened further the penetration of national administration in Kansas. Existing military bases expanded, and new ones sprung up as the state willingly enlisted to aid in national defense. Within two short decades public policies in agriculture, income security, and defense were dramatically broadened to serve national purposes, and policy change coupled with national administration of these arenas would have profound and lasting effects on state government and politics.

Kansas historians point to the monumental defeat of Governor Alf Landon in the presidential contest of 1936 as a critical turning point in the political consciousness of Kansans.[9] Kansas voters rejected their native son in favor of FDR, as did their counterparts in every state in the Union except for Maine and Vermont. Kansans began to wonder if their long-standing political passions were out of sync with the nation. Instead of cutting edge had Kansas become a political backwater?

The three decades of the postwar period accelerated the trends of the 1930s and 1940s in terms of nationalizing influences. The election of Kansan Dwight Eisenhower to the presidency restored a measure of home-state pride, but Eisenhower was a product of national and international experiences, not state politics. More important, the 1960s and 1970s spawned a flood of national initiatives on everything from preventing juvenile delinquency to controlling rats. By 1980 over five hundred grant-in-aid programs were on the books, compared to a dozen in 1950. Funding for these programs jumped forty-fold between 1950 and 1985. The availability of easy money from Washington diverted the attention of state and local officials to purposes outlined by Congress and specified across a raft of national agencies. By 1980 dollars from the U.S. treasury comprised nearly one-third of all revenues of state and local governments. Kansas officials chased after the easy money like their counterparts in other states.

The depression, the Dust Bowl, and the nationalizing impacts of income security and defense, among other influences, throttled political passions in Kansas, at least for a time. By 1983 *Washington Post* columnist Neal Peirce and coauthor Jerry Hagstrom in a book on the fifty states labeled Kansas the Eclipsed State.[10] Responding to White's statements in the 1920s, the authors concluded that Kansas "is scarcely the place where things happen 'first.' Indeed, nowhere on the continent can the eclipse of a region or a state as a vital force—a focal point of creative change or exemplar of national life— be felt so strongly and poignantly as in Kansas."[11]

Kansas may have moved out of the national political limelight, but it did not lose its zest for reform. In the 1950s and 1960s political leaders, socialized during the progressive era, began to follow a more active path, turning their attention to revitalizing state and local government by bringing the state's constitution up to date. Forty-three constitutional amendments were adopted by voters from 1957 through 1986. The political institutions of state government were transformed by unifying the judicial branch, consolidating executive powers, loosening restraints on legislative prerogatives, modernizing taxing authority, lifting limits on spending, allowing home rule for cities, and repealing the century-old provisions prohibiting liquor and gambling.

The constitutional reforms and the politics that followed set the stage for the modern era of state politics and government in Kansas. Augmented powers reenergized the political institutions of state government, and state policy makers began exercising new initiatives in public policy. The election of Ronald Reagan accelerated this trend by restraining Washington's domestic spending through substantial tax cuts and increased spending on national defense; it was a trend that would extend into the early years of the twenty-first century.

Leading the resurgence in state politics and government were activist governors, state courts, and legislative leaders. The governorship has become the prime source of political leadership in Kansas. Despite the state's domination by the Republicans, enterprising Democrats have been at the forefront of constitutional revisions; of decisions concerning taxing, spending, and borrowing; and of the restructuring of state government. In the early 1970s Democratic Governor Robert Docking in cooperation with legislative leaders promoted sweeping structural reforms through revisions to the state's constitution. In the early 1980s Democratic Governor John Carlin championed an ambitious expansion of the scope of state government in spurring economic growth through constitutional amendments and newly empowered agencies funded by a newly authorized state-sponsored lottery. Republican Governor Mike Hayden followed in the late 1980s with initiatives in highway and environmental finance and fundamental reform of the state income tax. In the early 1990s Democratic Governor Joan Finney under pressure from state courts worked with legislative leaders to raise state taxes, to shift school finance away from reliance on property taxes, and to substantially equalize funding between rich and poor, urban and rural school districts. In the early 2000s Democratic Governor Kathleen Sebelius successfully navigated state finances through the aftermath of 9/11, and again prompted by the intervention of state courts, she assembled a bipartisan coalition of moderate legislators to increase school aid by $750 million over a four-year period. These actions over the past fifty years took shape through a healthy competition of ideas that were attributable in large measure to a renewed vitality of the state's political institutions.

The resurgence in the political institutions of state government has taken place within a shifting political environment. Evangelical Protestants and orthodox Catholics, both groups energized by abortion politics in the 1970s and nurtured by Ronald Reagan in the 1980s, have become a powerful force

in Kansas Republican politics. These newcomers to state politics first focused on abortion but eventually shifted their attention to evolution, gambling, gay marriage, stem cell research, and other issues they believe to be
critical in restoring a good society. They began with protests in the 1970s
and 1980s in front of Planned Parenthood offices across the state, coalesced
their forces to descend on Dr. George Tiller's abortion clinic in Wichita in
the summer of 1991, and thereafter focused on gaining political power and
have done so with great success. Over a fifteen-year period these partisans
have gained control of local and state Republican party organizations, challenged incumbent Republican officeholders who do not share their vision,
gained positions of leadership in the state legislature, and taken control of
the Kansas State Board of Education for two terms.

These political developments have split the Republican Party into two
camps, one championing an aggressive agenda on moral and economic issues and one seeking a more moderate middle ground. With the Republican
Party divided, the governorship—the crown jewel of state politics—has escaped the grasp of these newly energized party activists. Republican candidates carrying the activist banner were overwhelmingly defeated in elections for governor in 2002 and 2006 as moderate Republicans abandoned
their party's ticket. Indeed, in both elections Governor Sebelius persuaded
high-profile moderate Republicans, including a former state party chairman, to desert their party, cross over, and join her on the Democratic ticket
as lieutenant governor. Further, in the 2006 contest for attorney general,
another crossover to the state Democratic ticket, former Johnson County
attorney Paul Morrison, defeated by a landslide a leading protagonist of the
activist faction, Republican Attorney General Phill Kline.

The success of the partisans of a moral agenda has been mixed. They did
secure a constitutional ban on gay marriage and civil unions in 2005 and
through legislative action succeeded in restricting abortion practices at the
University of Kansas Medical Center. However, their moves to otherwise
limit abortion have largely stalled. They delayed but could not block casino
gambling, which was authorized in the 2007 legislative session, while their
attempts to ban Darwin from high school biology classrooms have moved
to and fro, gaining Kansas national headlines but falling short of eliminating
the teaching of evolution from the state's science standards.

The policy advances of those promoting moral order have been limited,
this movement has added much fluidity to party politics in Kansas. Republican Party leaders try to patch over the chasm in their party's ranks. Their top
nominees lick the wounds of stunning defeats. Despite all this, U.S. Senator
Sam Brownback's plans to run for governor in 2010 provides these parti-

sans a measure of hope that one of their own will finally be elected governor and that state policies will begin to reflect their values more fully.

The politics of the late twentieth and early twenty-first centuries have ushered in a new era of "it happens first in Kansas." Twenty years after Peirce and Hagstrom's broadside, Thomas Frank contended that Kansas had again become the epicenter for national politics.[12] His modern and revised book-length version of William Allen White's 1896 editorial, "What's the Matter with Kansas?" also took a decidedly negative view of the state's political landscape. Frank concluded that social issues such as abortion, homosexuality, and evolution act as a smoke screen that is used by Republican politicians to align religiously inclined working class voters with the interests of Wall Street.

DEMOGRAPHIC AND ECONOMIC CHANGE

As this volume will show, the clashes of political cultures explain much of the historic and current dynamics of Kansas politics and government. Within the political environment shaped by such cultures, changing demographic and economic conditions in Kansas also produce opportunities for episodic coalitions that form around urban versus rural interests.

When Kansas was settled in the latter half of the nineteenth century, most of the population made their homes in rural areas and earned a living from farming and ranching. For the entire twentieth century the industrialization of agriculture has led to larger farms and fewer farmers. Exacerbating this trend were events like the Dust Bowl in the 1930s and the agricultural downturn of the mid-1980s. As the population of farmers and ranchers has declined, so too have the populations of many rural communities. Counterbalancing the loss of rural people is the growing population in a small number of urban counties and counties immediately adjacent to these urban centers.[13]

These demographic and economic changes have on occasion placed other strains on state politics, creating what many interpret as an urban-rural divide. Those who focus on this characterization of Kansas politics tend to emphasize that two-thirds of the state's one hundred and five counties reached their peak population in 1930 or before and that the population of the state's five urban counties now exceeds that of the other one hundred. Further, they point out that Johnson County in the Kansas City metropolitan area, has a population of five hundred thousand, which equates to that of sixty rural counties in western Kansas.

These statistics, however, fail to recognize the complexity of Kansas'

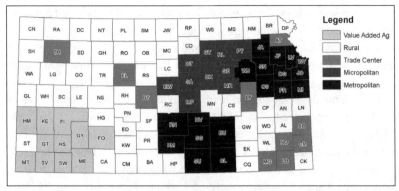

Fig. 1. Classification of Counties

Value-added Counties (3): population chg. 65%; per capita income $25,605; adjacent value-added rural counties (9); population chg.11.1%; per capita income $28,960.

Rural Counties (55): per capita income $27,812; population chg. 19.4%.

Trade Center Counties (10): per capita income $28,180; av. population chg. –4.2%.

Micropolitan Counties (2): per capita income $31,465; population chg. 19.2%; adjacent rural counties (8); per capita income $31,509; population chg. –1.4%.

Metropolitan Counties (5): per capita income $40,240; population chg. 48.7%; adjacent rural counties (13); per capita income $30,011; population chg. 25.4%.

Note: Per capita income data taken from 2006 Census; population change is measured for years 1971 to 2007. *Source: Kansas Statistical Abstract, 2008.*

demographic and economic characteristics. Figure 1 captures some of this complexity by viewing Kansas counties from a framework of economic clusters. This perspective emphasizes that growing counties have one or more clusters of economic activity that stimulate employment, raise the standard of living, and boost population in the county and its contiguous areas due to spillover effects.[14] Counties without such economic clusters or counties that are not close to those with a cluster tend to be losing population.

Kansas counties can be divided into five economic categories drawing upon this framework of economic clusters.[15] First, the fifty-five mostly smaller rural counties that depend primarily on extractive industries related to farming, ranching, and oil and natural gas are the most economically distressed. In these counties government jobs in public schools and county courthouses have become a major source of employment, and transfer payments such as Social Security have become a primary source of personal income. The per capita income of these counties in 2006 was about $27,812, and their population decline for the period 1971 through 2007 was 19.4 percent.

The five largest urban counties (Douglas, Johnson, Shawnee, Sedgwick, and Wyandotte) and the thirteen adjacent rural counties that surround them comprise the second category. The per capita income of the five urban counties was $40,240 in 2006, and their population growth for the thirty-six-year period was 48.7 percent. In the thirteen counties surrounding the large urban centers, the per capita income was $30,011, and the population growth was 25.4 percent.

Closely related to these metropolitan counties is a third group, two "micropolitan" counties, Riley and Saline, and their adjacent rural counties. Neither Riley nor Saline qualifies as a metropolitan area, but both are approaching this designation. Their per capita income in 2006 was over $31,000, while their population growth over the thirty-six-year period approaches 20 percent. In contrast, the adjacent counties are comparable to the micropolitan counties in personal income, but their population has declined slightly by 1.4 percent.

Fourth are counties in the southwestern corner of the state that dramatically dispute the myth that all rural Kansas counties are losing population. In this region three counties, Finney, Ford, and Seward, have economic clusters based on value-added meat processing. On the positive side their population growth between 1971 and 2006 was 64.5 percent. However, the work force associated with meat processing tends to be composed of more transient and immigrant laborers. The pay scale of these jobs is typically lower than other industrial classifications, and working conditions are more dangerous.[16] Thus the per capita income in these three counties was less than $26,000 in 2006. The real winners of the value-added agricultural complex in the southwest are the nine adjacent rural counties. Because of the spillover effects counties surrounding Finney, Ford, and Seward had per capita income of $28,960 in 2006, while their population increase between 1971 and 2007 was 11.1 percent.

Making up a fifth group of Kansas counties are trade centers generally formed around one town with populations between ten and thirty-five thousand and a large employment basis in retail, government, and services. Ten of these counties dot the Kansas landscape, mostly in the central and eastern half of the state. Their per capita income was $28,100 in 2006, but over the past thirty-six years their population declined by 4.2 percent. Their populations have remained stagnant because these counties depend on the smaller rural counties adjacent to them for trade dollars, and as noted above, those counties have fallen on hard times. As the population of counties adjacent to the trade centers declines, so does the economic viability of the trade centers unless they can find another source of external dollars.

While the mix of economic clusters across Kansas tempers urban-rural conflicts, important episodes have thrown urban and rural interests into contention. The most divisive are the battles over rectifying the historic malapportionment of the state legislature. In 1964 and 1966 reapportionment based on one person–one vote forced a dramatic loss in legislative representation for rural Kansas and a redirection of state budgetary resources to address urban issues related to transportation and schools. However, unlike some states where the retribution against rural areas was swift and severe, this effect was less in the case in Kansas as a majority of the state's population at the time still lived outside of the urban centers.

Another major urban-rural battle occurred over public school consolidation. As a reflection of demographic changes noted above, Kansas lawmakers over a twenty-year period consolidated over 5,000 rural school districts into 348 unified school districts. This gut-wrenching affair profoundly diminished hundreds of smaller rural communities and their residents throughout the state, and for these rural residents the word consolidation became, and continues to be, the longest four-letter word in the English language.[17]

Urban and rural interests collided again in the mid-1980s over the issue of liquor by the drink. Governor Carlin assembled an almost purely urban coalition primarily from the Wichita and the Kansas City metropolitan areas to support the constitutional amendment, but after passage, this alliance vanished.

Resource and environmental issues are yet another source of occasional conflict between urban and rural Kansas. In the 1980s Governor Carlin proposed and lawmakers passed a severance tax, which urban legislators from the northeast supported and which many rural legislators opposed, particularly those in the oil and natural gas counties of the western half of the state. However, business interests in Wichita, tied closely to the oil and natural gas economy of the state, persuaded many Wichita area legislators to oppose the legislation.

In addition, for the past thirty years there has been an ongoing policy debate regarding the overappropriation of the Ogallala Aquifer for irrigated crops in southwestern and northwestern Kansas. Despite calls by academics and environmentalists to resolve this issue, Democratic and Republican administrations alike have kept the issue contained within the Kansas Department of Agriculture.[18]

Finally, in the 2008 legislative session Governor Sebelius's administration ignited a political storm with rural western Kansas after her secretary of the Kansas Department of Health and Environment denied an air quality permit that prevented Sunflower Electric from building two seven hundred megawatt coal-fired plants near Holcomb in southwestern Kansas. This decision aligned the governor with eastern urban interests concerned with carbon emissions and their environmental impact on public health, and it infuriated western Kansas legislators who believed this project would open doors for greater rural economic development, wind farm expansion, and population growth.

Except for malapportionment and liquor by the drink, few of the aforementioned issues have divided Kansas along a strictly urban-rural cleavage. During the 2008 legislative session, for example, Republicans from all parts of the state lined up in favor of passing legislation allowing the coal-fired plants to be built in Holcomb, while mostly Democrats, except for the few from western Kansas, opposed this legislation.

The intermingling of urban and rural interests across the state tend to make political conflicts along these lines episodic in character. In most years this cleavage is more like a semidormant fault line in the earth's crust. Occasionally the fault line sends rumbles through the political landscape, as, for example, when the state welfare agency proposes to consolidate county offices in rural areas. Nonetheless, in an average year this fault line remains largely inactive.

There are signs, however, that pressure along this political fault line will build. Simply put, providing a full range of government services to a widely dispersed, aging population costs dearly and confronts a growing demand by taxpayer groups like Americans for Prosperity to cut taxes and curb the growth in government spending. These pressures to cut government spending may yet ignite a movement to consolidate governmental services in rural communities ranging from schools to courts to public health, to perhaps even county governmental units. Another round of consolidation would trigger a divisive period in Kansas politics that would rival all others. But this day has not yet arrived and is not likely to arrive as long as the dominant Republican Party maintains its bases of support in both rural and suburban areas of the state.

ORGANIZATION OF THE BOOK

The balance of this volume focuses on explaining the modern era of Kansas politics and government in the context of the state's history and political cultures. In chapter 1 the passions of state politics are viewed and interpreted through the prism of political cultures. The political cultures associated with Kansans' preferences for liberty, order, and equality are traced over time, and their impact on contemporary state politics is analyzed. This framework of political cultures is then used when appropriate in the remaining chapters in order to examine in more depth the cultural context of state politics and government with respect to political parties, political institutions, federalism, and fiscal behavior.

Chapter 2 outlines the development of the state's constitution from a typical nineteenth century state constitution with a limited state government to a state constitution that reflects many of the principles espoused by the model state constitutions movement of the 1950s and 1960s. This chapter also examines the major amendments to the constitution and the influence of political cultures in pursuing these amendments.

Chapter 3 analyzes patterns of partisan strength across Kansas counties in terms of alignments that shape the political topography of the state's party system. This chapter assesses the validity of many of the traditional notions that describe these patterns and finds them in need of revision. In addition, this chapter examines the development of party organizations in terms of their ability to be candidate-centered organizations.

Chapter 4 analyzes the historical development of the state legislature from an institutional perspective and focuses on the influence of political cultures on institutional innovations designed to maintain the legislature's status as a citizen legislature. This chapter also analyzes the effects of the current political situation in the state legislature that was brought on by the factionalization of the majority Republican Party.

Chapter 5 reviews the evolution of the Kansas governorship and its transformation in the modern era. Selected Kansas governors are also examined in cultural context, that is, in terms of their contributions in building and sustaining cultural coalitions.

Chapter 6 discusses the development of interest group politics in the state. It focuses on the growing diversity of lobbying interests represented in the legislative process and the impact of this diversity on the way in which lobbyists interact with state legislators.

Chapter 7 examines the impact of the federal structure on politics and state and local governments in Kansas. The evolution of federalism in Kansas, both nation-state and state-local relations, is interpreted from the perspective of political cultures.

Chapter 8 tracks the profound transformation in state taxing, spending, and borrowing from a cultural perspective. Attention is given to major components of state taxation and expenditures and the recent ballooning of state debt.

Chapter 9 highlights major themes in Kansas politics and government. And finally, suggestions for further reading are provided after the notes section.

KANSAS POLITICS AND GOVERNMENT

CHAPTER ONE

Political Cultures

An array of forces shape state politics. Reflecting the diversity of these political influences, observers of Kansas politics draw from various theories
to explain the state's political history or its current politics. Unfortunately,
the explanatory powers of these theories fade as new political occurrences
or movements arise. For example, explanations of the populist movement
in Kansas have scant bearing on the recent rise of evangelical politics in the
state. An examination of urban-rural divisions may be helpful in explaining
the politics of school finance but sheds little light on conflicts over issues
such as abortion or gambling. Interest group theory gives insight into policy
disputes between business and organized labor but falls short in explaining
election outcomes. This chapter makes the case that the politics of Kansas
may best be understood, both historically and presently, as the clash of the
political cultures, that is, as the ebb and flow of the underlying cultures of
individualism, order, and equality.

THE PRISM OF POLITICAL CULTURES

The historic contradictions in Kansas politics do bewilder. Within the state's
first fifty years, for example, Kansas gave the nation crusading abolitionists,
fervent prohibitionists, insurgent populists, and progressive reformers. The
state led the nation in railroad building while at the same time prohibiting
state government from building roads. State lawmakers granted business
and town boosters free rein while prohibiting the sale of intoxicating liquors
and even cigarettes. State officials prided themselves on being debt free
while allowing local jurisdictions to borrow into bankruptcy.

Current state politics also mystify. Kansas was recently recognized as
number one among the fifty states in economic freedom but also led the

nation in the growth of state debt. State lawmakers mandated uniform state-wide property tax levies for schools and later freed a few thousand other local governments to levy property taxes at will. Kansas gained national attention for an unprecedented civil disturbance in which antiabortion protesters blocked clinics, and in which local police made twenty-six hundred arrests; meanwhile, voters in jurisdictions across the state embraced casino gambling.

Political cultures may be the best way to understand the conflicts, the contrasts, and the motives and methods of Kansas politics. Deep-seated cultural preferences energize the body politic of Kansas and have sparked extraordinary moments in Kansas political history. At these times political cultures give rise to movements that dominate state politics, frame state issues, and leave long-standing imprints on state government. But political cultures have vulnerabilities as well as strengths. Contending cultures temper these political shifts. The moments pass, but underlying political cultures remain largely intact to reengage new issues and again to reshape the state's future. Current political behavior in Kansas may in large measure be traced to political cultures of long standing.

Three cultural strains find fertile soil in Kansas politics. In their most elemental form these cultures evolve from the core political values of liberty, equality, and order. Cultural theorists deduce political cultures from a two-dimensional group-grid typology, as shown in figure 2.[1] The group dimension measures the degree to which an "individual's life is absorbed in and sustained by group membership." The grid dimension characterizes external regulation that prescribes the "scope for personal choice." Weak group-weak grid defines an individualistic political culture that prefers liberty; strong group-strong grid defines a political culture of hierarchy that prefers order; and strong group-weak grid infers an egalitarian political culture that prefers equality.[2] This framework may be applied to a wide range of political phenomena and in this volume is used to aid in understanding Kansas politics.

Cultural theorists assert that cultural preferences underpin distinct patterns of political behavior and that core values justified and sustained by political relations comprise political cultures. These cultures conflict and indeed compete for partisans. Alliances across cultural divides are occasionally constructed to address emerging issues, but such alignments do not fundamentally change political cultures.

A political culture of individualism represents a dominant cultural strain in Kansas and evolves from a preference for liberty. Individualists believe that social relations characterized by free markets—bidding, bargaining,

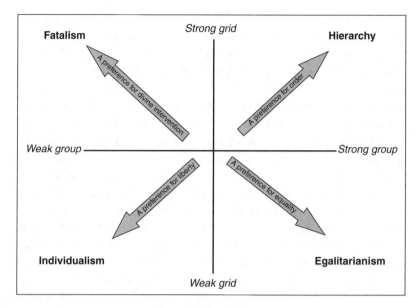

Fig. 2. Political Cultures

and bartering—provide the best assurance of individual liberty. Competitive individualists view nature as wonderfully forgiving and natural resources as unlimited and therefore embrace a laissez-faire approach to this natural world. When things go wrong, poor judgment, personal incompetence, or just bad luck are to blame.

In politics individualists are by nature self-seeking, prefer self-regulation, and desire to minimize the scope of governmental regulation. In their view political competition and limits on political authority best guarantee individual liberty. Cooperation is secured through deal making in one-on-one negotiations. Innovation, trial and error, and experimentation are encouraged. Individualists believe that the pursuit of self-interest in combination with limited government will naturally result in social progress.

An egalitarian political culture represents another cultural strain and evolves naturally from a preference for equality. Egalitarians prefer social relations based on equal status and are accordingly suspicious of any structure that gives one person more authority than another. In their view differences in established authority should be diminished and power relations equalized. As a result egalitarians promote cooperation through direct participation and consensus among participants with equal status—a position that makes the resolution of conflict difficult.

Egalitarians believe that "human beings are born good but are corrupted by evil institutions."[3] Therefore human nature may be good but is also "highly malleable" and susceptible to institutional influences. Evil institutions, external forces, "the system," the establishment, or some alliance of government and business are likely to be blamed when things go wrong. To egalitarians the natural world is fragile and is easily subject to degradation and possible ruin and thus must be managed with special care and timidity.

Egalitarians seek to equalize conditions in human affairs. They concern themselves with inequities and injustice in society and consequently promote measures that produce equality of results, such as redistribution of wealth, progressive taxation, and quotas based on sex, race, or other divisions.

A political culture of hierarchy represents another dominant cultural strain in Kansas and evolves from a preference for order. Hierarchs seek collective order through social relations characterized by the rule of law, hierarchical structures, division of labor and specialization, and standards based on scientific methods and expertise. Individual sacrifice is believed to be essential for collective order, and therefore duty, obligation, deference, and service for the benefit of the whole are emphasized. If cooperation among individuals is needed, those in authority ordain it by defining and if necessary enacting laws to enforce the collective good. When things do go wrong, blame is likely placed on social deviants who do not know their place.

Those with a preference for order believe that human beings "are born sinful but can be redeemed by good institutions. This conception of human nature helps sustain a way of life rich in institutional constraints."[4] Such collectivists rely on the power of conscience and reason to restrain the baser passions and impulses of human beings. Nature is viewed as tolerant and forgiving but vulnerable to unusual occurrences and therefore in need of regulation to assure order.

Viewing Kansas politics and government through the prism of political cultures begins with the state's political history. Defining moments in Kansas political history vividly reveal the state's political cultures; those cultural preferences for liberty, equality, and order; and political practices associated with these preferences. These moments have left indelible marks on Kansas politics and find expression in current state politics as well. Their imprints may be found in most every arena of state policy as well as in the structure of government.

A PREFERENCE FOR LIBERTY

Kansas grew up in the nation's Gilded Age when the politics of individualism ran rampant.[5] Industrial capitalism was enveloping the nation. National policy promoted free, unrestrained enterprise. Individual initiative was encouraged; governmental regulation was discouraged. John J. Ingalls, a founding father of Kansas and three-term U.S. senator from Kansas (1873–91), gave voice to the Darwinian vision of economic progress and limited government prevalent in Kansas as well as the nation at the time:

> I belong to the school of politicians who think that government should interfere as little as possible in the affairs of its citizens. I have no sympathy with the paternal idea, but believe that the best results are attained when people are left to settle the great questions of society by individual effort. All that legislation can do is to give men an equal chance in the race of life. We cannot make poor men rich, or rich men poor, except by making the natural capacities of men exactly alike. The difficulties in society arise from the fact that Providence has established unequal conditions, making some men wise and others foolish; some men provident and others thriftless; some men industrious and energetic and others idle and self indulgent.[6]

The Kansas-Nebraska Act opened the Kansas Territory in May 1854 and brought the politics of individualism into Kansas. The act ignited a contest for land, for capital to develop and build on the land, and for people to occupy the land. The Homestead Act of 1862 opened the opportunity for free land and, according to one Kansas editor at the time, "dedicates forever the unoccupied public domain to Freedom."[7] The frenzy for open land and possibly free land continued in fits and starts for thirty years or more. Imagine the visions of railroaders, speculators, settlers, town boosters, entrepreneurs, squatters, and others who rushed madly into Kansas: Fifty million acres becoming available. Beautiful wide-open spaces, moderate climate, fertile soil, and potential for mineral resources. Easy financing. Government yet to be established by self-determination. Come and stake your claims!

With the passage of the Kansas-Nebraska Act a new political party also came into being to address the issue of slavery. Based in the northern states, the new Republican Party attracted former Whigs and alienated northern Democrats as well as factional and third-party partisans opposed to slavery. The Kansas conflicts over slavery in the late 1850s propelled this new party to national prominence, and territorial Kansans became Republicans. In their first presidential election Kansans gave Abraham Lincoln seventy-nine percent of their votes, and with Lincoln's election and the secession of six southern states, Kansas entered the Union as a Free State in January 1861. For most of the next thirty years Kansans would vote overwhelmingly Republican and would embrace this new national party that advocated "free men" and "free soil"—an end to slavery and homestead legislation—as well as promoting aggressive national development through railroad expansion, internal improvements, and banking. The Republican Party, undergirded by a culture of individualism, would put down deep roots in the body politic of Kansas.

The political culture of individualism dominated Kansas politics through the Gilded Age and occasionally brought the state to the edge of political chaos. Deal making characterized the times, in politics and in business, and nearly everyone was open to making deals for land, for town sites, for a railroad, for immigrants, and for personal advantage. The line between politics and business blurred. State officials headed commercial enterprises; businessmen held political office. Both usually benefited from the arrangements. Competition was fierce, and tactics were raw, occasionally violent. Alliances were fragile and short lived. Survival of the fittest characterized Kansans' practice of politics in the state's early days.

Railroad entrepreneurs led the land grab in Kansas, and lawmakers were most compliant. State officials granted four railroads all of the five hundred thousand acres the state received for internal improvements upon its entry into the Union. State charters for railroad companies were freely granted, and by 1910 eleven hundred railroad charters had been filed, though most were never built.[8] Railroad investors often played town against town in mapping routes, and town boosters responded most often by generously authorizing local bonds in order to attract railroad construction. Railroad builders formed alliances with state and local leaders to wrest Indian lands from national control. Historian Gene Clanton estimates that over ten million acres of Kansas land, one-fifth of the entire state, passed through the hands of the railroads in this period.[9]

Most folk came to Kansas seeking their fortunes and the promise of a better life, and in the resulting competition for land, capital, and people, Kansas boomed. A confluence of self-interest fueled the boom. Settlers came for opportunity. Squatters wanted verification of their claims. Farmers sought not self-sufficiency but cash for crops transported to distant markets. Railroad investors sought competitive advantage and quick returns. Land speculators wanted a quick buck. Town boosters desired thriving businesses. Creditors wanted to loan money on strict terms and excessive rates. Hucksters abounded. According the John Hicks, anyone with cash became a deal maker.[10]

Individualism pervaded local politics as well. Scott McNall observes that "Kansas was a state of small entrepreneurs" and found that "the politics of the community revolved almost exclusively around the issue of how to boost business. . . . [People] arrived in town with capital, or a skill, or just an idea for making money, and stayed to do so. . . . [M]ost people took their business to be business: they wanted to participate in the growth and expansion of the town."[11] People and things were judged in terms of this "business ideology."

In this early period the belief in limited government profoundly shaped the structure of Kansas government. The Wyandotte Constitution of 1859, with which the state entered the Union in 1861, severely restricted state government's ability to engage in state development. State government was prohibited from direct participation in internal improvements of any kind and could borrow no more than one million dollars without consent of the voters. State lawmakers were, however, committed to laissez faire and skirted restraints by granting others free rein to make improvements and to build the state. Local citizens were given rights of self-government to organize counties, towns, townships, and schools. Unrestrained by constitutional strictures, cities and counties were given broad authority to borrow in order to make community improvements and to attract business. This freedom of local self-government diffused political authority and spawned vigorous competition for any opportunity whether securing a business, a railroad, a county seat, or a state facility.

Enthusiasm for individual and community prosperity generated expansive investment. Farmers borrowed to buy and operate farms. Cities and counties borrowed to grow. By 1890 farmers had mortgaged over two hundred thousand acres and had incurred debts of $175 million—twice the levels of their Nebraska neighbors. With restraints on state government the financing of any public improvement fell upon local governments that borrowed for roads, public buildings, water supply, parks, sanitation, and other public facilities as well as for inducements for private enterprise. In addition to substantial railroad subsidies, public incentives were authorized for woolen, flour, sugar, and sorghum mills; starch works; coal, oil, and gas prospecting; manufacturing enterprises; and cheese factories, among others. Municipal debt mushroomed to $37 million by 1890 while state debt was under a million.

Diffusion of political and financial authority nurtured home rule in Kansas and deferred for some time any necessity for an active state government. At the dawn of the twentieth century state services in Kansas consisted of hardly more than a university; an agricultural college; a normal school; schools for the insane, blind, and deaf; a penitentiary; and two reform schools. Essential public services such as law enforcement, fire protection, public education, roads, assistance to the poor, public health, administration of justice, tax administration, and elections were carried out at the local level. By 1890 local governmental spending exceeded state spending by a factor of nine; the ratio of local debt to state debt was 46 to 1.

The raw politics of individualism gave Kansas an extraordinary boost. By 1890 1.4 million immigrants had flooded into Kansas; most of the state's fifty-two million acres had moved from the public domain into private hands; two hundred thousand farms were opened; nine thousand miles of railroad track had been constructed; and 106 counties, 1,509 townships, 329 cities, and 9,284 school districts had been organized across the state. But markets rise and markets fall. The boom of the mid-1880s was followed by a bust. By the late 1880s the vulnerabilities of an individualistic political culture had become more visible. Deal making in business and politics spawned corruption. Farmers faced foreclosures. Excessive borrowing brought on municipal bankruptcy. Overconfident town boosters left ghost towns. Those affected fomented insurrection.

A PREFERENCE FOR EQUALITY

After the mid-1880s boom the bust came to Kansas. A drought set in, and crops failed. Grain prices fell. Land values plunged. Yet rail and interest rates stayed high. Foreclosures began. Farmers were hammered, and numbers of new settlers picked up and left their debts behind. However, most farmers persevered, and Kansas became a national hotbed for the populist revolt. Kansas farmers demanded justice, an end to economic and political inequities.

The economic chaos of rampant individualism had been a source of discontent among new settlers from Kansas' early days. In the 1870s third party movements gave expression to this distress both in Kansas and nationally and tested various ideas for economic and political reform but failed to gain political traction.

The populist movement was different. A populist political party, a genuine people's party, emerged in the 1890s to voice farmers' disgruntlement and to challenge Republican hegemony in Kansas. As their chief goal Kansas populists sought economic and political equality. They wanted more than Ingall's "equal chance in the race for life." They wanted equality of conditions and championed measures that would rectify the inequities resulting from the dominant political culture of individualism.

Populist leaders took direct aim at the prevailing political culture. As one Kansas protest publication aptly stated, "there never was, nor can there be, a more brutal, utterly selfish and despicable doctrine than the Darwinian 'struggle for existence,' when applied to the social relations of man. It justifies oppression, the aggregation of wealth in the hands of those able to grasp it, the occupation of everything the 'fittest' are able to gain and keep." According to Topekan John Grant Otis in his campaign for congress on the People's Party ticket in 1890, populists envisioned a culture grounded in cooperation, not competition: "We are emerging from an age of intense individualism, supreme selfishness, and ungodly greed to a period of co-operative effort. Competition is giving way to united action."[12]

Populists looked to government as the vehicle for ending competitive individualism and for securing equality and justice. Frank Doster, a leading thinker of the populist era, believed that equality "must be realized through the process of human government, and it is the business of government to discover and enforce those laws of harmony which raise man above the barbarous antagonisms of the natural state into relationships of social unity and fraternity."[13] In his inaugural address of 1893 the newly elected populist governor Lorenzo Lewelling foresaw a government guided by human brotherhood and justice: "The 'survival of the fittest' (or strongest) is the government of brutes and reptiles, and such philosophy must give place to a government which recognizes human brotherhood. It is the province of government to protect the weak. . . . I appeal to the people of this great commonwealth to array themselves on the side of humanity and justice."[14]

To secure equality and justice, the populists sought broad economic and political reform, and their agenda grew with time. The populist cause was energized by distressed farmers who demanded equity of money, land, and transportation.[15] On money issues farmers saw their livelihoods at stake. State and national policies were being dictated by creditors against borrowers. The money supply was being constricted, and usurious interest rates were still being charged. Loans were being called, and farms foreclosed. Farmers demanded credit and currency reforms that included abolition of national banks, expanded currency, easy credit, caps on interest rates, mortgage principals reduced in line with falling farm values, laws that provided farmers more time in which to pay debts and thus avoid foreclosures, and government loans at favorable rates.

Farmers also believed that tariff and tax policies were unjustly skewed to benefit capitalists at the expense of farmers. Tariffs protected manufacturers and drove up prices on farm goods but left farm products at the mercy of free markets. Property taxes fell heavily upon farmers while railroads and financial interests were either exempted or lightly assessed. Farmers demanded repeal of tariffs and called for redistribution of the tax burden through a graduated income tax and taxes on bondholders.

Farmers had become dependent on railroads in moving crops to market, and railroads had now become the scourge of farmers. Railroads were charging exorbitant rates and manipulating state and national politics to the detriment of farmers. At the same time political parties had become captive to railroad interests. When all attempts to regulate rail rates fell short, populists demanded a radical solution, government ownership, specifically demanding railroads and telegraphs "owned by and operated in the interest of the people, as is the postal system." Further, to free state politics and parties from the corrupting grip of railroads, populists advocated the Australian ballot that assured public oversight of voting and secrecy of the ballot.

Farmers also demanded land reform. Over the prior thirty years as a result of state and national land policies, railroads had come to control large sections of the best land. Other lands had fallen into the hands of creditors through foreclosure and to interests outside the state through purchase. The supply of good land for homesteading had been exhausted. Farmers could no longer acquire lands on favorable terms and called for a ban on all alien ownership of Kansas lands. In addition, farmers wanted laws that would allow them to redeem homestead lands lost through court orders and repossess lands owned by aliens and foreign syndicates.

In sum rebellious farmers championed a radical and genuinely egalitarian agenda: graduated taxation, government ownership of railroads, government loans, and confiscatory land reform. In general populists wanted to turn the free market on its head and end a political culture of dog eat dog. Just how did the populists intend to accomplish this revolution?

Populist leadership and organization were fluid at best. There were many leaders, at times no leaders. Spokesmen came and went. Organization appeared and then disappeared. When holding power, populists became factious. Even under this cloud of diffusion, however, distressed farmers and populists exercised grassroots power at the ballot box over four election cycles, 1890 though 1896, and undermined Republican hegemony—at least for a time. In this period the People's Party in Kansas elected a U.S. senator and two of four governors, won seventeen of thirty-two contested seats in the U.S. House, controlled at different times the state house and the state senate for four of eight years, gave two presidential candidates aligned with the populist party the state's electoral votes, and elected numerous partisans to other state and local offices.

The beginnings of a populist political party emerged in the late 1880s. Simultaneous political activity was occurring at various levels. Farmers energized the grassroots through large gatherings across the state. At the state level self-appointed organizers with experience in earlier third-party movements in Kansas struggled to refine the populist program and to solidify populist organization. Other partisans met in order to create a political force at the national level.

Populist leaders took steps to devise a new party that would become "the strongest organization in America." Lecturers were dispatched to organize the grassroots and to recruit new members. Organizers were instructed to exclude from party membership merchants and those associated with mercantile businesses such as lawyers, stockholders, and anyone owning shares in a banking association. A solemn, secret ritual, prescribed for those initiated into the "common brotherhood" of party membership, called for a commitment to reducing inequality: "our purpose is to exert an influence in opposition to the glaring and shameful vices which degrade mankind, lower him in the scale of human existence and bring despair and woe to the dearest creatures he has on earth."[16]

By the fall elections of 1890 the new party had slated candidates for each of the 125 seats in the Kansas House, and populist leaders would claim two thousand local organizations and one hundred thousand members. Anger at the ruling Republican oligarchy further energized the populist challenge as Republican lawmakers in 1889 reneged on their platform of agrarian reform. Election results were jolting: irate populists overturned Republican control of the Kansas House by winning 93 seats, dramatically reducing Republican House seats from 123 in the 1889 legislative session to 25 in 1891. Populist voters fell just short of unseating the incumbent Republican governor, but in the 1891 session their legislative representatives ousted the leading defender of the prevailing political culture, three-term Republican U.S. Senator Ingalls. In his place populist legislators elected former Republican state legislator William Peffer who as editor of the *Kansas Farmer* for nearly twenty years had emerged as the most articulate spokesman for the demands of alienated farmers.

In the next election populist success in securing power ended in a debacle. Populists came close to taking complete control of state government. In 1892 they swept all state executive offices: governor, lieutenant governor, attorney general, secretary of state, and treasurer. They won five of eight seats in the U.S. House. They elected a majority in the state senate, but in the state house fell short of a majority. Rather than govern with near complete control and exalt in their rule of the executive branch, legislative populists chose to challenge the election results of the state house and thereby ignited an historic "legislative war" for control of the house. To gain physical control of the house chamber, the contesting sides brought guns and barricades to bear in a battle of wills that would consume most of the legislative session. By the time the matter was resolved, populist legislators had not only failed in their attempt to control the state house but were labeled anarchists in papers throughout the state and nation. Their cause had been undermined.

The egalitarian character of the populists became even more vivid as they began to govern after the disruptive legislative war of 1893. As egalitarians populists were inherently distrustful of authority, even when their own partisans held power. They demanded political change but offered little in political support. Actions of the populist governor were viewed with suspicion and questioned as to their purity of purpose. Populists broke ranks on political strategy and tactics, fought publicly on issues, and they freely branded their own as traitors to the cause. They even undermined their governor's reelection bid. Kansas historian James Malin observed that populist reformers "failed to find adequate leadership. . . . [P]ersonality conflicts were numerous. . . . The turnover of personnel in party offices and committees of the various reform organizations was so rapid. . . .[that] [f]ew of the early leaders of [Populism] survived a decade of prominence. . . . The big-named leaders of Populism simply could not consistently get along with each other. . . . No one outside the Populist party said any harsher things about Populist leadership than Populists themselves."[17] As a result of internecine warfare populists wasted two years in which they held near complete control of the state government.

The opportunity of populists to rule by themselves had been lost. In the 1894 elections populists lost all state executive offices, held only one of eight seats in the U.S. House, and saw their state house minority shrink further to 31 of the 125 seats. Two years later, the populists fused with the Democrats and returned to power, but fusion diminished their passion and watered down their agenda. Fusion was defeated in the 1898 election and again in 1900. Shortly thereafter, the populist party disappeared forever from the political scene. Some populists became socialists and some Democrats. Lifelong Republican farmers who had been able to vote for the populist cause in earlier elections could not stomach an alignment with Democrats and returned to the Republican fold.

Despite their short-lived hold on power, Kansas populists claimed a few modest legislative successes. In the 1891 state legislative session, with the cooperation of a Republican state senate, populists saw the enactment of two new regulatory laws of agrarian interest, specifically regulation of banking and grain warehousing, that with updating have continued to the present day. Two other adopted measures, prohibition of alien ownership of land and of anticompetitive combinations in the marketing of livestock, gave populists symbolic victories if not actual effective enforcement. Although populists could claim little in the debacle of the 1893 session, they did see the adoption of two election laws, one sponsored by Republicans prohibiting corrupt election practices and the other, the Australian ballot, sponsored by populists.

After the election of 1894 populist accomplishments were meager. In the 1895 legislative session most measures advanced by the populist senate died in the state house. In the 1897 session populist success through fusion resulted in little from the populist's original reform agenda being enacted except for a law prohibiting trusts that was another symbolic but unenforceable populist measure. Populist congressional representatives saw little accomplished nationally, and the radical egalitarian platform of the early 1890s was repudiated in the national election of 1896.

After the populist uprising of the 1890s some egalitarians turned to the Socialist Party, an alliance of equality and hierarchy. Through the first half of the twentieth century they organized socialist tickets for state and city offices but with little success. Deep in the national depression of the 1930s, John Brinkley, Kansas' infamous goat-gland doctor, campaigned for governor in 1930 and 1932 promising "pensions for the aged, a lake in each [county], free state medical care for those otherwise unable to afford it, a state hospital for Negroes, [and] free textbooks," among other egalitarian measures and garnered thirty percent of the vote in both three-man contests including a total of 244,000 votes in 1932. Francis Schruben documented the similarities in voting patterns between the Brinkley and the populists of the 1890s.[18] According to William Allen White, the Brinkley campaign represented a call for "a more equitable distribution of the common wealth."[19]

Populism did work as a tonic on Kansas politics as it called attention to the inequities resulting from the prevailing political culture of individualism and as it challenged the protagonists of individualism. At their core Kansas populists were genuine egalitarians, blaming the system for injustice and championing measures to rectify inequities. The populist movement thus tempered Republican rule and left an egalitarian imprint. When the Republican Party reasserted control, it had been changed. Republicans would usher in a progressive movement and become the trust busters, trade regulators, and political reformers of the early twentieth century. They moved in this new direction, however, more because of a preference for achieving political order than for equality.

A PREFERENCE FOR ORDER

Amid the chaos wrought by the politics of individualism and later egalitarianism, another countervailing cultural force emerged. Alongside those seeking their fortunes in Kansas were others desiring to give order to the politics and morals of the new state. The Kansas-Nebraska Act of 1854 had opened the possibility that Kansas could become a slave state through the self-determination of settlers and triggered New England Puritans to organize and aid immigrants desiring to counter proslavery forces on the slavery issue. The struggle brought national attention to Bleeding Kansas and ultimately set the stage for sparks that ignited the Civil War. In the end free-state forces prevailed, and Kansans prohibited slavery by constitutional decree, entering the Union in 1861 as a free state.

Free-state crusaders brought to Kansas not only a desire to abolish slavery but also ideals for achieving a more perfect moral and political order. Their moral beliefs had roots traceable to the evangelical foment of the early nineteenth century. They believed that social harmony and morality could be achieved through reason and conscious design. Their desire for moral improvement, originally focused on redemption through individual action, began to shift toward social control through politics, rule of law, and the exercise of governmental powers. Their preference for political order, which began with the slavery issue, gained momentum at the turn of the twentieth century as progressives sought to restructure state politics. Moral and political reformers coalesced to dominate state politics for the first two decades of the twentieth century, and Kansas experienced a hierarchical political culture in full bloom. The story begins much earlier, however, for no issue reveals Kansans' hierarchic instincts more vividly than the state's century-long struggle to achieve moral order through restraints on human vulnerabilities with respect to intoxicating liquors.[20]

The prohibitory movement in the United States had New England roots, its first major victory being the enactment of statutory prohibition by Maine in 1851. Prohibitory laws had spread throughout New England and even beyond by 1855. From the beginning free-state immigrants coming into Kansas cited temperance as one of their missions and almost immediately resorted to the rule of law in order to achieve their aims. In 1854–55 those organizing town associations in the free-state strongholds of territorial Kansas—Lawrence, Topeka, Ottawa, and Emporia, among others—wrote bylaws banning the sale of intoxicating liquor. In 1856 free-state women petitioned the territorial legislature to lay "the foundation for a new society" by enacting laws prohibiting the sale of liquor. The Wyandotte convention debated prohibition, but organizing for statehood, later a civil war, and eventually a land rush pushed aside early attempts to order and enforce an outright ban on liquor sales.[21]

In an era dominated by disorder and a cultural preference for individual liberty, the energy for temperance and prohibition in Kansas was rekindled by evangelical religious denominations. Methodists, Congregationalists, Presbyterians, Baptists, Disciples of Christ, Scandinavian Lutherans, United Brethren, and Friends resorted to politics and law to curb the liquor traffic. Women became independently engaged, as did assorted revivalists and temperance organizers. These disparate forces came together in the late 1870s to espouse prohibition by constitutional edict. Their unique prohibitory idea was championed by Republican Governor John St. John, a temperance leader who helped gain legislative support to place the measure on the ballot. Further, in 1880 St. John campaigned throughout the state, both for constitutional prohibition and for reelection as governor. He won reelection, and Kansas voters adopted the amendment with 52.3 percent of the popular vote, making Kansas the first state in the Union to prohibit through constitutional language the "manufacture and sale of intoxicating liquors."[22] Opponents viewed the unprecedented amendment as "a radical change of policy, trespassing upon personal liberty and right of property."[23]

Kansans could accomplish moral order with respect to slavery by constitutional decree. Constitutional language, however, could not similarly control human frailties with respect to booze. This Kansan resort to the organic law—the state constitution—for achieving the moral ideal of temperance revealed the hierarchic instincts of the citizens of Kansas. Kansans' attempts to enforce prohibition over the next forty years would unveil the trappings of a hierarchical political culture in more vivid terms: with the adoption of constitutional prohibition Kansans began a steady climb to enforce prohibition, invoking with each step broader state powers to realize their vision of moral order.

State lawmakers' initial steps toward enforcement of prohibition were moderate. In 1881 they simply shifted responsibility to the local level, charging local law enforcement officials with controlling any traffic in booze. Saloon keepers, however, defied the law, particularly in the state's larger cities, and local officials often turned a blind eye to this defiance of the law. A cultural divide on the issue surfaced. The Republican Party, though not unanimous, became the party of prohibition calling for stricter enforcement; the Democrats labeled prohibition tyrannical and, hoping for repeal, called for the prohibitory amendment to be resubmitted to voters. A Republican majority consistently prevailed.

Citizens outraged by conspicuous violations of prohibitory laws demanded tougher enforcement. In 1885 state lawmakers passed additional laws bolstering enforcement and armed law enforcement officials with extraordinary powers to conduct search and seizure, to convene grand juries in response to citizen complaints, to shut down and place liens on offending places, and to destroy illegal goods. Local prosecutors were authorized special fees for obtaining successful convictions, and citizens were authorized to hire attorneys to assist local prosecutors. The state's attorney general was given full authority of enforcement if local officials failed to do the job. Any person could demand that a pharmacist stop selling intoxicating liquor to a family member for "medicinal" purposes. Another law mandated "temperance education" in the public schools and also required that all teachers pass an examination on "effects of alcohol stimulants" as a condition of certification.[24]

These measures failed to satisfy antiliquor forces who demanded even more aggressive action. In 1887 state lawmakers responded once again by passing the Police Government of Cities Act, which was characterized by one local scribe as "obnoxious, Russian-police-surveillance." This extraordinary measure allowed two hundred householders in Kansas' larger cities to petition for the establishment of a state board of police commissioners with authority to take control of city police and all police facilities in order to enforce the prohibitory laws in an offending city. In smaller cities complaints by fifty householders could trigger the state's attorney general to commence ouster proceeding against a city's mayor and council for the city's failure to enforce prohibition. Upon ouster a state board of police commissioners would take control of city police operations.[25] Temperance organizers, particularly women, successfully petitioned state and local prosecutors for stricter enforcement. State rule of local police was activated in a half dozen of the larger Kansas cities, and hundreds of saloons were closed down. By the end of the 1880s Governor John Martin could proudly observe that Kansas "is today the most temperate, orderly, sober community of people in the civilized world."[26]

The force of the state, however, failed to dry up the wet problem. Enforcement of prohibitory laws waned in the 1890s, slowed by court actions, allegations of collusion between violators and police commissioners, and the diminishing enthusiasm of top state officials.

At the turn of the twentieth century another force emerged and gave new life to ideals of prohibition. Carrie Nation took enforcement into her own hands and began shutting down joints with the force of her own personality. She attacked and demolished, and she prodded women to join her army of "home defenders" and her extralegal enforcement of prohibition. Her direct action sparked similar attacks on joints throughout the state. In response state lawmakers again strengthened enforcement authority in 1901 by granting yet broader powers to conduct search and seizure, enjoin offending places, and subpoena witnesses.[27]

At this same time moral reformers allied with a newly emerging progressive constituency—business and professional leaders also seeking community improvement—to dominate Kansas politics. These reformers shared hierarchic instincts and envisioned "God's plan for democracy" based on the idea that "every ordinary individual could be made into a perfect citizen through the agencies of the state, and that a perfect citizenry would, perforce, produce perfect democracy."[28] This progressive alliance continued and expanded its moral agenda but extended that agenda to include economic and political reforms, bold measures to regulate the economy, reorder state and local politics, and augment state authority. These initiatives exhibited supreme confidence that through the power of rational thought and conscience and with the help of experts the authority of state government could be applied to cure the ills of society.

Moral reformers continued their pursuit of strict enforcement of prohibition but branched out seeking to achieve a broader moral agenda: the outlawing of abortion, slot machines, cigarettes, solicitation of prostitutes, and indecent post cards, among other perceived evils.[29] Laws were passed authorizing various state and local officials to suppress vice and immorality through the regulation of theaters and dance halls and the censorship of moving pictures.[30]

To aid prohibition, lawmakers passed tougher laws against repeat violators, authorized state and local prosecutors to initiate ouster proceedings against *any* offending public officer, and further broadened inquisitorial powers of enforcement.[31] In 1917 Kansas lawmakers took the ultimate step in enforcing prohibition by passing the "bone-dry" law making "possession" of intoxicating liquor a crime.[32] Along the way Kansas lawmakers would declare with unanimity that due to prohibition "Kansas is cleaner, better, more advanced in mental culture, and stronger in moral fiber and conviction; her homes are happier . . . children better educated . . . [and] crime is less prevalent and poverty less general."[33] The nation apparently concurred with Kansas' model of moral order. By 1920 prohibition had become the law of the land.[34]

Kansas progressives then sought a political makeover, much as the populists before them had. The motives of this emerging class of business and professional men, however, were political order rather than political equality. They sought to cleanse state politics, to wrestle control of the Republican Party from the pernicious grip of the railroads, and to protect main street businesses from domination by corporate monopolies.

This reform movement was led by a series of progressive Republican governors—Ed Hoch, Walter Stubbs, Arthur Capper, and Henry Allen—

who all served two consecutive terms beginning in 1905 and ending in
1923, this period being interrupted only once for two years by the Bull
Moose debacle of 1912. These progressive-era governors embraced measures seeking moral order, but more important, they sought to reshape the
political landscape of Kansas and to reform the Republican Party. Their
activism in office would leave a lasting imprint on the Kansas governorship for both Republicans and Democrats that would follow for the balance of the new century. Most important, they established a standard for a
Republican governorship in Kansas and imparted a legacy of progress, yet
moderation, in pursuing the ideals of liberty and order for those Republican
governors who followed.

In contrast to the populists, however, progressive lawmakers achieved
over the first two decades of the twentieth century dramatic results and
unleashed a flood of new laws that reformed state politics, regulated the
economy, and augmented the authority of state officials. Political reforms
included significant changes in the state constitution: a line-item veto for
the governor (1903), removal of the state printer from election by the legislature (1903), voting rights for women (1911), and recall of any elected
public official (1913). Kansas lawmakers also quickly ratified amendments
to the U.S. constitution, authorizing the income tax (1911), direct election
of U.S. senators (1913), and women's suffrage (1919). In addition, laws
were enacted requiring primary elections (1908–9), abolishing party labels
in city elections (1909), providing for the ouster of public officials in cases
of misconduct (1911), eliminating a ballot option for straight party-ticket
voting (1913), and authorizing city electors to replace political administration of city government with a city manager selected on the basis of administrative ability (1917).

State initiatives designed to regulate the economy were extensive and
represented a dramatic departure from a culture of laissez faire. Most early
attempts at regulation were primitive as states and the nation as a whole
experimented with regulatory regimes. In Kansas numerous laws were
aimed at rectifying the excesses of turn-of-the-century Kansas industries, as
for example, owners operating dangerous mines, unscrupulous merchants
preying on farmers, speculators defrauding investors, and railroads levying
unfair rates and exerting undue influence. While a number of states including Kansas were following a parallel course in addressing workplace safety
and working conditions, workmen's compensation, child labor, and food
and drug regulation, among other issues, Kansas progressives were in the
forefront in regulating public utilities and "blue sky" securities and guaran-
teeing bank deposits.[35] State lawmakers took over state printing and built

a state printing plant, started a twine business at the state penitentiary, and even tried without success to compete with Standard Oil in the oil refinery business. In 1920, as a final act in Kansas' play to control the economy, lawmakers created the Kansas Court of Industrial Relations with authority to intervene in labor-management disputes and to force the parties into compulsory arbitration. After two years of rocky operations the U.S. Supreme Court ruled this state action to be an unconstitutional violation of the rights of both business and labor.

At the turn of the twentieth century most government in Kansas was local. Cities, counties, and schools accounted for nine out of every ten tax dollars being spent, but this picture began to change during the new century's first two decades. An array of state officials and agencies was added to regulate the economy. New state offices were created to examine and certify those seeking to practice emerging new professions. Lawmakers sanctioned new disciplines at the agricultural college and state university and authorized the skeletal beginnings of what would become two regional state universities. Environmental protection, public health, road building, state hospitals, and numerous other services that would in time become major components of state government were initiated or augmented. State actions were also taken to reform tax administration.

Terms such as management, economy, and efficiency entered the lexicon of state lawmakers, who established a committee to investigate "the business management of every institution and department in Kansas" and recommended "more economical administration or management of public affairs." A state business manager was later authorized and charged with "full authority to manage and control" all the educational, benevolent, and penal institutions of the state. Cities were authorized to appoint a city manager responsible for "administration of all the affairs of the city" including hiring and firing of all employees and preparing the annual budget. The first calls for a state budget were issued. At both gubernatorial and legislative insistence numerous study commissions were authorized to examine the management of state services and to recommend more efficient and economical operations.[36]

Kansans' preference for order in the early twentieth century also revealed vulnerabilities in a hierarchic political culture. At the height of the progressive era, for example, Kansas officials became enamored of the eugenics movement that was sweeping through the nation. They sterilized hundreds of residents in state institutions based on their belief in the superior wisdom of state officials and professionals who could by this procedure benefit society as well as those who deviated from society's mainstream. In a broader sense these hierarchic impulses nurtured the growth of state institutions in Kansas. This particular institutional solution to isolate and treat those who deviated from community standards set deep roots after the turn of the century and would shape state policy for most of the century.

As noted in the introduction, the passions of Kansas politics were dampened in the 1930s and 1940s by a number of factors that included the national depression, the Dust Bowl, and the nationalizing trends of federal grants-in-aid and national defense. The iconic images of Kansas' political fervor—Senator Peffer, Carrie Nation, and Doc Brinkley—were replaced in the post–World War II era by a new era of leadership that was connected to the progressive penchant for political order and strong sense of public service. A postwar progressive resurgence was led by figures such as Frank Carlson, George Docking, Bill Avery, Bob Docking, and a host of legislative leaders such as Paul Wunsch, Glee Smith, Bob Bennett, and Pete McGill. The politics of this new brand of leadership was calmer, less combative, more moderate, and often bipartisan. Resurgent progressives would initiate fundamental constitutional reforms of the political institutions of state government in the 1950s through the 1980s and usher in a modern era of state politics.

POLITICAL CULTURES IN THE MODERN ERA

The political cultures that enlivened the state's political history still operate within Kansas politics today. The deep-seated preferences for liberty, order, and equality that underpin these political cultures and cast Kansas politics onto the national stage on issues such as abolition, prohibition, populism, and progressivism continue to frame contemporary issues, energize political competition, and shape the state's future.

For example, a political culture of individualism is alive and well in present-day Kansas. An analytical fifty-state study conducted in 2004 by Pacific Research Institute, a public policy center dedicated to individual liberty and free markets, ranked Kansas number one in economic freedom based on greater fiscal restraints on government, less regulation of the economy, more limits on judicial intervention, smaller government, and lower welfare spending. Today, a number of well-funded groups advocate on behalf of a culture of individualism. The Flint Hills Center for Public Policy, a think tank promoting open markets, limited government, and individual freedom, offers civic education and policy papers. Kansas Taxpayers Network, Americans for Prosperity Kansas, and Kansans for Growth work actively in the state capitol and in the state's larger communities to forestall any tax increase and to restrain governmental spending. These lobbies have demonstrated success in securing no-tax pledges from legislative candidates and targeting the reelection campaigns of state and local lawmakers who have supported tax increases.[37]

A political culture of hierarchy striving for moral order is also alive and well in modern Kansas. Religious activists in the state work through various organized groups to restrict abortion, prohibit gay marriage, preclude any state sponsorship of expanded gambling, and question the teaching of evolution in public schools. In 1991 Operation Rescue, an antiabortion group, targeted Wichita for a national rally and found friendly territory among Protestant evangelicals and orthodox Catholics in the state. This extraordinary display of civil disobedience continued for six weeks, resulted in twenty-six hundred arrests for blocking access to local abortion clinics and culminated in a massive rally of twenty-five thousand on a hot Sunday afternoon in August on the campus of Wichita State University. Moral fervor has energized grassroots activists to gain control of the Republican Party apparatus and to elect their partisans to a controlling majority in the Kansas House of Representatives as well as to the State Board of Education.

Finally, in today's Kansas an egalitarian political culture finds expression in diverse demands for equality of conditions: in the funding of public welfare and education, in state taxation, and in appointments to state office. However, beginning with the arrival of the New Deal, egalitarians have more often looked to national rather than state authority for a redress of grievances and have not mounted a concerted attempt for elective state office. National assistance to agriculture and for income security initiated in the 1930s addressed Kansans confronting desperate conditions during the Great Depression. The introduction of Medicaid and Medicare in the 1960s further deepened the nation's commitment to equalizing conditions, and these programs comprise a steadily growing portion of Kansans' economic life. From the 1960s to the present federal courts have commanded state governments to provide equality for citizens in the exercise of their various rights, most particularly in the weighting of their votes for state legislators.

Kansas courts have in some measure provided a state vehicle for equalizing conditions. Beginning in the 1970s and continuing through the present day, poorer school districts that are heavily reliant on property taxes have brought suit to force the state legislature to provide an equal education for every child in the state. These districts claimed that the quality of a child's education should not depend upon the wealth of a district in which a child resides. In a series of court cases, as well as threats by state judges, the state legislature has taken repeated steps toward equalizing funding for school

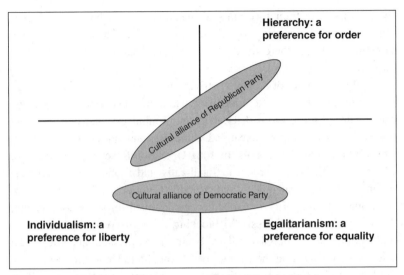

Fig. 3. Cultural Alliances of National Political Parties

districts. Most recently, school districts with a disproportionate number of at-risk students appealed to state courts and won an infusion of over seven hundred and fifty million dollars in additional funds.

In their moments of brilliance political cultures also reveal their vulnerabilities, with other political cultures working as a counterforce to temper these excesses. Populists and later progressives served to rectify the inequities and the chaos of rampant individualism of the late nineteenth century. The disorganization of populists gave way to the preference for order in the progressive era. A preference for individual liberty eventually eroded the force of state coercion in behalf of prohibition and later gambling.

POLITICAL CULTURES AND PARTY POLITICS

Political cultures help understand the dynamics of party politics. Historically the Republican Party found footing as an alliance of political cultures grounded in liberty and order, as shown in figure 3. Abraham Lincoln brought this "establishment" alliance into national life after the middle of the nineteenth century as a party that embraced liberty in terms of "free enterprise aided by subsidies" and "free land for homesteaders" and that championed order and national union through national banking, internal improvements, and tariffs.[38] In Kansas, for most of state history, the party has shifted to and fro on the liberty-order axis, as illustrated graphically in

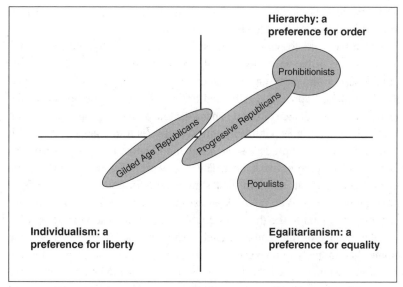

Fig. 4. Cultural Placement of Historic Political Forces in Kansas

figure 4. In the Gilded Age the party prominently tilted toward economic liberty with strict limits on state government, yet at the same time it embraced prohibition and indeed became the party of prohibition. During the progressive era the party repositioned itself fundamentally toward order, becoming the vehicle for governmental intervention in behalf of economic, political, and moral reform. In the 1920s and 1930s the party again adjusted course, urging reduced spending and tax cuts during the depression years, and its center of gravity shifted back toward economic liberty.

Historically Republican Party factionalism may also be understood as a struggle between those partisans favoring liberty and those favoring order. At any single point in time party leaders and their followers leaned more toward one cultural pole than the other. In the early years control for the center of the party was fought out among partisans in nominating conventions for elective and party offices; more recently, contests unfolded in primary elections and legislative caucuses. Tension between liberty and order defined factions, and majority factions shifted with the party's center of gravity. From time to time the factions engaged in fierce struggles for party control, with these struggles occasionally leaving deep fissures and losing elections to the Democratic opposition. But party leaders could quickly regroup, mend fences, redefine their center, return to battle, and reclaim office. In the state's first forty-eight gubernatorial elections, 1861–1954, five

Democratic gubernatorial candidates won office following factional rup-
tures, but none was reelected to a second term.

Progressive-era Republicans, most particularly the Republican governors serving in the early decades of the twentieth century, left an indelible stamp on the party and its leadership for the balance of the century.
Hoch, Stubbs, Capper, and Allen led the way in testing the bounds of the
party's cultural alliance of liberty and order and defined a progressive strain,
a middle ground in Republican politics, that lives to the present day. With
political ties to their predecessors, Reed and Landon, and later Ratner, followed under a progressive banner. The next wave of Republican governors,
Schoeppel, Carlson, and Arn, had similar links in politics and beliefs to
their predecessors. With possibly an exception or two this progressive legacy may be found in the thirteen Republican governors serving after Allen
for the balance of the century.[39] Each negotiated the liberty-order alliance
somewhat uniquely in response to the demands of the times, but as a group
these governors defined the Republican Party as a moderate, progressive
party with a distinct center of gravity that resisted being pulled to the ideological extremes by those preferring either more liberty or more order.

The progressive strain of Republican Party politics faced a serious challenge in the aftermath of *Roe v Wade* in 1973. The Reagan era transformed
party dynamics, and Republican Party politics realigned on its cultural axis.
Reagan championed a return to smaller government, tax cuts, and less regulation while appealing to Christian hierarchs distressed over the Supreme
Court's abortion decision. Following Reagan's lead, opportunistic party
leaders of the recent era abandoned the party's historic footing between
liberty and order and sought to position the party on both cultural poles as
an alliance drawn to issues on the party's fringes. As a result party leaders
espoused freedom from government intervention on economic matters such
as taxing, spending, and regulation while demanding governmental intervention in social matters such as abortion, marriage, and gambling.

The exact motives for this alliance appear mixed. True-believing Christian hierarchs demand governmental control of individual choice on social
issues while also wanting to restrain governments biased against their beliefs on matters such as prayer in schools, sex education, or the teaching
of evolution. Party hierarchs could embrace individualist preferences for
cutting taxes as a means for throttling government on social issues. On the
other hand, true-believing individualists more likely view the alliance as a
marriage of convenience that attracts political support for their belief in limited government but requires them to stomach infringements on individual
freedom.

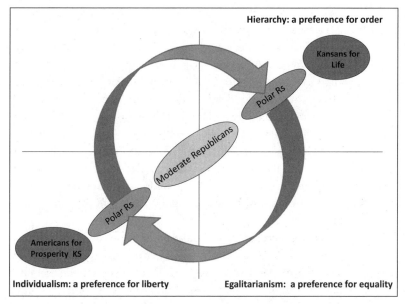

Fig. 5. Cultural Alliances of Kansas Republican Factions

Whatever the motives, a unique "polar" alliance, a party faction based on contradictory ideas, has emerged.[40] This alliance of the party's cultural poles draws political energy from those attracted to the core values of liberty and order as well as from organized interests aligned with one cultural preference or the other. This alignment also prompts litmus tests such as no-tax pledges in behalf of liberty and obligatory positions on abortion in behalf of order. Polar Republicans make the pledge, while centrist Republicans may embrace a tax increase for a compelling cause or hold disparate positions on abortion. This party dynamic has fostered two Republican factions, polar alliance Republicans on the one hand and moderate Republicans on the other. The polar alliance has abandoned the center and those party faithful preferring to find a middle ground. Figure 5 graphically displays the cultural alliances of these Republican factions as well as groups aligned on the cultural poles.

A series of events energized this party dynamic. In 1974, only a year after *Roe v Wade*, the campaign of U.S. Senator Bob Dole used the abortion issue to galvanize pro-life supporters in his reelection contest with U.S. Representative Bill Roy. Pro-life groups aligned with Dole accused Roy, an obstetrician from Topeka, of performing abortions and on Sunday mornings prior to the election blanketed cars in church parking lots with leaflets.

Pro-life forces also ran negative ads against Roy in major newspapers in the state. In 1980 Reagan successfully bucked nearly fifty years of Democratic hegemony at the national level with his call for tax cuts, spending reductions, and decreased regulation while also opening the party's door to opponents of abortion. In 1988 Reverend Pat Robertson carried this message into Kansas politics during his presidential bid as he challenged native son Bob Dole in party caucuses and lured a large contingent of dedicated evangelical Protestants and orthodox Catholics into the GOP. Then in 1990 moderate Republican Governor Mike Hayden, a supporter of abortion rights, was challenged from both flanks in primary and general elections on issues of taxes and abortion. Finally, in 1991 Operation Rescue's Summer of Mercy brought a national protest of thousands into Wichita and fully politicized the movement.

The 1994 elections became the seminal event in establishing the legitimacy of polar alliance Republicans in Kansas. A covey of Republican moderates won the state's top elective offices, with Bill Graves and running mate Sheila Frahm winning the governorship, Carla Stovall becoming attorney general and Ron Thornberg secretary of state. However, the newly elected members of the Kansas House did not share the moderate banner and immediately showed their intentions by dumping moderate House Speaker Bob Miller. Further, in the primary elections of the prior August, these newly energized partisans quietly and systematically infiltrated the party at the precinct level and eventually took control of the state party organization. They threw moderate Republicans out and elected as the state party chair in 1990 David Miller, who had run on the ticket challenging former Governor Hayden and who was also a vocal critic of the newly elected Republican governor.

A new Republican majority was born and immediately staked its claim to power. Newly elected House Speaker Tim Shallenberger issued a "Declaration for Change," whose goals were "to find ways to cut government . . . to put money back in the pockets of the taxpayers . . . to call for less government intervention." The Speaker's House majority would focus on the "size and growth of government, the spiraling taxes."[41] In taking control of the party organization, Republican party chair David Miller thanked "almighty God" for his victory. His partisans were adamant as to their purpose. Mark Gietzen, president of the Kansas Republican Coalition for Life and chair of the Sedgwick County GOP, declared total victory: "A clean sweep. Absolutely. Spic-and-span pro-lifers have taken over the Republican Party." The antiabortion wing had campaigned to establish a new social order through the force of organic law: "our mission is to keep the Republican Party firmly pro-life . . . and work toward eventual passage of a Human Life Amendment to the U.S. Constitution." Those on the outside of the polar alliance were stunned. Longtime State Senator Ben Vidricksen expressed alarm: "The thing that bothers me is the fact that a good share of these people I haven't ever heard of before, and they haven't been in the party that long. I'm basically pro-life. But I'm not a single-issue person. If these people have just one mission in mind, it will be the demise of the Republican Party."[42]

Kansas Republican politics has thus split into two camps, a polar alliance that controls the party organization and the House Republican caucus and moderates who claim the party's middle ground and the Senate Republican caucus. The polar alliance finds support from passionately motivated partisans who demand loyalty through litmus tests on taxes and abortion. They do not easily tolerate dissent. The moderates espouse a pragmatic big-tent party that avoids litmus tests on single issues and is willing to compromise to achieve results.

While polar alliance Republicans have for the most part controlled the party apparatus over the past fourteen years, they have failed in three concerted attempts to claim the governorship, the big prize of state politics. Party chair David Miller challenged incumbent Republican Governor Graves in the 1998 gubernatorial primary and was overwhelmingly defeated by a margin approaching three to seven. In the 2002 primary moderates split votes between competing candidates allowing Shallenberger to be nominated, but he was handily defeated by Democrat Kathleen Sebelius in the general. In 2006 Sebelius defeated another polar alliance standard bearer in a landslide. In each of these elections moderate Republican voters defected from their party's candidates who positioned themselves on the extremes of the liberty-order axis.

In contrast to Republicans, Kansas Democrats have been continually searching for footing. The national Democratic Party from its beginnings with Jefferson and Jackson has found a political base in an alliance of political cultures grounded in liberty and equality (see figure 3), but the Kansas party failed to gain firm traction on this cultural axis. Throughout the state's first hundred years Kansas Republicans were able to undermine Democrats as weak on grounds of moral order by waving the "bloody shirt" symbolic of Democrat complicity in the Civil War and national disunion and by maligning Democrats as the party of booze which desired to abandon prohibition. As noted above, Democratic success in claiming the governorship from statehood through the mid-twentieth century resulted more from Republican factionalism than from building a stable party base.

Beginning with the New Deal, Democrats have been more competitive in winning and holding the governorship. During the 1930s, in the midst of the Great Depression, Harry Woodring (1930) and Walter Huxman (1936) won election. George Docking won in 1956 and in 1958 becoming the first Democrat to be reelected to the office. His son Robert Docking won an unprecedented four successive elections, beginning in 1966 running through 1972. John Carlin and most recently Kathleen Sebelius have also won successive terms. Indeed, beginning with the 1956 election Democrats have prevailed in eleven of the last eighteen gubernatorial contests.

While cultural conflicts within the Republican Party help explain the recent success of Democrats in winning the governorship, agile, entrepreneurial politics better explains Democratic ability to hold onto the office. In the initial gubernatorial victories of the Dockings and Carlin, Republican candidates lost support in the liberty-leaning wing of the party; in the case of Sebelius the moderate middle defected. The Dockings held onto office by beating Republican challengers on Republican cultural turf. Robert Docking in particular championed economic liberty through tax cuts, tax lids, and budget freezes while aligning with Nixon on law and order and cracking down on campus unrest. Carlin and Sebelius both succeeded through savvy reelection campaigns that claimed the middle ground.

Even with their effective claim on the office of governor, Democrats remain the minority party in Kansas. While they have garnered two thin majorities in the Kansas House over the past thirty years (1979–81 and 1991–93), their legislative numbers have barely risen to the level necessary to sustain a gubernatorial veto over the past twelve years. Their winning of statewide executive offices, other than the governorship, is the exception rather than the rule. In cultural terms their weakness in Kansas may be due to the party's inability to develop its egalitarian base as the national party has done. For the first half of state history Kansas Democrats ended up on the wrong side of the leading egalitarian issues. They suffered with the national party in their opposition to the abolition of slavery, and the party's sectional strength in the South drove African Americans into the Republican Party. They viewed women's suffrage in Kansas as a means for preserving prohibition and therefore opposed extending the franchise to women. Kansas Democrats did fuse with egalitarian populists to win statewide elections in 1896, but this electoral coalition went no further.

Beginning with the New Deal, egalitarians increasingly turned to the national level, that is to the presidency, the Congress, and federal courts and to the national Democratic Party as well as to the national media, for a redress of their grievances. A New Deal coalition of organized labor, urban ethnic minorities, and African Americans represents a minority of Kansas voters, and egalitarians did not come to view state government and state politics as an active venue for addressing their issues. Robert Docking, for example, studiously avoided alignment with the national party or its leaders and discarded most suggestions of an egalitarian bent.[43]

Governor Kathleen Sebelius (2003–2009), has demonstrated savvy and versatility in attacking the political strategy of polar alliance Republicans. In 2002 she persuaded moderate Republican John Moore to switch parties and to join her ticket as lieutenant governor. After winning the governorship by beating Shallenberger, an original leader of the polar alliance, she asked high-ranking appointees from the moderate Graves administration, including former governor Hayden, to stay on in her administration. As governor in the aftermath of 9/11, Sebelius steered a cautious centrist course, avoiding tax increases, protecting education spending, and gaining fiscal breathing room through extension of state debt obligations. More recently, she has preempted Republicans by championing tax cuts for business. Then in her 2006 bid for reelection she audaciously recruited Mark Parkinson, former Republican state party chairman during the Graves administration, to the Democratic Party and made him her new running mate. Moderate Republicans abandoned their polar alliance ticket in droves, giving Sebelius a landslide reelection with fifty-eight percent of the popular vote. However, with her departure to join the Obama Administration and Parkinson's refusal to run for governor in 2010, Sebelius's strategy to woo Republican moderates into the Democratic fold has stalled, at least for now.

Extraordinary moments in Kansas political history demonstrate the vitality of Kansas politics and the strength of three active political cultures that undergird the body politic of Kansas. A political culture of individualism fosters a profound belief in individual liberty and limited government and has produced Kansans characterized by initiative, productivity, and entrepreneurship. A political culture of hierarchy nurtures the belief that government can and should play an affirmative role in the moral improvement of all Kansans and in the political improvement of Kansas communities and the state as a whole. An egalitarian political culture serves as a tonic for the body politic, calling attention to inequities and injustice in the state and deflating the pomposities of both free markets and coercive governments. Even against the potent forces reshaping life in the twentieth century—the rising preeminence of national authority, economic globalization, the mass media, and individual mobility—these political cultures frame today's issues, compete for partisans, shape party politics, and guide the state's future.

CHAPTER TWO

The Constitution

Following the prevailing political winds of the dominant political cultures, the Kansas Constitution has been interpreted, reinterpreted, revised, and amended to reflect the needs of the state's citizens. In the early years of statehood its articles mirrored the wishes of free-soil Republicans who dominated the Wyandotte Convention in 1859. In the late nineteenth century and early twentieth century, prohibitionists and progressives took turns influencing the constitution's structure and shaping its restrictions. From the 1950s through the 1970s good government hierarchs passed broad sweeping reforms making the judiciary more independent, elevating the leadership role of the governor at the expense of state legislative power, and providing home rule powers to local governments. In the late twentieth and early twenty-first centuries polar alliance Republicans sought to amend the constitution in order to reflect their values. Perhaps no recent amendment to the constitution expresses these values more than the 2005 ban of marriage and civil union for gay and lesbian couples. This chapter documents the historical development of the state's constitution, discusses the major attributes of the constitution, and compares Kansas' constitution with other states.

HISTORY OF THE KANSAS CONSTITUTION

The early history of the constitution reflects the trials and tribulations of the territory that became known as Bleeding Kansas. The 1854 Kansas-Nebraska Act precipitated much of the violence over the slavery question because it allowed settlers to vote in a referendum on the acceptance of slavery. Passed by a proslavery Congress and president, the act destroyed the 1820 Missouri Compromise, which dictated that new territories and states north of thirty-six degrees latitude would be free. As a result the Kansas-Nebraska

Act the abolitionist forces from states like Ohio, Indiana, Illinois, and Massachusetts competed with proslavery forces mainly from the slave-holding state of Missouri to populate the state. Abolitionists settled in towns like Lawrence, Topeka, and Manhattan, while proslavery forces settled in towns like Atchison, Lecompton, and Leavenworth.[1]

From 1855 to 1859 different factions of settlers wrote no less than four different constitutions for the Kansas Territory. The most infamous of these was the 1857 Lecompton Constitution, written by proslavery Democrats and ratified in a September referendum boycotted by abolitionists. In October 1857 abolitionists took control of the territorial legislature and called for a new vote on the Lecompton Constitution. This time, proslavery forces stayed home, and the Lecompton Constitution failed. In 1858 Congress ordered a new vote on the Lecompton Constitution, and in October 1858 abolitionists defeated it again.[2]

In March 1859 voters approved a referendum calling for a constitutional convention to draft a new constitution. In June they elected convention delegates, thirty-five Republicans and seventeen Democrats, who met in July in Wyandotte County. In addition to setting the boundaries of Kansas, a hotly contested issue, the new constitution copied the basic outlines of the Ohio and Indiana constitutions, including a bill of rights, a weak chief executive, a strong bicameral legislature, and a judiciary. Most important, the constitution prohibited slavery, and for this reason Kansas was not accepted into the union until 1861 after the Southern states had seceded from the Union.[3]

Even though all thirty-five Republican delegates to Wyandotte Convention were men, women did participate in discussions. The most prominent of these women was Clarina Irene Howard Nichols, "an activist in abolition, temperance, and women's rights."[4] Only two years after moving to the Kansas Territory, the Vermont native became one of the major organizers of the Wyandotte Convention and was allowed to participate in discussions but not to vote.

Nichols's adeptly promoted women's rights on the basis that women are the "guardian angels of the home," and thus she argued that she should have the "power [to protect] myself and my children, because I do not possess the power which ought to belong to me as a mother."[5] Her use of Christian motherhood to justify women's rights was a bold stroke in a convention dominated by abolitionist men. Due to her influence, the convention granted women "control of real and personal property, their earnings, divorce under certain circumstances, child custody, and a homestead exemption naming women as equal partners."[6] Even though the Wyandotte Constitution did not grant suffrage to women for fear that the U.S. Congress would reject the document, it did give women the right to vote at school meetings.[7]

Reflecting the predominant political culture of the time, which emphasized individual liberty and a distrust in government, the Wyandotte Constitution included only two means to revise or amend it: legislative initiative and constitutional convention.[8] Although the structural aspects of the Wyandotte Constitution survive to this day, most of its sections have been revised over the years, including Article 14, Section 1, outlining the amendment process via legislative initiative.

Through the years Kansas voters have ratified over ninety amendments to the state's constitution.[9] Most of the ninety plus amendments represent relatively small revisions, meant to address court rulings or administrative convenience. However, some are major alterations that change either state government's structure or its powers to regulate citizen actions. Even though there are periods in which cultural forces promoting equality have successfully won constitutional revisions, most of the major modifications are the product of struggles between the political cultures of liberty and order.

MAJOR PERIODS OF CONSTITUTIONAL CHANGE

The Wyandotte Constitution mostly reflects the values of those with a preference toward liberty. For example, the Wyandotte Constitution contained a balanced budget provision and a limitation of one million dollars for debt that could be incurred for public improvement. These provisions meant that libertarians had little reason to propose revising the constitution and many reasons to oppose amendments offered by the prohibitionists, populists, and progressives. Still, those with a preference for liberty did pass a couple of amendments, both designed to limit the activities of the state legislature. In 1875 voters ratified an amendment that limited the state legislature to meeting only every other year (biennial sessions), and in 1901 they ratified an amendment to limit these biennial sessions to ninety days. After WWII voters repealed both of these amendments, thus, allowing the legislature to meet every year starting in January.

Prohibition

Prohibitionists took the lead in demanding constitutional revision in the 1870s. The prohibitionists' actively promoted using state institutions to forbid or restrict the sale and consumption of alcohol. Prohibitionist sentiments were common among abolitionists who migrated from the northeastern states in the 1850s. Delegates at the Wyandotte Convention in 1859 discussed a provision forbidding the production, sale, and consumption of alcohol but in the end decided against it. By the mid-1870s supporters of prohibition became an integral part of the Republican Party and Governor John St. John's base of support. By 1879 prohibitionist forces in the state legislature mustered the two-thirds majority needed to forward the amendment to voters. And in the following year a slim majority of voters approved the amendment, making Kansas the first state to ban the production and sale of alcohol by constitutional amendment.[10]

As noted in chapter 1, the politics of prohibition ebbed and flowed over the years, with much of the attention focused on enforcement issues. In 1934 Kansas voters' preference for order on the issue of alcohol remained strong, clearly rejecting the repeal of prohibition. By 1948, fifteen years after the rest of the nation had passed the 21st Amendment repealing prohibition, Kansas ended its efforts to ban the manufacture and consumption of alcohol by ratifying an amendment to Article 15, Section 9. This revision repealed prohibition but not without a major concession to the forces for moral order. The amendment expressly forbade "open saloons." To get around this provision, the legislature soon passed laws enabling liquor by the drink in "private clubs," which then sold "reciprocal" memberships enabling members to patronize a multitude of clubs.

The debate over the regulation of distilled and fermented liquors is responsible for some of the more colorful personalities from Kansas history. Carrie Nation and the Women's Christian Temperance Union at the beginning of the twentieth century gained national attention for her extralegal vigilante enforcement of prohibition. In the late 1960s her successor emerged in the form of a Methodist minister, the Reverend Richard Taylor, who led the United Dry Forces that after 1971 became Kansans for Life at its Best.[11] The sole purpose of Taylor and his group was to prevent the expansion in Kansas of vice, particularly liquor by the drink and all forms of gambling, including bingo. In 1970 Taylor and the United Dry Forces beat back a constitutional amendment to allow open saloons.

Supplemented by the United Dry Forces newsletter called the *Issue* (circulation 75,000), Taylor used all the tools of mass media to keep Kansas from giving into the temptation of alcohol. He appealed to Kansans' reason by noting the relatively low percentage of alcohol-related traffic fatalities; he enlisted the well-respected conservative radio news anchor Paul Harvey to promote keeping Kansas dry; and of course, he prayed all over the state, including at the state house, that Kansas lawmakers would not give into the forces of sin.[12]

Taylor, however, was fighting an uphill battle. In the 1970s and 1980s Kansas received a black eye in national news outlets for its alcohol restrictions. In some cases the wounds to the state's national image were self-inflicted. For example, in the early 1970s Attorney General Vern Miller, a Democrat, boarded trains traveling through the state to prevent the serving of liquor by the drink. He also unsuccessfully tried to force airlines to stop serving cocktails while flying over the air space of Kansas. The negative backlash from Miller's activities helped to change public opinion. In the late 1970s the wet forces, many of whom were those with a strong preference toward liberty, won surprising victories in the state legislature, and by 1986 the legislature passed, and the voters ratified, an amendment to the Kansas Constitution allowing open saloons.[13] Much to the chagrin of Reverend Taylor, Kansans ratified two other sin amendments in 1986, the lottery and parimutuel betting at horse and dog tracks.[14] But even as Kansas put to bed over one hundred years of strict regulation of alcohol, these new amendments made small but significant concessions to communities favoring moral order. For example, counties in which a majority voted against the amendment in 1986 are allowed to ban open saloons within their county.

Populists and Progressives

Other demands to amend the constitution began to surface with the populist movement, which developed over the decade of the 1880s and peaked in the mid-1890s. The populists promoted a range of constitutional and statutory proposals aimed at instilling equality into Kansas institutions by reforming the party system (primaries, direct election of U.S. senators, and recall), by embedding progressivity into the tax system (progressive income tax and estate tax), and by promoting labor and social reforms (labor unions and child labor laws). Even though the populist were less than successful in enacting their egalitarian agenda, the progressive movement, which gained full strength shortly after the demise of the populists, adopted many of the movement's ideas and added several of their own. Progressives, however, supported many of the populist reforms in the name of establishing a new moral order rather than promoting egalitarian principles. Progressives endorsed fair and efficient government, government decision making in the best interests of the people, and the weakening of political parties, the primary purveyors of political disorder and corruption.

By the early 1900s the "boss-buster" progressives infiltrated the GOP. Over the next thirty years they fought a series of pitched battles with machine Republicans (the "standpatters") who maintained strong ties to railroad interests.[15] Progressives successfully amended the constitution to establish the office of state printer (1904), to provide the governor with the line item veto for appropriations bills (1904), to grant women the right to vote (1912), and to allow for the recall of state officers (1914).

Those with a preference toward liberty maintained a strong presence in the body politic, even at the height of the progressive movement. Thus not all progressive proposals passed the first time they were proposed. In fact, a number of progressive amendments only passed after several years of trying, in some cases long after the progressive movement had faded into the history books. Some of the more interesting long-term battles where progressive ideas eventually won include:

> On five occasions from 1902 to 1930 voters rejected progressive amendments to increase the pay for legislators (the Wyandotte Constitution set these rates, and they had not increased with inflation). Voters would finally approve a pay raise in 1948 and agreed to allow legislators to set their own pay in 1962.[16]
>
> In 1914, 1920, and 1930 voters rejected the progressive's attempts to institute a state income tax. Only with the economic calamity of the Great Depression in 1932 did voters finally approve it.[17]
>
> Progressives proposed a series of measures to introduce a property-tax classification scheme in the early twentieth century. Finally, in 1986 voters ratified the scheme.[18]

No other period of reform in Kansas history matches the breadth of political impact that the progressive movement on Kansas politics had. Like other midwestern states with strong progressive movements (Wisconsin, Iowa, Minnesota, and Nebraska), the ripple effects from this period still linger, influencing the manner in which parties act, leaders are chosen, and public business conducted. Echoes of the progressive movement resounded throughout the twentieth century, with the most significant emerging in the series of "good government" constitutional reforms passed in the 1970s by a new generation of progressives.

The Progressive Resurgence

The good government revisions of the 1970s restructured the state's constitution by modernizing it and eliminating statutory, or legislative sections. The revisions took place in a flurry of nineteen amendments ratified by voters in 1970, 1972, and 1974.[19] Unlike prior periods of reform that often had a strong partisan flavor, bipartisan cooperation marked this period. The reform effort's leaders promoted the revisions in the name of good government, with many of the ideas emanating from a larger national movement to modernize state constitutions. In the 1950s and 1960s the National Municipal League and national commissions such as the Kestnbaum Commission (1955) promoted revising state constitutions in order to better enable states to deal with the expanding scope of national and state governments' activities in the wake of the Great Depression and WWII. With its focus on good government this period of reform follows a path blazed by the progressives sixty years before by seeking to establish political order through changes in the structure of government institutions.

In Kansas the pressure for constitutional revision first started developing momentum in 1957. Democratic Governor George Docking was the first to call for a constitutional convention to address the malapportionment of the state legislature. His call fell on the deaf ears of the mostly rural legislators. In lieu of a convention Docking appointed a committee that included former Governor Alf Landon.[20] However, the committee's report was largely ignored. In the early 1960s Republican Governor John Anderson also appointed a blue ribbon committee, which justified its recommendations based on the 1955 Kestnbaum Commission Report. This committee's report also found little traction with legislative leaders.

Until the mid-1960s the malapportionment of the legislature to favor rural constituencies and legislators was a major stumbling block to constitutional change (see chapter 4 for a more extensive discussion of the urban-rural dimension of malapportionment). Rural legislators viewed all attempts to revise the constitution as a potential threat to the status quo that clearly favored them over the interests of growing urban areas. The U.S. Supreme Court's rulings in *Baker v. Carr* (1962) and *Reynolds v. Sims* (1964) effectively removed this impediment. Together, these rulings dictated that state legislative districts in each respective chamber would be apportioned by an equal number of constituents and that reapportionment would occur at least once every decade after the census is taken. By 1966 both chambers of the state legislature reapportioned districts to meet the requirements of the Supreme Court's rulings. Wichita, Kansas City, Topeka, and other mid-sized towns such as Salina, Lawrence, and Hutchinson won new seats, while sparsely populated counties in north central, western, and southeastern Kansas lost representation.

Like his father, Democratic Governor Robert Docking also called for a constitutional convention shortly after his election in 1966. The request was ignored by legislative leaders. However, unlike in the 1957, legislative leaders decided to appoint their own Citizen's Committee on Constitutional Revision in order to develop a set of recommendations. Because this committee was a legislative creation, it was viewed as more legitimate by state legislators. Most important, the committee decided to support many of the revisions recommended by the two previous gubernatorial commissions.

One of the key questions before the committee was how to pursue so many sweeping revisions to the state's constitution without calling a state constitutional convention? The committee's answer was twofold. First, it assumed the constitutionality of revising an entire section using the legislative initiative process. Indeed, in 1966 voters ratified a revised education article, setting up the Kansas State Board of Education. Second, the committee decided to revise Article 15, Section 1, of the state's constitution to allow up to five amendments to be considered by voters in one election and to allow the legislature to call a special election for the purpose of ratifying amendments to the constitution.

The open saloons amendment and the revision to Article 15, Section 1, appeared on the 1970 general election ballot along with a third amendment to revise a minor aspect of the executive article and the related state militia's article. The open saloons amendment failed, but voters ratified the other two amendments.

After the ratification vote a "taxpayer's court challenge" questioned the validity of these two amendments. The Kansas Supreme Court unanimously ruled in *Moore v. Shanahan* that simultaneously revising two subjects (two articles) with one amendment was a violation of the amendment process. This invalidated the ratified amendment to the executive and the state militia articles. However, by a five to two vote the court upheld the wholesale revision of Article 15, Section 1, using the legislative initiative process. This decision opened the flood gates for other proposed constitutional revisions.[21]

Table 1 summarizes the flood of amendments passed in 1972 and 1974. In 1972 voters ratified eight amendments, the most significant of which revised the executive and judiciary articles. The executive branch revision reduced the number of elected statewide officers from six to four (governor and lieutenant governor, elected together; attorney general; and secretary of state), expanded the terms of office from two to four years with elections occurring during the midterm congressional elections, and gave the governor the power to reorganization cabinet-level agencies. The revision of the judiciary article established a unified state court system and allowed each judicial district to choose between nonpartisan appointment with periodic retention votes for district judges versus partisan elections for district judges. Appendix 1 provides a brief history and description of Kansas' uni-

Table 1: Constitutional Revisions Adopted in 1972 and 1974

Article Revised	Revision Adopted
Amendments Adopted in 1972	
1. Article 1	Revised the entire Executive Article, 4-year term, ERO, and Cabinet
2. Article 3	Revised Judicial article to create a unified state court system, optional appointment of district judges
3. Article 5, Sec 5	Eliminated antiquated dueling provision
4. Article 7	Eliminated statutory language for public institutions and welfare & established tax levy authority for building fund
5. Article 15, Sec11	Eliminated antiquated provision on homesteads for WWI veterans
6. Article 2, Sec 26	Repealed state census
7. Article 10, Sec 3	Repealed provisions on apportionment of legislature
8. Bill of Rights	Repealed antiquated provision for underground railroad
Amendments adopted in 1974	
1. Article 2	Eliminated one representative per county rule and several minor revisions
2. Article 4	Eliminated statutory language associated with recalls
3. Article 5	Eliminated antiquated provisions regarding suffrage of women, minorities, and immigrants
4. Article 10	Provided for apportionment rules and procedures, equality among districts
5. Article 12, Sec 3	Eliminated antiquated language for properties of religious organizations
6. Article 15, Sec 3a	Authorized state regulation of bingo
7. Article 15, Sec 14	Provided for oath of state officers
8. Article 14, Sec 4	Eliminated state printer
9. Article 11	Authorized classification and taxation of motor vehicles

Source: Francis Heller, *The Kansas State Constitution: A Reference Guide* (Westport CT: Greenwood Press, 1992), 32–35.

Table 2: Constitutional Revisions Adopted between 1976 and 1988

Article Revised	Revision Adopted
Amendments Adopted in 1976	
1. Article 11, Sec 12	Revised assessment and taxation of agricultural lands
Amendments Adopted in 1980	
1. Article 14, Sec 1	Made minor revisions to the amendment process
2. Article 13	Eliminated statutory language governing banks
3. Article 11, Sec 9	Authorized the acceptance and expenditure of federal funds for internal improvements
Amendments Adopted in 1986	
1. Article 11, Sec 1	Established of property tax classifications
2. Article 11, Sec 9	Authorized the expenditure of state funds for economic develop projects
3. Article 14, Sec 10	Authorized liquor by the drink
4. Article 15, Sec 3c	Authorized state lottery
5. Article 15, Sec 3b	Authorized pari-mutuel betting
Amendments Adopted in 1988	
1. Article 10, Sec 1a	Authorized federal census data for apportionment, but adjusted numbers to redistribute students and military personnel to hometowns for purposes of state legislative representation

Source: Francis Heller, *The Kansas State Constitution: A Reference Guide* (Westport CT: Greenwood Press, 1992), 32–35.

fied court system. In 1974 voters ratified nine more amendments, the most significant of which addressed the apportionment of the legislature, requiring it to reapportion seats once every ten years.[22]

The reformers also promoted a number of revisions after 1974. Table 2 summarizes the revisions passed between 1976 and 1988. In 1976 and in 1986 voters ratified amendments regarding differentiated property tax assessments for residential, businesses, utilities, and agricultural property. Also in 1986, in addition to the ratification of the three sin amendments (lottery, parimutuel betting, and open saloons, none of which were a part of the progressive agenda), voters approved the expenditure of state and local funds for private sector job creation (economic development).[23]

The Kansas Constitution emerged from this twenty-year period of reform as a modern political document. In making these revisions, the reformers established political order by supplementing powers of the governorship, by unifying the court system, by establishing a property-tax classification system, by removing restrictions on amending the constitution, and by deleting statutory and archaic provisions. The new political order created by these reforms stands in stark contrast to the laissez-faire distrust of centralized state government power exhibited by the framers of the Wyandotte Constitution. A preference for order superseded the individualistic political culture, which had clearly dominated the framers' thoughts when fashioning the state's institutions.

Nonetheless, evident in many of these changes are compromises with the dominant individualist political culture. For example, the judicial amendment allows each judicial district to choose its own method of judge selection (partisan elections versus appointment-retention vote). The gubernatorial article still maintains two other constitutional statewide offices in addition to the governor and lieutenant governor positions, and the governor may only stand for reelection once. Thus while these reforms centralized power and establish order, progressives made concessions to individualistic political culture in order to protect against too great a centralized governmental authority.

The Cases for Equality

The populists, the first and perhaps only major movement for equality to influence state politics, had little success in amending the constitution. Those who have since inherited the mantel of equality continue to struggle to pass amendments to the constitution. Despite this failure, egalitarians are successful in pursuing the enforcement of their values via the court system. In no area is this success more evident than in the area of school finance.

The major earthquake that fundamentally altered school finance in Kansas did not occur until 2005; however, for three and a half decades state courts operated along this fault line. Responding to the *Serrano v. Priest* decision in California and an impending case in Kansas (*Caldwell v. State*, 1972), the Kansas legislature enacted the Kansas School District Equalization Act of 1973.[24] Even though the act did improve the equality of funding among Kansas school districts, many issues remained. In the early 1990s forty school districts filed suit claiming that the School District Equalization Act led to large funding disparities among school districts (*Mock v. Kansas*, 1991). Prior to the scheduled hearing Judge Bullock informed Governor

Joan Finney and legislative leaders of the likely outcome of the case, thus giving the legislature a chance to enact new legislation to remedy funding inequalities among school districts before the Mock case was heard.[25]

In 1992 the state legislature passed the School District Finance and Quality Performance Act. This act established a baseline state aid to school districts that was a weighting formula to take into account the higher cost of educating rural (fewer economies of scale) and special needs (physical and learning disabilities and language) students, a uniform statewide property-tax mill levy for schools, and a Local Option Budget (LOB) for localities to supplement state aid.[26]

A number of school districts, especially those in communities with populations between eight and fifty thousand and those with a large number of at-risk students, felt the new act treated them unfairly. This perception led to another set of court challenges culminating in the second major case *Montoy v. Kansas* (2005). In *Montoy* the court ruled that the weighting formula should be based on actual costs of providing a "suitable" education to all children, especially those who are at risk. The court found that what the legislature had provided was inadequate because funding is based "on former spending levels and political compromise." In its unanimous decision the court ordered the state legislature to "increase" funding for school districts to reflect the "actual costs."[27]

The court rejected the legislature's first attempt to address its ruling in *Montoy*. This rejection led Governor Sebelius in the summer of 2005 to call a special session of the legislature, during which moderate Republicans and Democrats forged a bill that met the demands of the court and provided a total funding package of $290 million in 2005 and $541 million over three years beginning in 2006.[28]

In 2003 Judge Bullock described the legal framework established by the Mock and Montoy cases: "If our Constitution requires the Legislature to establish, maintain, and finance free public schools from public funds for all the school children of Kansas what kind of educational opportunity would you expect the Legislature to be constitutionally required by our courts to provide each individual child? This Court believes the answer you would get is: EQUAL!"[29]

Polar alliance Republicans view these court decisions as the latest example of liberal activist judges illegitimately using the bench to promote liberal values, in this case by funding public schools and the teachers' union. Representative Frank Miller's (R-Independence) reaction is typical of this point of view. He stated that "the only way he would support increasing school spending was if the legislature offers $5,000-per-year vouchers to allow parents to send their children to private schools. Vouchers . . . would inject competition into the education system to force public schools to be more accountable with their money." Miller continued, "The schools very much need reform. . . . I'm talking about major, major reform."[30]

Funding for K–12 education represents over fifty percent of the state's general fund spending. Given this, the forces for equality won a major victory via the courts. There may be other court-based victories for the forces of equality in the offing, but none of these victories will match the magnitude or scale of the *Montoy* decision.

Polar Alliance Amendments

Following in the well-worn path of the prohibitionist and progressive movements, the polar alliance Republicans see amending the constitution as the only viable means for enshrining and protecting their values from being manipulated by activist judges. Polar alliance Republicans promote two types of revisions to the constitution. One type of revisions consists of amendments that ensure the preservation of polar alliance moral values. In 2004 polar alliance Republicans proposed to amend the constitution to ban marriage and civil union between gay or lesbian couples. Surprisingly, this amendment failed to obtain the necessary two-thirds support in the Kansas House during the 2004 legislative session. However, in the aftermath of the 2004 elections, which increased polar alliance Republican numbers in the Kansas House, the amendment passed in the 2005 legislative session. It was then placed on the 2005 municipal elections ballot and was ratified by voters with seventy percent support.

Thus far this is the only polar alliance amendment that is designed to enshrine polar alliance values and that has been forwarded to the voters and ratified. But polar alliance forces have other amendments working their way through the process aimed at limiting what they see as a liberal activist state government. In reaction to two Kansas Supreme Court rulings, the first commuting the death sentences of all death row inmates in Kansas because of incorrect sentencing instructions to jurors (overturned by the U.S. Supreme Court in 2006) and the second declaring the school finance formula unconstitutional, a host of state senators, led by Susan Wagle (R-Wichita), pushed for a constitutional amendment to include senate approval of all gubernatorial appointments to the Kansas Supreme Court. Kansas currently uses the Missouri Plan for selecting supreme court justices. The proposed amendment's stated purpose is to provide a check against the appointment of activist judges by the governor and the Kansas Bar Association. In 2005 the proposed amendment stalled for lack of two-thirds support in the Kansas Senate.

Polar alliance Republicans also promote limiting the authority of the state legislature to pass tax increases beyond a prescribed restriction without voter approval. Commonly referred to as the Taxpayers Bill of Rights, or TABOR, the idea is to limit the growth of state government to the rate of inflation and population increase. Other similar constitutional initiatives regarding taxation propose requiring a two-thirds majority of both legislative chambers to enact any tax rate increase. This proposed amendment has not made it out of committee so far; proponents like Americans for Prosperity promise to keep trying.

Other Major Amendments

Over the course of many years there have been other major amendments to the Kansas Constitution that do not fit easily into any of the reform periods described. Some of these amendments can be classified as simply tinkering with the system in response to immediate political or economic needs. Another set of amendments represents attempts to modernize the constitution in order to address the expanding role of government.

An example of the former occurred in 1873 when legislators and voters ratified an amendment that permanently set the number of senators at 40 and the number of house members to 125 (one representative for each of the 105 counties plus 20 distributed by population). In 1875 voters ratified a constitutional amendment that limited county treasurers and county sheriffs to two consecutive terms of office. In 1931, during the Great Depression when jobs were scarce, voters ratified another amendment eliminating this term limitation.

There are any number of examples of voters ratifying amendments to allow the state to engage in new activities related to governments' expanded role in society. In 1917 and 1928 voters approved special tax levies devoted to building new facilities on university campuses and to supporting the expanding network of roads for automobiles. In 1936 voters ratified an amendment to allow Kansans to participate in federal unemployment programs and Social Security and to enact a sales tax in support of these programs. In 1954, after it became apparent that the biennial ninety-day state legislative session was insufficient to address the state's growing volume of business in the wake of the explosion of federal grant-in-aid programs, voters ratified an amendment to allow the legislature to meet annually with the session on even years limited to a sixty-day budget session. In 1966 voters ratified another revision to allow for a longer session during even years and to allow nonbudgetary legislation to be introduced in even years. In the same amendment voters authorized legislative committees to meet between sessions.

In response to the growing complexity of large urban areas, the legislature passed and the voters ratified home rule for larger cities in 1954. Six years later, an amendment was ratified granting general home-rule powers to all cities.

Of course, political shenanigans also provide the impetus for constitutional change. This motivation was behind the amendment ratified in 1957 that changed the method for appointing supreme court justices. The 1957 amendment was the product of a controversial gubernatorial appointment to the court. After losing the GOP gubernatorial primary, Governor Fred Hall resigned his office, allowing Lieutenant Governor John McCuish to succeed him. Governor McCuish then proceeded to appoint Hall to the supreme court. Smelling a political deal, legislative leaders, editorial writers, and informed citizens cried foul. As a consequence, the legislature and voters accepted a constitutional amendment based on the Missouri Plan for the appointment of supreme court justices. This plan dictates that a nonpartisan committee, comprised of five members of the American Bar Association of Kansas and four gubernatorial appointees, nominates three possible replacements, one of whom the governor must choose. After serving one full year on the court, the new justice faces a retention vote in the next general election. Thereafter the justice faces a retention vote every six years for as long as he or she serves. Since enacted, no supreme court justice has lost a retention vote; however, as noted above, there are some polar alliance Republicans who believe that this court is now displaying too much judicial activism-independence.

The Last Vestiges of 1859: The Bill of Rights

Sections 1 through 20 of the Bill of Rights from the original Wyandotte Constitution remain intact. These twenty sections include equal rights, the right to bear arms, prohibition of slavery, religious liberty, freedom of press and speech, bail, trial of accused, habeas corpus, search and seizure, speedy trial, and trial by jury. Most of these rights are inherit in the federal bill of rights and are common fare in other state constitutions. Francis Heller's *Kansas Constitution* provides a good summary of the major Kansas court cases associated with interpreting these sections.[31]

CONTRASTING THE KANSAS CONSTITUTION WITH OTHERS

State politics scholars typically use two standards to assess state constitutions. The first standard is a normative prescription for a model state constitution (MSC). Model state constitutions gained popularity after WWII as state governments became key players in implementing federal grant-in-aid programs for highways, social welfare, public health, environment, and education.[32] Simply put, these new programs created additional responsibilities and demands on state governments. State institutions designed to meet the demands of the Eighteenth and Nineteenth centuries were inadequate for those of the twentieth.

The second standard is to contrast state constitutions by examining new rights and restrictions as well as by looking at other special governing provisions that have become common place among many states. These rights and provisions are not a part of the U.S. Constitution and as such apply only to citizens within the state.

Some analysts accurately note that a (MSC) is a moving target. What may have seemed like a good idea in 1948 may not be a great idea fifty years later. For example, in 1948 the Committee on State Government's *Model State Constitution* recommended that states adopt the initiative process, thus enabling voters to organize a petition process to place a constitutional amendment on the election ballot. But given California's experience over the past thirty years with the initiative process (starting with Proposition 13), few would recommend this provision today.[33] A further example comes from conservative commentators who add that judicial independence, a characteristic recommended by these models, leads to what they consider to be liberal judicial activism.[34] In this same vein others argue that these models have very limited use because there is limited agreement on what the "model should be."[35] Despite the academic discord regarding the relative merits of a MSC, there are a number of themes that pervade the various models, which have withstood the test of time and thus provide useful benchmarks for evaluating the Kansas Constitution.

Table 3 compares the basic provisions of the model state constitution with the Kansas Constitution. Given the extensive number of revisions in the 1970s, the Kansas Constitution meets many of prescriptions of a MSC, but the Kansas Constitution does fall short in a number of ways. Kansas governors serve four-year terms but are limited to two successive terms. Kansas governors do have cabinet-level agencies with broad appointment powers, but Kansas still elects other statewide officials, and there are many independent boards and commissions.[36] The powers of the governor's office are improved, but they still do not meet MSC standards.

Table 3: Model State Constitution and Kansas Constitution

Model Constitution	Kansas Constitution
Executive Branch	**Executive Branch**
4-year term, unlimited	4-year term, 2 terms
Veto & line-item veto, 2/3rd override	Veto & line-item veto 2/3rd override
Governor w/ Lieutenant Governor only elected state officials	Governor w/ Lieutenant Governor, Secretary of State, & Attorney General constitutionally elected offices
Cabinet w/ broad appt powers Executive Reorganization Orders	Cabinet w/ broad appt powers Executive Reorganization Orders
Few independent boards	Many independent boards and commissions
Legislative Branch	**Legislative Branch**
Annual sessions, no day limit full-time w/ appropriate pay	Annual sessions, 90-day limit part-time w/ minimal pay
Bicameral, minimum number of legislators	Bicameral, 40 senators & 125 representatives
Legislative Coordinating Council	Legislative Coordinating Council
Judicial Branch	**Judicial Branch**
Qualified judges appointed by governor, senate approval optional	Superior and appellate court judges selected by Missouri method w/ retention votes
	District judges selected by gubernatorial appointment or partisan election
Unified court system	Unified court system
Constitution	**Constitution**
Bill of Rights	Bill of Rights
Structure of institutions	Structure of institutions
No statutory provisions	Few statutory provisions
Short length	About 12,000 words

Sources: Committee on State Government, *Model State Constitution*, 5th ed. (New York NY: National Municipal League, 1948); Francis Heller, *The Kansas State Constitution: A Reference Guide* (Westport CT: Greenwood Press, 1992).

Table 4: Rights and Restrictions in Other States and Kansas (2005)

New Rights & Restrictions	Adoption by Other States	Adoption in Kansas
Privacy	8-Constitution, 16-Statute	None
Sexual Discrimination	19-Constitution, 21-Statute	None
Disabled Persons	6-Constitution, 35-Statute	Statute
Crime Victims Rights	26-Constitution, 21-Statute	Constitution
Taxpayer Rights	2-Constitution, 27-Statute	None
Gay Marriage Restriction	19-Constitution, 23-Statute	Constitution

Sources: Robert L. Maddex, *State Constitutions of the United States* (Washington DC: Congressional Quarterly Press, 1998) xxxvi–xxxviii; Wikipedia, "Same-Sex Marriage in the United States," http://en.wikipedia.org/, May 17, 2005), and updated by authors.

With regard to the legislative branch Kansas falls very short of the MSC. Kansas maintains a citizen-legislator model rather than the professional legislator model. The Kansas legislature meets once a year, but even-year sessions are limited to ninety days while odd-year sessions are not limited but by tradition generally adjourn after ninety to one hundred days. While the Kansas Senate has 40 members, the Kansas House has 125, a number the MSC considers too large for smooth operation.

An MSC usually prescribes that the selection and retention of state judges should ensure the independence of the judicial branch from the whims of partisan politics. Amendments passed in 1957 and in 1974 dictate that supreme court justices are selected via the Missouri Plan, while district state court judges can be chosen by partisan election or gubernatorial appointment with periodic retention votes.

Finally, the state constitution has all of the basic components suggested by the MSC and generally does not enshrine statutory laws in constitutional super majorities. A simple but effective indication of how well the Kansas Constitution follows the MSC is to count the number of words contained in the constitution. With just over twelve thousand words, the Kansas Constitution is one of the shortest in the United States, well below the average of thirty-thousand words.[37]

As noted above, states have been adding new rights and restrictions that go beyond the Bill of Rights of the U.S. Constitution. Table 4 shows a breakdown of these new civil rights and restrictions according to how many other states have adopted each provision (by constitutional amendment or by statute) and the status of its adoption in Kansas.

Table 5: Constitutional Provisions in Other States and Kansas (2005)

Constitutional Provisions	Adoption by Other States	Adoption in Kansas
Balanced Budget	39-Constitution, 6-Statute	Constitution
Popular Initiative*	18-Constitution	None
Term Limits**	13-Constitution, 3-Statute	None
Home Rule	39-Constitution, 7-Statute	Constitution

* Initiatives to amend the Constitution.

** Term limits in California, Massachusetts, Nebraska, and Oregon were struck down by their state supreme courts. Idaho's state legislature repealed its term limits in 2002.

Sources: Robert L. Maddex, State Constitutions of the United States (Washington DC: Congressional Quarterly Press, 1998); National Conference of State Legislatures, "The Initiative and Referendum States" (www.ncsl.org/programs/legman/elect/irstates.htm, October 10, 2002); Thomas R. Dye, Politics in States and Communities, 10th ed. (Upper Saddle River NJ: Prentice Hall, 2000), 47; U.S. Term Limits, "State Legislative Term Limits" (http://www.termlimits.org/Current_Info/State_TL/index.html, May 26, 2005).

Of the six new rights and restrictions the Kansas Constitution includes only two: A crime victims' bill of rights and a restriction prohibiting gay and lesbian marriages. In 1992 voters ratified the crime victims' rights amendment as recommended by the Victims' Rights Task Force (Article 15, Section 15).[38] The gay marriage amendment passed in the legislature and ratified by voters in 2005 defines marriage as only applying to "one man and one woman" and prohibits the legal recognition of civil unions for gay couples. By state statute Kansas has laws protecting the rights of disabled individuals.

States have also been active in reforming the manner in which they govern. Table 5 examines the adoption of a balanced budget requirement, popular initiative, term limits for state legislators, and home rule for localities. Term limits in states are tied to whether the voters can directly amend the state constitution through the initiative process.[39] Kansas has not adopted an initiative process, so it is not surprising that it also does not have term limits. Since becoming a state, Kansas has required a balanced budget and has limited the types of debts the state may incur. Finally, Kansas adopted home rule for large cities (as designated by the legislature) in 1954 and extended home rule to all cities in 1961. The state legislature by statute granted home rule powers to counties in 1974.

The Kansas Constitution follows many of the basic prescriptions laid out in the MSC framework. Over the past fifty years more power and independence have been vested in the gubernatorial and judicial levels, and the constitution has become relatively free of the statutory language that typically plagues other state constitutions. From a comparative state constitutional perspective, Kansans ratified two amendments that are common among states, restrictions on gay marriage and crime victims' rights. However, other amendments such as a taxpayers' bill of rights, privacy rights, or a prohibition against sexual discrimination are still working their way through the process.[40]

POLITICAL CULTURE AND THE FUTURE
OF THE KANSAS CONSTITUTION

The Kansas Constitution is constantly evolving so as to fulfill the governmental requirements of each succeeding generation of Kansans. Prohibitionists, progressives, new progressives, and now polar alliance Republicans have each taken their turns amending and revising the constitution to better reflect their values.

The future of the relationship between the Kansas Constitution and the state's dominant political cultures may be shaped by two cultural forces, each using its own method to pursue change. Those with a preference for equality will most likely continue to use the state court system to enforce equality, especially in the area of school finance. Polar alliance Republicans, on the other hand, will pursue constitutional amendments to enshrine their moral and economic values in the constitution.

Polar alliance Republicans, however, are not likely to be the last group to press its case for constitutional revision. As each successive generation moves through the body politic, it will shape the Kansas Constitution and thus the ability of state government to enact and execute policies. As in the past some of these amendments may reorganize state institutions to become more modern. Other amendments may add rights such as the crime victims' bill of rights or prohibit individual liberty like the prohibition of intoxicating drink and of gay marriage. Still other amendments may act to reverse the handiwork of a previous generation (prohibition, term limits, biennial legislative sessions). No matter, the constitution will continue to evolve, reflecting the values of those who must live under its rules.

CHAPTER THREE

Elections and Political Parties

Since Kansas became a state in 1861, the Republican Party has dominated the state's political landscape by winning the vast majority of county, state, and national offices. For many, Kansas is the epitome of a "red" state.[1] The state is so dominated by the GOP that neither of the major parties' presidential hopefuls bother to campaign in Kansas. This portrayal, however, is akin to the depiction of Kansas as a "flat" state. It's an easy shorthand description that in some places is accurate but that for much of Kansas misses the true variability of the state's topography.

Far from being a one-party red state, Kansas is more accurately a one-party state with episodes of two-party competition.[2] To be sure, with the exception of two short interludes, Democrats have always been in the minority. Nonetheless, Democrats do win elections in Kansas, especially at the gubernatorial level when intraparty feuds break out within the Republican Party. This chapter examines elections and political parties in Kansas by analyzing the development of the Kansas party system. This analysis focuses on the influences of Republican factionalism and national party alignments on the state party system. The analysis suggests that national party alignments play a more important role than previous scholarship suggests. The chapter concludes by analyzing the historical development of the state party organizations in Kansas. The data for this chapter come primarily from historical election returns.

PREVIOUS SCHOLARSHIP ON KANSAS ELECTIONS

Beset by factionalism, Kansas Republicans have a tradition of providing openings for Democratic gubernatorial candidates to win. Republican factionalism erupted during prohibition (1880s), the populist (1890s) and progressive (1900–1930) uprisings, and over right-to-work legislation (1950s), all leading to the election of Democratic governors.[3] The outcome of the 2002 gubernatorial election seems to represent another example of this political pattern. In 2002 Kansas Democrats nominated for governor Kathleen Sebelius, the sitting insurance commissioner. Although the insurance commissioner's office is not a port that has launched a thousand successful gubernatorial campaigns, Sebelius was the sole Democratic statewide officeholder remaining after a decade of Republican dominance in the 1990s. Despite the GOP's successes, factionalism once again afflicted the Republicans, this time over the abortion issue, the role of religion in public life, and the teaching of evolution in public schools. Many moderate Republicans felt uncomfortable supporting their nominee Tim Shallenberger, the former speaker of the Kansas House and a leader of the polar alliance Republicans. Thus in September and October of 2002 ominous yard signs popped up reading "Another Republican For Sebelius." Sebelius won by a comfortable margin (about fifty-four percent). In an replay of 2002 she won easily again in 2006, this time over Republican State Senator Jim Barnett.

Over the years only a handful of scholarly treatments have addressed elections in Kansas. The most prominent and systematic of these studies is the historical analysis of Marvin Harder.[4] Harder, writing in 1989, suggests that two eras divide Kansas' electoral history: the pre-1950s period and the post-1950s to late 1980s period. GOP domination and Democratic marginalization marked the pre-1950s period. The Democrats only won a few gubernatorial contests when factional conflict erupted within the GOP.[5]

Harder argues that during the period between the 1950s to the late 1980s, Kansas became more like the rest of the United States. Voters moved away from the parties, developing weaker party attachments or becoming independent. At the same time candidate characteristics became more important for determining election outcomes. Some scholars refer to this process as a party dealignment, which in Kansas made the state more competitive. Democratic candidates for governor and other offices started competing with Republicans on their own merits.

From Harder's historical framework one can extrapolate that the Kansas party system entered a third electoral era, also characterized by Democratic marginalization, albeit perhaps a milder version compared to the first era. The rise of polar alliance Republicans in 1994 restructured party dynamics. As early as 1974 Republican U.S. Senator Dole appealed to a newly emerging pro-life movement to win a close election against Representative Roy, a Democrat and obstetrician. In 1980 Reagan officially opened the Republican Party to pro-life forces at the national level, while Rev. Robertson's

Table 6: Election Defeats of Republican Candidates for Governor, 1859–2006

1882 John St. John (R) loses to George Glick (D)	German-speaking Republicans are disillusioned with incumbent St. John for supporting the constitutional amendment on prohibition, ratified by voters in 1880. Still other Republicans are upset with St. John for seeking an unprecedented third term. Glick loses reelection bid in 1884.
1890s Populist uprising: Lorenzo Lewelling (P) wins in 1892; John Leedy (P/D) wins in 1896	Farmers' Alliance mobilizes around commodity prices, railroad fees, mortgage rates, and the gold standard. New populist party forms, siphoning off GOP support among farmers. Republican gubernatorial candidates lose in both 1892 and 1896. There is also a pitched battle between Populists and Republicans for control of the state legislature in the 1890s.
1912 Authur Capper (R) loses to George Hodges (D)	Republicans are divided into progressive and "standpat" camps, the latter group often aligned with railroad interests. Progressive Republican Capper loses to Hodges as standpatters abandon the GOP ticket. Democrats also take control of both houses of the state legislature for first and only time in state history. William Allen White, upset with the standpatters, promotes the development of the Progressive Party following lead of Teddy Roosevelt, but Capper stays in the GOP and defeats Hodges in 1914 rematch.
1922 William Morgan (R) loses to Jonathan Davis (D)	Davis's win attributed to farm recession, aggravation over incumbent Republican governor Allen's Industrial Court, and lingering progressive-standpatter disputes. Newspaper editor Morgan of Hutchinson is aligned with standpatters. Davis loses reelection bid in 1924.
1930 Frank Hauke (R) loses to Harry Woodring (D)	Woodring wins a three-way race in which Dr. John Brinkley runs an independent write-in campaign for governor by appealing to the downtrodden and growing numbers of unemployed and by promoting an array of social reforms in the aftermath of the stockmarket crash and the beginning of the Great Depression. Standpatter Hauke defeats progressive Republican governor Reed in the primary as the incumbent's arrogance alienates most GOP leadership. In 1932 Woodring is beaten by Republican Alf Landon, with Brinkley again in the race.
1936 Will West (R) loses to Walter Huxman (D)	Huxman aligns himself with FDR and benefits from FDR's national landslide over native son Alf Landon. GOP factionalism does not factor into West's loss. Huxman loses in 1938.
1956 Warren Shaw (R) loses to George Docking (D)	Progressive Republican Governor Hall vetoes "right-to-work" legislation supported by the Republican legislature and sparks other intraparty feuds. Shaw beats Hall in the GOP primary, and the fis-

sure allows Docking to win. Docking wins reelection in 1958 and becomes the first incumbent Democratic governor to do so in the state's history.

1966 William Avery (R) loses to Robert Docking (D)	Governor Avery promotes increased taxes to support expanded education and social services. Robert Docking, son of George Docking, wins by campaigning against tax increases and for "austere but adequate" budgets. Docking succeeds in winning reelection three more times, becoming the first and only Kansas governor to win third and fourth terms in office.
1978 Robert Bennett (R) loses to John Carlin (D)	Incumbent Governor Bennett, an urbane and articulate Johnson County attorney, is perceived as distant by many voters, particularly in western Kansas. This perception, coupled with prospective utility rate hikes associated with the opening of Wolf Creek nuclear power facility, allows John Carlin, an underfinanced challenger, to pull off an upset. Carlin wins a second term in 1982 by promoting a severance tax, a position popular in eastern Kansas but not in western Kansas.
1990 Mike Hayden (R) loses to Joan Finney (D)	Moderate Governor Mike Hayden is challenged in the GOP primary by real estate agent Nestor Weigand over property tax increases resulting from property classification and reappraisal and support of abortion rights. Hayden wins the battle but loses the war. In the general election, anti-abortion supporters voted for pro-life Democrat Joan Finney. Democrats also take control of the Kansas House. Facing certain defeat, Finney chooses not to run for reelection in 1994, becoming the only governor to serve one term and not seek reelection.
2002 Tim Shallenburger (R) loses to Kathleen Sebelius (D)	House Speaker Tim Shallenburger leads polar alliance Republicans to control of the Kansas House in 1995, and in 2002, runs for governor and beats two moderates in the GOP primary. However, he is unable to rally moderate Republicans to support him in the general election and loses to Sebelius. In a repeat of the 2002 election, Sebelius easily beats Jim Barnett in 2006 with 58 percent of the vote, one of the most lopsided Democratic victories in the state's history, second only to Docking's reelection in 1972.

Sources: Marvin A. Harder, "Electoral Politics in Kansas: A Historical Perspective," in Marvin A. Harder, ed., *Politics and Government in Kansas* (Topeka KS: The University of Kansas, 1989); and authors.

1988 presidential campaign and Operation Rescue's Summer of Mercy in 1991 galvanized Christian conservatives into supporting the GOP. In 1994 polar alliance Republicans took control of the state house of representatives and the Kansas Republican State Party and elected two polar alliance U.S. representatives, Todd Tiahrt in the Wichita area and Vince Snowbarger in suburban Kansas City.

Table 6 summarizes Harder's historical analysis of Democratic gubernatorial victories and adds the most recent elections of Democratic governors to his analysis. From 1882 (St. John loses to Glick) to 1930 (Hauke loses to Woodring), Republican gubernatorial candidates lost only when significant factionalization divided Republicans or when third party candidates parsed the GOP constituency. Intraparty factionalization is evident in 1882 when prohibitionists and antiprohibitionists unseated St. John, and in 1912 and 1922 when the conflicts between progressives and the standpatters helped Democratic candidates win. The affects of third party candidates are apparent in the 1890s and 1930. In 1892 and 1896 the populist candidate (Lewelling) and the populist-Democratic candidate (Leedy) are the beneficiaries of Republican discord. In 1930 the infamous Dr. John Brinkley lured voters insecure about the emerging depression to his write-in campaign, splintering the GOP vote and enabling the election of the Democratic candidate Woodring.

In 1936, for the first time, Democrats won the governorship without the aid of a conflict among Republicans. Democrat Huxman beat Republican West by attaching himself to the coattails of FDR. A factional conflict within the GOP between Hall supporters (moderate Republicans) and anti-Hall opponents (conservative Republicans) over the issue of right-to-work legislation facilitated George Docking's election in 1956, but his reelection in 1958 marked the first time in the state's history that a Democratic governor won a second term. In 1966 George Docking's son Robert took advantage of a GOP dispute over taxes to win the first of four straight elections. In 1978 Democrat Carlin won office by taking advantage a Republican incumbent weakened by questions concerning utility rate increases related to the construction of the Wolf Creek Nuclear Power Plant. However, neither Docking nor Carlin won their elections because of intense Republican factional disputes (see chapter 5 for a more detailed discussion).

A GOP factional dispute did erupt in 1990 when Republican Governor Hayden lost his reelection bid. Signaling a major shift in the politics of Kansas, a coalition of right-to-life and antitax groups came together to support his primary challenger and then to support his pro-life Democratic opponent, Finney. Although the Democrats benefited in this election from the disaffection of Republicans, this gain would prove to be short-lived. After the Summer of Mercy in 1991 right-to-life forces made concerted efforts to infiltrate the organizational and primary election structures of the Kansas Republican Party. Their considerable success created a bifurcated Republican Party in which polar alliance Republicans occupy the economic and social conservative wings of the party and moderate Republicans occupy the middle.[6] Chapter 1 discusses the differences among moderates and polar alliance forces in the Republican Party.

The factionalism between polar alliance and moderate Republicans manifested itself in the 2002 GOP gubernatorial primary. The polar alliance candidate Shallenberger beat back the challenge of two moderate candidates to win the party's nomination. In the general election, however, Democrat Sebelius beat Shallenberger because of his inability to woo the support of enough moderate Republicans and independents.[7] The 2006 gubernatorial election repeated the 2002 election as conservative Republican Barnett failed to rally moderate GOP support to wage an effective campaign against the popular Democratic governor.

Even though GOP factionalization has a long history of influencing gubernatorial contests, this factionalism can influence elections in other arenas. In 1996 Democrat Moore beat 3rd district (Kansas City area) Republican U.S. Representative Snowbarger. Snowbarger, a prototypical polar alliance Republican, lost the support of independents and some moderates in Johnson County. Since 1996 polar alliance and moderate Republican challengers continue to face off in primary battles in which the main beneficiary is Moore. Despite being in an overwhelming Republican district, Moore won his first three reelection bids by less than fifty-three percent of the two-party vote. However, since 2004 his margins have grown more safe (fifty-five and sixty-five percent).

Harder's factional framework for understanding electoral politics seems appropriate at the gubernatorial level, but there is reason to question how well it applies to state legislature, U.S. Senate, and U.S. presidential elections in Kansas. Allan Cigler and Burdett Loomis examined a number of indicators of partisan change, including party registration data, a 1988 survey of 362 Kansans, and major election outcomes. They found electoral patterns that support Harder's analysis but also noted the influences of national forces on Kansas party politics. The New Deal in the 1930s led to a temporary increase in Democratic officeholding, and Reagan's popularity in 1980s led to an increase in GOP registrations and a decrease in the percentage of independents.[8]

Figures 6, 7, and 8 update some of the data analyzed by Cigler and

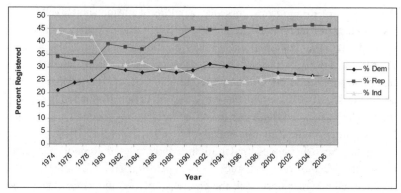

Fig. 6. Voter Registration by Party Identification, 1974–2006

Source: From Allan Cigler and Burdett Loomis, "Kansas: Two-Party Competition in a One-Party State," in Maureen Moakley, ed., *Party Realignment and State Politics* (Columbus OH: Ohio State University Press, 1992); and Kansas Secretary of State, 2007.

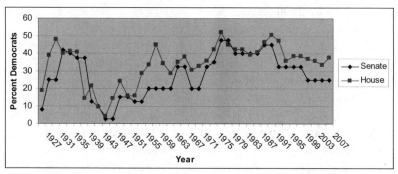

Fig. 7. Percentage of Democrats in the State Legislature, 1927–2007

Source: From Allan Cigler and Burdett Loomis, "Kansas: Two-Party Competition in a One-Party State," in Maureen Moakley, ed., *Party Realignment and State Politics* (Columbus OH: Ohio State University Press, 1992); and U.S. Census Bureau, *Statistical Abstract of the United States: 1987 to 2007* (Washington DC: Government Printing Office, 2007); and http://www.census.gov/statab/.

Loomis. Figure 6 focuses on party registration; figure 7 depicts the percentage of seats controlled by the Democrats in the state legislature; and figure 8 shows the percentage of Republican votes for presidential and gubernatorial elections.

Figure 6 illustrates that despite the election of Sebelius in 2002 and 2006 and Morrison in 2006, from 2000 through 2006 Democrats continued to lose ground in party registrations. This decline suggests that the oft-cited conversion of moderate Republicans to Democrats has not translated into change at the grassroots level.

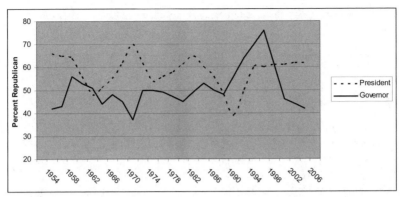

Fig. 8. Percentage of Republican Votes for President and Governor, 1956–2006
Source: From Allan Cigler and Burdett Loomis, "Kansas: Two-Party Competition in a One-Party State," in Maureen Moakley, ed., *Party Realignment and State Politics* (Columbus OH: Ohio State University Press, 1992); and Kansas Secretary of State, 2007.

Figure 7 underscores the ties between Democratic gains in the state legislature and FDR's victories in 1932 and 1936 and to the period between 1966 and 1991 when Kansas Democrats had a string of gubernatorial victories beginning with Robert Docking. Following these periods, the Democrats lost many of their gains and returned to levels of representation of below forty percent. Significantly, periods of GOP factionalism do not appear to benefit state legislative Democrats. In the mid-1990s and 2000s, the period coinciding with the rise of polar alliance Republicans, Democrats sustained a sharp decline in the percentage of Democratic state legislators in both chambers.

Figure 8 exhibits some support for Harder's contention that party attachments may have less significance in the modern era. Even when the Kansas GOP splits into factions for gubernatorial elections (1956, 1990, 2002, and 2006), Republican presidential voting percentages run in the opposite direction from the gubernatorial level. Taken together, all three figures suggest that the GOP factionalization hypothesis may primarily apply to the election of Democratic governors; presidential and state legislative election outcomes appear to be unaffected.

Table 7 takes a different perspective on the extent to which Harder's factionalization hypothesis applies to offices other than the governor and the U.S. House. The table lists the winners of each election, their winning percentage of votes, and their political party for the offices of the president, U.S. senator, and governor since 1912, the first year that senators were popularly elected. The list of senators and governors reads like a Who's Who of Kansas

Table 7: Gubernatorial, U.S. Senator, and Presidential Winners in Kansas, 1912–2006

Year	Governor	Party	Winning %	Senator	Party	Winning %	President	Party	Winning %
1912	G. Hodges	D	46.6	W. Thompson	D	49.3	W. Wilson	D	39.3
1914	A. Capper	R	39.7	C. Curtis	R	35.5			
1916	A. Capper	R	60.8				W. Wilson	D	50
1918	H. J. Allen	R	66.4	A. Capper	R	63.7			
1920	H. J. Allen	R	58.4	C. Curtis	R	64	W. Harding	R	64.8
1922	J. M. Davis	D	50.9						
1924	B. S. Paulen	R	49	A. Capper	R	70.1	C. Coolidge	R	61.5
1926	B. S. Paulen	R	63.3	C. Curtis	R	63.6			
1928	C. M. Reed	R	65.6				H. Hoover	R	72
1930	H. Woodring	D	35	A. Capper	R	61.1			
1930				G. McGill **	D	50			
1932	A. Landon	R	34.8	G. McGill	D	45.7	F. Roosevelt	D	53.6
1934	A. Landon	R	53.5						
1936	W. Huxman	D	51.1	A. Capper	R	51	F. Roosevelt	D	53.7
1938	P. Ratner	R	52.1	C. M. Reed	R	56.2			
1940	P. Ratner	R	49.6				W. Willkie	R	56.9
1942	A. Schoeppel	R	56.7	A. Capper	R	57.1			
1944	A. Schoeppel	R	65.7	C. M. Reed	R	57.8	T. E. Dewey	R	60.3
1946	F. Carlson	R	53.5						
1948	F. Carlson	R	57	A. Schoeppel	R	54.9	T. E. Dewey	R	53.6
1950	E. F. Arn	R	53.8	F. Carlson	R	54.3			
1952	E. F. Arn	R	56.3				Eisenhower	R	68.8
1954	F. Hall	R	53	A. Schoeppel	R	56.3			
1956	G. Docking	D	55.5	F. Carlson	R	57.9	Eisenhower	R	65.4
1958	G. Docking	D	56.5						
1960	J. Anderson	R	55.5	A. Schoeppel	R	54.6	R. Nixon	R	60.4
1962	J. Anderson	R	53.4	F. Carlson	R	57.9			
1962				J. Pearson **	R	56.2			

electoral politics. Starting in the early 1900s through the mid-1900s, Capper, Landon, and Curtis, all Republicans, dominated the state. Capper served two terms as governor (1915–19) and five terms as U.S. senator (1919–49); Curtis became vice president (1929–33); and Landon became the Republican presidential nominee (1936), only to lose in a landslide to FDR.

After WWII a new set of Republican leaders emerged at the U.S. senatorial level, including Carlson, Pearson, Kassebaum, and Dole. While all four had distinguished senatorial records, Dole rose above the others of his era. He became the vice presidential nominee for Gerald Ford in 1976. In the 1980s he became the chair of the Senate Finance Committee, then the

Year	Governor	Party	Winning %	Senator	Party	Winning %	President	Party	Winning %
1964	W. H. Avery	R	50.9				L. Johnson	D	54.1
1966	R. Docking	D	54.8	J. Pearson	R	56.2			
1968	R. Docking	D	51.9	B. Dole	R	60.1	R. Nixon	R	54.8
1970	R. Docking	D	54.3						
1972	R. Docking	D	62	J. Pearson	R	71.4	R. Nixon	R	67.7
1974	R. Bennett	R	49.5	B. Dole	R	50.9			
1976							G. Ford	R	52.5
1978	J. Carlin	D	49.4	N. Kassebaum	R	53.9			
1980				B. Dole	R	63.8	R. Reagan	R	57.9
1982	J. Carlin	D	53.2						
1984				N. Kassebaum	R	76	R. Reagan	R	66.3
1986	M. Hayden	R	51.9	B. Dole	R	70			
1988							G. H. W. Bush	R	55.8
1990	J. Finney	D	48.6	N. Kassebaum	R	73.6			
1992				B. Dole	R	62.7	G. H. W. Bush	R	38.9
1994	B. Graves	R	64.1						
1996				P. Roberts	R	62	B. Dole	R	54.3
1996				S. Brownback**	R	53.9			
1998	B. Graves	R	73.4	S. Brownback	R	65.3			
2000							G. W. Bush	R	58
2002	K. Sebelius	D	52.9	P. Roberts	R	82.5			
2004				S. Brownback	R	69.2	G. W. Bush	R	62
2006	K. Sebelius	D	57.9						

** Won in Special Election

Source: *Guide to U.S. Elections* (Congressional Quarterly Press: Washington DC, 2007).

minority leader of the Republicans in the Senate, and finally in 1995 the majority leader. In 1996 he won the GOP nomination for president, only to lose to President Clinton. Since Dole's retirement Pat Roberts and Sam Brownback have become national leaders. Brownback ran for president in 2008 but suspended his candidacy before the Iowa primary.

By comparison, the Democrats have had only limited success in winning a U.S. Senate seat. Since 1912 only two Democrats have won: Thompson, who served for one term beginning in 1913, and McGill, who won a special election in 1930 and reelection in 1932. Otherwise, Republicans dominate U.S. Senate contests. All of these results suggest that there may be another dynamic undergirding the electoral system in Kansas in addition to the factionalization of the Republicans.

A party alignment approach provides another means to understand the dynamics undergirding electoral politics in Kansas. A party alignment is defined as an extended period of relative political stability during which the competitive relationship between the major parties—defined along a continuum of Republican Party domination to two-party competition to Democratic Party domination—remains consistent and the coalitions of voters aligned with each party are dependable. Stability, consistency, and dependability are relative terms that imply if all variables predicting an election outcome are held constant (candidate factors, the economy, other issues), an election should follow the "normal" voting patterns associated with the existing party alignment.

Party alignment changes when a substantial and long-term shift in the party allegiance of the coalition of voters associated with the parties occurs. This shift usually alters the competitive balance of the two major parties and sometimes results in policy change, but neither of these two outcomes is required for a realignment to occur.[9] However, a one-time change in voting patterns does not constitute a long-term shift.

Party Systems in Kansas: New Framework

This theory of party alignments and party system change aids the analysis of county-level voting patterns for president, U.S. senator, and governor from 1900 to 2004.[10] For this analysis the GOP percentage of two-party votes is calculated by dividing the total votes cast for the GOP candidate in a county by the total votes cast in the county for the Republican and Democratic candidates.[11] The phrase "the structure of Republican voting" refers to consistent pattern of Republican two-party vote associated with each alignment era. The findings from this analysis are presented in this chapter through a series of county-level maps. Shades of blue represent Democratic leaning counties and shades of red represent Republican leaning counties. Green represents a county where there is strong two-party competition.

In analyzing these county-level data, a striking and important pattern emerges. The structure of Republican voting for president, U.S. senator, and governor in counties are very similar. The correlations among the Republican voting for all three are over eighty-five percent. Because of the im-

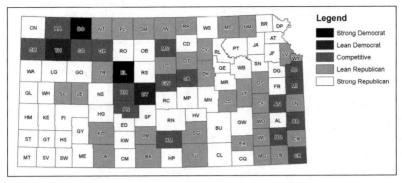

Fig. 9. Post–Civil War / Progressive Party Alignment
Source: ICPSR.

portance of Harder's previous work at the gubernatorial level, the findings of this analysis focus on gubernatorial contests.

Contrary to Harder's analysis, the structure of Republican voting for all three offices follows the ebb and flow of national party alignments. James L. Sundquist and others have defined these national alignments as well as the critical elections that signify the end of an old alignment and the beginning of a new one. From 1896 to 1930 the nation was in the post–Civil War / Progressive alignment. This party alignment also included the progressive era. Even though the progressives helped shape these politics, the basic structure of voting was established in the aftermath of the 1896 elections between the populist Democrat William Jennings Bryan and Republican William McKinley.

Figure 9 and table 8 show just how uncompetitive the Democrats were during the post–Civil War / Progressive alignment. As one would expect, the state is mostly Republican during this era. One region of Republican strength centers in the northeast corridor from Douglas County to Riley County. These strong Republican ties trace back to the settlement patterns of the Free Staters, primarily from New England.[12] The southwest part of the state tends to be the most Republican region, reflecting the party attachment of its rural agrarian population. Only a few counties, most notably Ellis and Decatur counties in the northwest part of the state, are Democratic strongholds. Democrats also have a foothold in Ellsworth, Barton, Rush, and Pawnee counties. All of these counties in the west had some combination of large enclaves of German and Volga-German immigrants and large railroad yards.

All of the major metropolitan counties lean Republican, but the Democrats show signs of being competitive in Sedgwick, Leavenworth, and Craw-

Table 8: Regression Analyses of Republican Normal Vote for Governor on Selected Demographic Characteristics, by Major Party Alignment

	b	Beta	t-stat
Post-Civil War / Progressive Regression with 1910 Demographic Variables			
Constant	**9.343**		**2.642**
% For Parents	-1.718	-0.126	-1.290
% Pop Change	0.003	0.141	1.457
% Urban	-0.289	-0.101	-0.636
Density per Mile	**-9.478**	-0.423	**-2.659**
% White	**-0.002**	-0.345	**-2.603**
Adj R-Square	**0.089**		
F-Statistic	**3.021**		
New Deal Regression with 1970 Demographic Variables			
Constant	**-2.698**		**-2.757**
% black	-0.016	-0.074	-0.875
% Hispanic	-0.056	-0.072	-1.017
% Pop Change	**0.047**	0.762	**8.017**
Avg. Age	**0.124**	0.553	**5.150**
Per Cap Income	-0.005	-0.081	-1.109
% Blue Collar	**-0.043**	-0.346	**-4.364**
% Urban	0.003	0.066	0.565
Adj R-Square	**0.666**		
F-Statistic	**30.691**		
New Right Regression with 1990 Demographic Variables			
Constant	-1.268		-1.466
% black	**-0.085**	-0.589	**-7.283**
% Hispanic	**0.087**	0.326	**5.133**
% Pop Change	-0.009	-0.153	-1.467
Avg. Age	-0.005	-0.016	-0.166
Per Cap Income	**0.111**	0.344	**3.487**
% Blue Collar	-0.010	-0.081	-1.230
% Urban	**-1.129**	-0.312	**-2.842**
Adj R-Square	**0.703**		
F-Statistic	**36.125**		

Bolded coefficients are significant at the .05 level.

All analyses are weighted by population. All analyses have an N = 105.

ford counties. The Democrats also maintain a foothold in Johnson County, which at the turn of the twentieth century was a lightly populated rural county southwest of Kansas City. One fact above all underscores the GOP domination of the state during this era: in 99 of the 105 counties the GOP could rely on greater than fifty percent of the two-party vote for governor.

Table 8 shows the demographic profile of the post–Civil War / Progressive alignment by regressing several variables from the 1910 U.S. Census for Kansas counties on the average level of GOP two-party support.[13]

The backbone of the GOP is found in the more rural communities with lower densities of population. The party of Lincoln also did well in counties with a larger percentages of blacks, a finding that explains the negative relationship between the percentage of whites and GOP support. The percentage of the population with foreign-born parents, population change, and the percent of urban population did not significantly relate to the structure of GOP voting in this alignment era.[14]

The establishment of the New Deal party alignment occurs after the onslaught of the Great Depression in 1929 and FDR's 1932 landslide victory. The precise end of the New Deal party system is a matter of some dispute. Carmines and Stimson claim it ended in 1964 when LBJ and the Democrats successfully passed the Voting Rights Act (1964) and Civil Rights Act (1965); others like Sundquist argue that Reagan's landslide victory in 1980 marks the end of the New Deal era and the beginning of the New Right party alignment.[15] The analysis here suggests that the New Deal alignment ends with the emergence of Reagan in 1980, a finding that corresponds with Cigler and Loomis's research that shows an increase in GOP party registrations in advance of the 1980 presidential primary.[16] While the civil rights era did not change the structure of GOP county voting in Kansas, perhaps because of the state's relatively small minority populations, the analysis does show signs of a dealignment evident in voting patterns from 1966 to 1978. These findings partially support Harder's analysis, although this dealignment started in 1966 rather than 1956 and lasted only until 1978.

Figure 10 illustrates how much conditions improved for the Democrats during the New Deal party alignment. First, more Democratic counties are evident and show a north-south split. The Democrats' regions of strength are found in the southeast around Crawford County, south central around Wichita, and the southwest around Dodge City and Ford County. The Democrats' success in the southeast is attributable to the large mining operations and the unions prevalent in this period. In south central Kansas manufacturing tied to the aircraft industry and unionization propelled Democratic success. New Deal Democratic candidates also appealed to agrarian interests in southwest Kansas, which was hit hard by the Dust Bowl of the Great De-

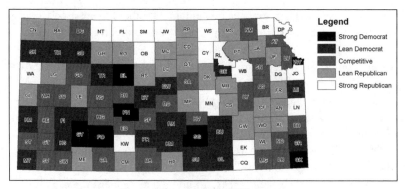

Fig. 10. New Deal Party Alignment
Source: ICPSR.

pression. Many farmers, especially of German descent, appreciated FDR's efforts to provide farm aid and subsidies in order to alleviate the effects of the Dust Bowl and the Great Depression.

Ellis County in north central Kansas remained a Democratic stronghold during the New Deal era. Consistent with trends at the national level, the more urban and diverse counties of Wyandotte (Kansas City) and Shawnee (Topeka) counties in the northeast aligned themselves more closely with the Democrats in this era, while Johnson County, a haven for white flight out of Kansas City after WWII, tilts heavily toward the Republicans.

The demographic profile of the New Deal alignment corresponds with traditional notions about this coalition. The middle section of table 8 shows the regression using census data from 1970. GOP support negatively relates with the percent of blue collar workers but positively to average age and percentage of population change. In Kansas rural counties tend to have aging populations. Kansas Republicans also do well in fast-growing suburban counties, particularly around the Kansas City area. Other variables, including per capita income, percentage of blacks, percentage of Hispanics, and percentage urban population do not predict GOP strength in the New Deal era. Racial factors represent large components of the New Deal coalition nationally but do not significantly relate to GOP support in Kansas.[17]

In 1980 the New Right alignment emerges. Figure 11 shows that under the New Right voting structure, the Democrats clearly lost ground. The north-south divide prevalent in the New Deal era is replaced by the U.S. 81 divide, separating the eastern more urban Kansas from the western more rural Kansas. The western half of the state along with the north central sections have the highest levels of rural populations and the strongest levels of GOP support. In addition, previous strongholds for the Democrats such as

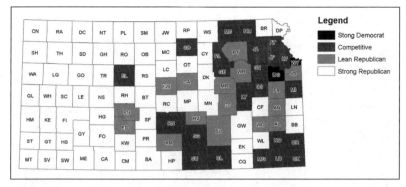

Fig. 11. New Right Party Alignment
Source: ICPSR.

Ellis and Sedgwick counties move significantly toward a more Republican disposition in the New Right era. This alignment continues to dominate Kansas' electoral politics.

At first glance a couple of aspects about figure 11 are surprising. First, the New Right voting structure begins in 1980 rather than the early 1990s when polar alliance Republicans first made their splash in Kansas state politics. Why is this? In the late 1970s the Moral Majority, headed by Rev. Jerry Falwell in Lynchburg, Virginia, came of age as a national movement to oppose abortion and to promote public school prayer. Even though Jimmy Carter successfully wooed born-again Christians to support him in 1976, by 1980 born-again Christians became upset with Carter's attempts to remove the tax-exempt status of many segregated white fundamentalist Christian schools in the South.[18] Candidate Reagan made explicit and implicit appeals to these Christian conservatives in his 1980 campaign.

In Kansas this awakening of the New Right appears in counties with fundamentalist Christian leanings that move toward the Republican Party. For the most part these counties are more rural and west of U.S. 81. However, Sedgwick County, with its large number of fundamentalist churches, also moved toward a more Republican disposition. Figure 12 shows party registration data for Sedgwick County. The shift toward the GOP begins in 1980 and continues throughout the 1980s, 1990s, and 2000s, making the GOP the majority party in Sedgwick County.

Even though national factors may help to provide an issue environment that facilitates the shift toward greater Republican dominance, state-level issues also figure prominently in this change. Governor Carlin's reelection bid in 1982 provides a case in point. In that year Carlin promoted the severance tax as a major campaign issue. In Kansas this issue pitted the rural

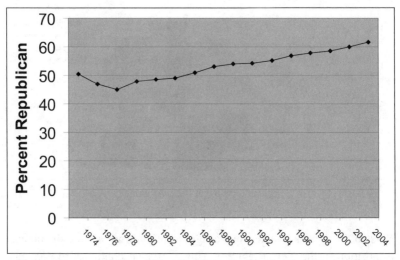

Fig. 12. Percentage of Republican Two-Party Registration in Sedgwick County

western counties, which were heavily dependent primarily on exploitation of oil and natural gas, against the more urban eastern counties. In 1978 Carlin won 49.3 percent of the vote in the western half of the state (forty-three counties west of U.S. 81), but in 1982 he dropped to only 38.9 percent in these same counties.

Some students of Kansas politics may still question the validity of these findings. Some will rightly note that polar alliance Republicans first appeared in the late 1980s and the early 1990s, bifurcating the Kansas Republican Party between moderates and social conservatives and thus laying the foundation for "three-party politics." This point of view, though alluring, does not stand up to empirical scrutiny. Most of the three-party characteristics are primarily manifested via party organizational infighting, that is, moderate versus polar alliance in GOP primary battles such as for the Kansas State Board of Education and in the structure of voting coalitions among members of the state legislature. However, analyses of party alignments focus on the structure of partisan voting patterns in general elections, and in this venue Republicans only produce one candidate, either a moderate, a polar alliance, or an unaligned Republican, to run against a Democrat. As noted in table 6, GOP factional disputes do bubble over into the electoral arena to help elect Democratic governors, for example Sebelius in 2002 and 2006, but not much else.

As early as 1974 pro-life forces played an important role in electing Republicans. As noted in chapter 1, Dole's reelection in 1974 is partly attributable to a negative ad campaign that smeared his physician opponent Democrat Roy as an abortion doctor. In 1980, at the genesis of the New Right party alignment in Kansas, the first signs of a split in the Kansas GOP bubble to the surface. In 1980 Reagan delegates to the national convention decertified a moderate Republican delegate for John Anderson after Anderson announced his independent presidential bid. This decertification left a bitter taste with moderate Republicans who had supported Anderson.

The demographic characteristics (see table 8) associated with the New Right voting structure differ from those prevalent during the New Deal era. The percentage of urban population and the percentage of blacks negatively influence GOP voting patterns, while percentage of Hispanics and per capita income are positively related. Percent of blue collar workers, average age, and percent population change all have insignificant effects. The strong negative relationship between blacks and GOP support reflects the Democratic Party's loss of a significant number of largely white communities to the GOP even as African American communities continue to elect Democrats. The positive relationship with the percentage of Hispanics reflects the voting patterns of whites in the large Hispanic-dominated counties in the southwest part of the state. Even though Hispanic immigrants represent a large component of the population in southwest Kansas, especially since the late 1970s when the meat-packing towns of Ford, Finney, and Seward counties grew dramatically, the political impact of Hispanics voters remains small because many Hispanic immigrants have not gained citizenship and the right to vote.

These findings lend some credence to the theory that the urban-rural split defines Kansas party politics in the modern era. Although the GOP is now the dominant force in rural areas, the party has also become the majority party in Sedgwick County while maintaining its dominance in Johnson County. If the Democrats regain strength in Sedgwick and make significant inroads in Johnson, the urban-rural split, noted in the introduction, will transition from being a semiactive fault line to a dominant fault line.

So what does all of this mean for the Kansas electoral system? The Kansas electoral system, at least with respect to the structure of GOP county voting, largely follows the contours of national party alignments. The manner in which these national alignments cut across Kansas and interact with the voting public leads to different outcomes than in other states. For example, the New Deal alignment improved the status of Kansas Democrats but did not result in their becoming the majority party in Kansas as they did in Michigan and Massachusetts. Unlike these other states, in Kansas the groups that comprise the New Deal Democratic coalition—urbanites, union members, Catholics and blacks—do not represent a large enough block of voters to overcome the GOP advantage in rural agrarian communities and communities with higher levels of per capita income.

The New Right alignment sinks Democrats into a decidedly competitive disadvantage, especially in comparison to the New Deal alignment. Democrats won on their own merits during much of the New Deal, but during the New Right alignment, Democrats such as Finney and Sebelius won in large measure because of GOP factionalization. In the New Right era the Democrats lost ground in their areas of strength, mainly Sedgwick County and other counties with a large contingent of blue collar workers, whereas the GOP strengthened its hand in rural agrarian counties. Even though the growth of the GOP has appeared to improve its competitive position during the past two decades by expanding its base, long-standing challenges for maintaining party unity plague the Republicans. These challenges are apparent in the party organization of the GOP. The remainder of this chapter addresses the party organizations of the Democrats and Republicans in Kansas.

PARTY ORGANIZATIONS IN KANSAS

David Mayhew in his exhaustive study of party organizations in all fifty states wrote that "nowhere in the slim literature on Kansas does traditional [party] organization make an appearance."[19] In 1996 Joseph Aistrup and Mark Bannister added to this slim literature by fleshing out the history of the development of the state political parties.[20] They note that from the early 1900s through World War II and until the late 1970s, both state organizations are largely temporary organizations, oriented toward electing governors.[21] When the gubernatorial term expanded to four years in 1974, the state parties were freed to build organizational capacity to pursue other activities supporting the election of candidates at other levels.

From the mid-1970s through the 1980s the Kansas Republican Party (KRP) refocused its efforts on lesser statewide offices, congressional elections, and state legislative contests. These candidate-directed activities began with the swapping of volunteer and contributor lists in the late 1970s, expanded to giving token monetary support to state legislative candidates in the early 1980s, and finally blossomed into a concerted effort to help state legislative candidates through training seminars for first-time candidates and vulnerable incumbents in the late 1980s.[22] Also in 1988 and 1990 the GOP began targeting its resources toward specific races in which Democratic incumbents were vulnerable and on open-seat contests. By 1990 this assistance included formal education about campaign finance laws and some political polling.[23]

Like most Republican state party organizations, a push by the Republican National Committee (RNC) to professionalize GOP state organizations in the wake of the Watergate affair aided the state party.[24] In the mid-1970s the RNC began funneling large sums of money to the organization, freeing resources to collect and disseminate donor, volunteer, and voter lists. Also during this time the RNC commissioned state polls to help state GOP candidates gauge the mood of the public.[25]

By the late 1970s Republicans possessed the resources necessary to conduct direct mail fund-raising campaigns. A Democratic Party fund-raising letter from the early 1980s lamented that the Republicans had a "10-year lead" in using computer technology.[26] The development of direct mail did much to ensure a steady source of income for the party. By 1990 the Republicans began to use telemarketing to enhance fund-raising efforts.

In contrast to the KRP, the Kansas Democratic Party (KDP) and its county organizations were all but meaningless up until the mid-1960s, existing only to dispense Democratic presidential patronage.[27] The KDP began to develop into a significant entity during Robert Docking's reign as governor. Docking used the KDP to organize county parties in order to turn out the vote and to organize other Docking campaign-related activities.[28] In 1970 the KDP's headquarters found a permanent home, and the organization started making moves toward a more professionally run operation and hiring a full-time executive secretary (later the position became executive director).

During the period between 1974 and 1985 the state organization began diversifying its operations to include other campaign and organizational activities. In 1981 state party chairman Thomas Corcoran raised funds to buy computers for direct mail fund raising.[29] In 1985, under the direction of Jim Parrish, the state organization assembled manuals for candidates on how to run campaigns and win elections. In the 1990s the state party made computer software available to mostly county-level candidates to facilitate targeted mailing and voter analysis.[30]

In the 2000s the KRP and the KDP continue to provide many of these candidate-center services. The key difference between the KDP and the KRP is that the former focuses more on the grassroots at the county level. The KDP continues to enhance its extensive Democratic voter registration database in each county, which it keeps as current as possible. Local Democrats use these lists for targeted funding raising and voter turnout. With fewer than thirty percent of all voters registered as Democrats, the KDP's tilt toward the grassroots is essential for the health of the Democrats in Kansas.

The KDP has a history of being more active in the recruitment of state legislative candidates than the KRP. Since the 1990s the KDP, county chairs, and committees work together to identify state legislative and county-level candidates. This focus recognizes that the Democrats are less likely to have complete candidate slates than the majority Republicans. In the late 1990s and early 2000s when the party lost control of all but one congressional seat and one statewide office, the Democrats typically fielded candidates in sixty to sixty-five percent of state house contests. Buoyed by Sebelius's popularity, the Democrats recruited candidates in seventy-nine percent of state house contests in 2006.

Intraparty Strife in the GOP

In 1995, barely two months after his landslide election, Governor Graves expected the KRP to elect his hand-picked party chair. However, over the course of the three previous years, polar alliance Republicans gained control of three of the four congressional district delegations and a majority of the Republican state central committee.[31] As a consequence, the KRP elected former state representative David Miller as state party chair without Graves's blessing. Miller, an ardent polar alliance Republican committed to pro-life issues as well as cutting taxes and government spending, opposed Graves's more moderate ways. In 1995 and 1996 Graves and Miller publicly disagreed over whether the party should write a platform for the 1996 election. Miller ignored Graves's wishes and drafted a party platform, replete with litmus test statements on polar alliance issues.[32] For the next two years their personal battle continued, culminating in Miller running in the GOP gubernatorial primary against Graves in 1998. Miller lost badly, giving Graves an opening to name a state party chair and to move the KRP back into moderate hands. Graves named Mark Parkinson the new state party chair. In 2006 Parkinson switched parties and became the Democratic candidate for lieutenant governor.

Even though moderate forces beat polar alliance Republicans in 1998, this battle was not the end of the story. In reaction to moderates controlling the KRP, Tim Golba, the director of Kansans for Life, in January 1999 organized a parallel state party organization called the Kansas Republican Assembly to assure that polar alliance views, particularly on issues like abortion, have a permanent and dominant voice within the GOP.[33] The Assembly plays a key role in pushing other polar alliance issues such as opposition to stem cell research, a gay marriage amendment, and the teaching of evolution in public schools. In the 2002 election the Assembly endorsed the candidacy of polar alliance stalwart Phill Kline of Overland Park for attorney general. Kline won a close and bitter primary battle with moderate Republican David Adkins and then barely beat largely unknown and underfinanced Democratic candidate Chris Biggs in the general election.

Not to be outdone by Assembly Republicans, moderate Republicans also organized in 2005 a parallel state party organization, mainly to nominate proevolution Republican candidates to challenge anti-Darwinist Republican candidates on the Kansas State Board of Education.[34] The new organization, Kansas Traditional Republican Majority, also known as TRIM, formally trifurcates the state GOP into three entities, each with its own agenda to nominate candidates and to control elective office. TRIM's efforts in 2006 were successful. Its endorsed slate of candidates won the seats of two Assembly-endorsed Republicans in the August 2006 GOP primaries for the Kansas State Board of Education. Both candidates went on to win their respective general election contests.

From a practical political perspective the existence of the Kansas Republican Assembly and the Kansas Traditional Republican Majority as parallel structures to the KRP shows that the factionalization of the Kansas Republicans remains at a critical stage. The existence of the Assembly Republicans underscores the perception by polar alliance Republicans that moderates are RINOS, "Republicans in name only," and lack true commitment on the fiscal and social issues that are required to govern and control the Kansas GOP. The existence of the Traditional Republicans underscores the opinion of moderates that polar alliance Republicans are not traditional Republicans but rather are interlopers who are infesting the party and driving it to the far right, out of the mainstream. The existence of both of these groups leaves the KRP as a fifth wheel. During the reign of Shallenberger as the KRP chair in the mid-2000s, the state party hit lows in terms of contributions to fund its activities. At least with respect to party organizations, Kansas has become a three-party state.[35]

This chapter addresses two major features of Kansas electoral and party politics. First, Kansas does follow the ebb and flow of national politics. National movements sweep through the state changing the underlying dynamics and coalitions of the Democratic and Republican parties. Thus Kansas experienced realignments in 1932 associated with FDR and the New Deal and once again in 1980 associated with Reagan and the New Right coalition. Even though Republican factionalization does help elect Democrats to the governorship, these election-specific conditions do not alter the underlying party dynamics defining the party alignment eras.

Second, Republican factionalism provides the minority Democrats regular opportunities to win elections, mainly at the gubernatorial level. Prohibitionists, progressives, and now polar alliance forces have all taken their turn leaving an indelible imprint on the body politic of Kansas and the nation. In the 2000s Republicans seem to be headed toward increased factionalization as Traditional Republicans (moderates) and Assembly Republicans (polar alliance) battle within the GOP for control. For their part Kansas Democrats in 2006 took advantage of GOP factionalization to elect two of four U.S. representatives, a governor, and an attorney general. But Kansas Democrats have yet to make significant gains in winning state legislative seats, picking up only five seats in 2006, or by registering Democrats registrants. All eyes are on Kansas Democrats in 2010 to see if the party can continue to win statewide offices in the face of the likely Republican nominee for governor, U.S. Senator Sam Brownback.

CHAPTER FOUR

The State Legislature

In many ways the Kansas legislature is the prototypical part-time citizen state legislature. Respecting the state's agricultural tradition, the first rap of the gavel starting each legislative session is on the second Monday in January, and the legislative session is limited to the winter and early spring months.[1] House members serve two-year terms, and senators serve four years both without term limitations. All 125 house seats stand for election in November in even numbered years. All 40 senate seats face the voters during presidential election years when the governor and other constitutional officers are not on the ballot. Legislative pay is poor, literally. Legislators are paid $84.80 per calendar day during the session and for interim assignments, $99 per day for expenses, an additional $6,775 per year for expenses, and 43 cents per mile for mileage, limited to one trip per week during the session. Thus for an average ninety-day session the pay is $22,317, excluding mileage.[2]

Just as Kansas' dominant political cultures mold other major institutions of state government, they also play a significant role in forging the institutional framework of the state's legislative chambers. Of the three the political culture of individualism, with its preferences for liberty and limited government, is the most influential in shaping or blocking changes that have pushed the Kansas legislature toward its current configuration.

This chapter charts the state legislature's historical evolution, focusing on the influence of the state's dominant political cultures. It explains how various institutional reforms and innovations bring order to a chaotic political environment while maintaining the traditions of a part-time citizen legislature. The chapter then shifts its focus so as to develop a more nuanced understanding of the current state of party politics in the Kansas state legislature. It moves beyond the familiar moderate versus conservative split in

Table 9: Classification of Professional and Amateur Legislatures in the U.S.

Professional	Semi-Professional	Between		Semi-Amateur	Amateur
California	Alaska	Alabama	Missouri	Georgia	Montana
Michigan	Illinois	Arizona	Nebraska	Idaho	New Hampshire
New York	Florida	Arkansas	North Carolina	Indiana	North Dakota
Pennsylvania	Ohio	Colorado	Oklahoma	Kansas	South Dakota
	Massachusetts	Connecticut	Oregon	Maine	Utah
	New Jersey	Delaware	South Carolina	Mississippi	Wyoming
	Wisconsin	Hawaii	Tennessee	Nevada	
		Iowa	Texas	New Mexico	
		Kentucky	Virginia	Rhode Island	
		Louisiana	Washington	Vermont	
		Maryland		West Virginia	
		Minnesota			

Source: *National Conference of State Legislatures*, "NCSL Backgrounder"
http://www.ncsl.org/programs/press/2004/backgrounder_fullandpart.htm, October, 2005.

the GOP in order to illustrate how the latest round of factionalization in the GOP affects leadership selection, primary challenges, and political conflict. The data used in this chapter come from public records and newspaper accounts assembled by the authors.

THE LEGISLATURE IN CULTURAL CONTEXT

Although Kansas has a part-time citizen legislature, other state legislatures have evolved into more full-time and professional bodies similar to the U.S. Congress. Tables 9 and 10 compare the Kansas legislature with the other forty-nine state legislatures in the United States using information collected by the *National Conference of State Legislatures*.[3]

The average Kansas legislator spends just over fifty percent of his or her time being a legislator compared to about eighty percent for a member of the more professional legislatures. The level of compensation for the average Kansas legislator is $22,323 (2007) as compared to $68,599 for professional legislators. Finally, the level of staff support for Kansas legislators is weak. Most Kansas legislators share a secretary who is employed only when the legislature is in session. Professional legislatures employ about nine full-time staff positions per member.

The Kansas legislature's intransigence against the pressures to evolve into a more professional legislature stands in stark contrast to the historical

Table 10: Average Job Time, Compensation, and Staff Size
         by Category of Legislature

Category of Legislature	Time on the Job	Compensation	Staff per Member
Most Professional	80%	$68,599	8.9
Between	70%	$35,326	3.1
Most Amateur	54%	$15,984	1.2

Notes: 1. Estimated proportion of a full-time job spent on legislative work including time in session, constituent service, interim committee work, and election campaigns.
2. Estimated annual compensation of an average legislator including salary, per diem, and any other unvouchered expense payments.
3. Ratio of total legislative staff to number of legislators.

Source: *National Conference of State Legislatures*, "NCSL Backgrounder"
http://www.ncsl.org/programs/press/2004/backgrounder_fullandpart.htm, October, 2005.

development of other state legislatures. In the wake of the Great Depression, the New Deal era, and WWII, large urbanized states such as California, New York, and Michigan led the movement toward the establishment of more professional bodies. Many other states followed, adopting aspects of a professionalized legislature in the form of higher salaries, more staffing, and greater legislative time commitment.

Why does the Kansas state legislature remain a part-time citizen-dominated body? Part of the answer lies with Kansas' populist past, which saw professional politicians as the root of most political evil. Another part of the answer lies with the influences of Kansans' preference for liberty that gives rise to a political culture that has a long tradition of distrusting legislative bodies that meet for inordinate periods of time. Individualists who seek every way possible to "keep theirs" see a long legislative session as a threat to their personal liberty. The less often the legislature meets, the less likely that laws will be drafted threatening personal liberty and freedom and the better for all concerned.[4] Thus from the very first efforts to limit legislative sessions and legislative pay in the 1880s, adherents to the political culture of individualism have exerted influence so that the Kansas legislature remains a citizen-based, amateur institution.

Legislative Sessions and Pay

Even though the current constitution limits a session's length, the original Wyandotte Constitution of 1859 did not. Over the course of the first 113 years of statehood, constitutional amendments would first shorten and then extend legislative sessions. In the early years of statehood the emphasis was on keeping the legislature citizen-based as opposed to professional.[5] The dominant individualist culture of the 1870s viewed professional politicians—those who made their living from being legislators—as open to corruption. Using this logic, in 1875 a constitutional amendment was proposed and passed curtailing the legislative sessions to only odd years. In the late nineteenth century the populists with their penchant toward the political culture of equality also had little use for full-time legislatures and professional politicians. They thought professional politicians were bought and sold by corporate robber barons and bankers.[6] Accordingly, the populists initiated the push for a constitutional amendment that was finally passed in 1900 to limit the number of days the legislature could meet in regular session to ninety.[7]

In addition to session length, the issue of legislative pay was also a concern for individualists. The Wyandotte Constitution set the base pay for legislators at three dollars a day with fifteen cents a mile reimbursement for round trips between their homes and Topeka.[8] Even in the 1870s this amount was not a king's ransom. By the early 1900s three dollars per day was clearly inadequate. Nonetheless, voters would not take pity on the state legislators' plight. Coming on the heels of voters changing the constitution to decrease the legislative sessions to a maximum of ninety days every other year, a majority of voters may not have seen the need to increase pay for a part-time public service. Between 1901 and 1929 voters rejected five constitutional amendments to increase the base pay for legislators.[9] The individualists were more concerned about preventing government actions than facilitating them. A poorly paid citizen's legislature with a high degree of turnover that met only every other year for a short legislative calendar was more likely to serve the individualists' interests while neglecting the clarion calls of do-good interest groups seeking government regulation of everything from cigarette ads to safety and sanitation devices on farms.[10]

After the Great Depression and WWII the scope of activities of state government dramatically expanded; this expansion led to a need for the legislature to meet more frequently. Even under these conditions, reforms came sparingly. Voters finally agreed to increase the daily pay for legislators in 1948 and in 1961 to allow legislators to set their own pay. The constitution was previously amended in 1954 to allow the legislature to meet on even years for sixty-day "budget sessions" and in 1966 to open these even-year sessions to nonbudgetary issues. In the batch of "good government" constitutional reforms passed in the 1970s, the length of even-year sessions was expanded from sixty to ninety days, and all restrictions were removed from odd-year sessions.[11] In addition, with the constitutional amendments passed in 1974, bills and concurrent resolutions introduced in either chamber during an odd-year session can be carried over to the next even-year session.[12]

Although Kansas legislators can now set their own pay, old traditions die hard. As noted earlier, Kansas legislators continue to be paid poorly. This low pay has another side effect, a high turnover rate. The average turnover rate in the house for the six elections between 1994 and 2004 was twenty-five percent. In the senate the turnover rate was even higher: for the three elections between 1994 and 2002 it was forty-six percent. As one recent study of the Kansas legislature concluded, the legislature's low pay means that Kansas does not need a term-limits amendment.[13]

Apportionment and Representation

A political tug of war over the apportionment of the state legislature ensued shortly after Kansas became a state. Initially the controversy was over how to accommodate the state's westward expansion. In 1871 the Kansas attorney general issued an opinion that every new county should be allotted at least one house seat. This opinion was followed in 1873 with a constitutional amendment setting the number of house seats at 125 and senate seats at 40.[14] This amendment, however, did not stop legislators from regularly exceeding these limits.[15] The apportionment debate would continue to rage for the rest of the nineteenth century until finally in 1909, after all 105 counties had been settled and recognized by the state, the legislature apportioned one house seat to each county and distributed the remaining twenty seats among the most urban counties at that time. This action effectively institutionalized malapportionment favoring rural landholders at the expense of the growing towns and urban centers of the northeast and south central parts of the state.[16] The historical basis of the urban-rural divide in Kansas discussed in the introduction begins with the malapportionment of the state legislature.

Not surprisingly, the malapportionment of the legislature combined with the limitations on salary to influence the type of people who became legislators. Under these conditions citizens needed an independent source of income to become a legislator. Historically in rural Kansas two occupational groups fit this description: farmers-ranchers and attorneys. During a number of sessions of the Kansas legislature, almost three-fifths of Kansas legislators fit into these two occupational categories.[17] If not members of these occupations, legislators were generally businessmen, bankers, real estate agents, or insurance brokers. Less common were laborers, retired individuals, and professional full-time politicians.[18]

Except for two brief periods, the populist era when farmers and ranchers pursued more egalitarian policies and the progressive era when business professionals and some attorneys actively pursued governmental reforms consistent with the culture of hierarchy and order, these occupational groups generally united behind a more individualist political culture and promoted smaller, more limited government. Thus, in addition to limiting the session length, these legislators kept intact many of the Wyandotte Constitution's original limitations on taxing, spending, and borrowing until well into the mid to late twentieth century (see chapter 8).

Although the forces for equality rarely won a battle in the chambers of the state legislature, this was not the case in the federal court system and Congress. The Kansas legislature was forced to abandon its malapportionment and aversion to reapportionment in the 1960s as a result of *Baker v. Carr* (1962), *Reynolds v. Simms* (1964), the Voting Rights Act (1965), and several other related court cases.[19] This need for reapportionment triggered a long and somewhat painful process of implementing the principle of one person–one vote for the district lines in both chambers.

Under the scrutiny of federal courts the senate reapportioned in 1963, 1964, and 1968. A court challenge led to a special session in 1966 to draw new boundaries for the house. In 1974 Kansas voters approved a constitutional amendment to reapportion the legislature once every ten years, starting in 1979 and using the state's census data. At that time the state required county clerks to conduct its own census at the end of each decade. In the 1980s the legislature voted to discontinue the state's census, relying instead on the U.S. Census.[20]

From a purely descriptive standpoint the implementation of one person–one vote dramatically altered the nature of representation in Kansas, shifting once rural districts into urban areas. Moreover, since the mid-1960s representation has continued to shift away from rural areas as the population of rural communities continues to decline. Rural counties in the southeast, northwest, and the northern tier of counties along the Nebraska border have all lost seats mainly to the urban clusters around Johnson County and Wichita.

Table 11 shows how the occupational background of legislators has changed since 1977. Even in 1977 more than a decade after the implementation of one person–one vote rules, farmers-ranchers and attorneys were still pluralities in the state legislature. However, over the course of next thirty years the number of farmer-ranchers in the house and the senate declined from thirty-eight in 1977 to twenty-one in 2007. For attorneys the decline is from twenty-eight to eighteen. While farmer-ranchers and attorneys have

Table 11: The Occupations of Kansas Legislators, 1977 and 2007

Occupation	1977 House	1977 Senate	2007 House	2007 Senate
Farmer/Rancher	30	8	11	10
Business	18	5	23	4
Attorney	16	12	13	5
Banking/Finance	2	2	4	4
Real Estate/Insurance	12	3	9	1
Manager/Director	6	1	11	2
Arch/Eng/Contractor	6	1	3	1
Educator	5	1	16	1
Publisher	1	2	1	0
Laborer	5	0	2	1
Homemaker	4	1	0	1
Legislator*	3	0	9	0
Student	3	0	0	0
Retired	4	0	3	0
Health Care	na	na	5	4
Information Tech	na	na	5	0
Other	10	4	10	6

Notes: na = not available.

*Self-Employed were classified as Legislators.

**Legislators who specified they were retired from a specific occupation were classified into the occupation they listed. In addition to the 3 house members in 2006 who stated they were retired (only), 18 other house members stated they were retired from a specific occupation.

Sources: The 1977 data were reported in Marvin A. Harder, "The Participants," in *Politics and Government in Kansas* (1989), p. 136. The 2007 data are collected by the authors from each state legislator's Web site.

decreased in numbers, other occupational groups have increased. Reflecting the growth of the new international economy and the urbanization of the Kansas, legislators with occupations in health care and information technology are more prevalent. In addition, perhaps indicating the vested interest that teachers have in state government, the number of educators serving in the house is greater (five in 1977 compared to sixteen in 2007).

Many assume that the emergence of one person–one vote has only acerbated the urban-rural divide in Kansas as urban legislators exacted a measure of retribution against rural legislators. Those promoting this argument point to the continued decline in rural populations to support their contention and suggest that these population losses are the product of the decline in government services and funding.[21]

It is, however, important to note that while most rural communities have lost population since the mid-1960s, the reality is that this population loss started in the 1920s and 1930s, long before the 1960s and one person–one vote. Further, even though in some major urban states the retribution of urban legislators against rural communities was swift and severe, such retribution was less the case in Kansas. For example, rural school consolidation, which adversely affected many small communities, was passed in 1966 prior to the 1966 special session reapportioning house districts based on one person–one vote. Moreover, almost thirty years after the end of malapportionment, the state legislature's 1992 weighted-funding formula for K–12 school finance was so generous to rural school districts that the state supreme court ordered the legislature in 2005 to change it to a more equitable distribution.[22]

Finally, it is true that transportation monies and sales and liquor-tax dollars began to flow more freely to urban areas after the mid-1960s.[23] Still, the state maintains a road system that is ranked fourth in the nation in paved miles, ranking only behind California, Texas, and Illinois. Since the late 1980s the state legislature has passed two major state highway programs to maintain and enhance this road system, including the rural highway system (see chapter 7).

One of the better possible explanations for the continued support of rural areas, despite the shift in representation to urban communities, is provided by the Kansas Senate majority leader, Senator Derek Schmidt from Independence. Schmidt noted to a group of students that while "there are several senators who represent purely urban or suburban constituencies, many are like me, representing both mid-sized towns and small towns. This means that many of us don't have a purely urban or rural district, but districts that are a combination. So, it's hard for us to support policies like changing the school-funding formula. Yes, it may free resources for our larger schools, but it may do so by endangering the viability of our rural school districts."[24]

Interestingly, Schmidt's comments may be pointing to a new era of egalitarian politics in Kansas. His words suggest that the state should be seeking equal outcomes for school funding as well as for the providing of other governmental services among urban and rural communities. This is an expensive proposition given the higher per capita costs of schools, roads, health programs, and the like for rural communities.

Of course, this type of equality of outcome was a primary value of rural populists in the late nineteenth century. In the early twenty-first century most individualists and polar alliance Republicans reject this idea, instead promoting cuts in government spending in order to lower taxes. To the extent these groups are successful, pressure will mount to reduce government spending in rural communities for schools and other programs. If education and other state programs follow the lead of SRS, which consolidated rural offices in the early 2000s, the combination of these forces may usher in a new era of rural populism and political conflict between urban and rural communities.

INSTITUTIONAL INNOVATIONS AND REFORMS

Given the less than nurturing environment for a more professionally based legislative body and the added demands for governance in the post–New Deal, WWII era, the Kansas legislature, hemmed in by a short session length, poor pay, high turnover rates, and an unsympathetic dominant political culture, has been forced to evolve—in sometimes innovative ways—in order to manage demands for its time more efficiently. These innovations include, but are not limited to, the Legislative Coordinating Council, the Legislative Research Department, more efficient budgeting procedures, and strong leadership.

Legislative Coordinating Council

In 1933 Kansas was one of only a few states to form a legislative council. During this period the legislature met only during odd years for ninety days. The council's job was to work during the interim in order to assure the preparation of a program of legislation before each legislative session. Composed of ten members of the senate and fifteen of the house, the council divided into subcommittees to draft legislation in several policy arenas.[25]

Over the years two major changes enhanced and facilitated this interim process. First, in 1966 voters ratified Article 2, Section 3, of the constitution allowing the legislature to set its own pay and per diem reimbursement. This constitutional revision enabled legislators to set reasonable rates of reimbursement for expenses incurred during interim committee work. Second, in 1971 the legislative council reorganized and renamed itself the Legislative Coordinating Council. With the name change came a major reorganization of its membership and the way it conducted business.[26]

Under the 1971 reform the leadership of the house and senate serves on the council with the chair and vice chair rotating between the house speaker and the senate president. The council's charge is to be the central coordinating committee of the state legislature. As such, it hires the director of the Legislative Research Department, the revisor of statutes, and the legislature's legal counsel. The most important activity of the council is appointing interim committees of legislators to study, and if necessary, to draft legislation for a variety of pressing issues. With a few minor exceptions the interim committees are joint committees, comprised of members from both chambers. In most cases the joint committees represent legislators who already serve in the relevant standing committees from both chambers. This arrangement allows the work of the legislature to continue in the summer and fall months, even though the legislature is not in session. Compared to the previous incarnation of the council, the current council engages a much wider array of legislators to serve on the interim committees.[27] Through the work of these interim committees, about one-third to one-half of the Kansas legislators are effectively working three-quarter time.

Legislative Research Department

Also in 1934 the Kansas legislature created the Legislative Research Department (LRD). The purpose of the LRD is to provide legislative committees, subcommittees, and individual legislators objective nonpartisan research. The LRD also provides staff services to committees and subcommittees. Only the director of the LRD is appointed by the Legislative Coordinating Council. Legislators from both parties concur that the LRD effectively provides nonpartisan research services for committees and legislators, effectively meeting its mission.[28]

The research function of the LRD is especially important given that the staffs of most legislators consist of a shared secretary and college interns. Except for the leadership, most lack professional staffs to research pending legislation or to draft bills. On the other hand, all legislators are inundated with information from citizens and interest groups. The LRD helps to fill the void created by the dearth of paid professional staff, thus providing an important institutional check on the information supplied from special interests.

The LRD is important for another reason. As noted earlier, the Kansas legislature has a high turnover rate. By contrast, the turnover rate of the LRD is much lower. Michael A. Smith and Brenda Erickson note that because of the high turnover rate among legislators, the legislature's institutional memory tends to reside in the LRD.[29] Long-term staffers have researched a variety of policy issues, many of which recur from year to year. They know which ideas have floated through the legislature in the past and why these proposals failed.

Appropriations Process

Each year the main task of the legislature is to pass appropriations bills. Even in a state of about 2.8 million people, this is a long and arduous process. No matter the intent, the process invariably ends in the final days of the legislative session with the governor and legislative leadership negotiating an omnibus appropriations bill, which contains the unpassed budgets for a multitude of agencies and the salary increases for state workers.[30] As chaotic as this appropriations process may seem to outside observers, it could be worse. Legislators could spend so much time on appropriations issues that there would need to be full-time versus part-time legislators just to pass the budget.

Three key reforms, passed over half a century, have made the appropriations process more efficient. In 1925 a new statute delegated to the governor the power to prepare and submit an executive budget for state government to the legislature (see chapter 5). Instead of each agency and department submitting separate budget requests to the legislature, the governor is given the responsibility of collating these requests and making budget recommendations for all the state agencies, departments, and boards. The governor's budget director also provides staffing for the appropriation process in the legislature. These are the first and most important steps in pulling together pieces of a fragmented, decentralized process.

The appropriations process became even more focused at the gubernatorial level when Governor Docking used executive reorganization orders (EROS) to create a cabinet system of administration (1972–75). Prior to this time agency governing boards appointed lead administrators for state agencies and departments, effectively delimiting the power of governors to hold agencies directly accountable. This system also complicated the budget process. State agency directors, who received an unfavorable recommendation in the governor's budget, would appeal directly to the relevant legislative committee, effectively going over the head of the governor. This behavior concentrated power into the hands of legislative leaders but made for a chaotic and less than efficient appropriations process.[31]

From 1972 to 1992 fourteen EROS effectively consolidated many of the existing agencies and departments into a smaller number of cabinet-level agencies.[32] Except for a few select agencies such as the Department of Agriculture and the Department of Education, the governor appoints each cabinet-level secretary for each agency.[33] This change made the agency heads directly accountable to the governor, thus consolidating and centralizing the budgeting process in the governor's office. Although this action took some power away from the House Appropriations and the Senate Ways and Means committees, it also alleviated a chaotic appropriations environment and relieved time pressure on legislators.[34]

In response to the consolidation of budgetary authority in the executive branch, the legislature established its own fiscal staff in 1974 to conduct research and to advise the appropriations committees in both chambers. In addition, the legislature also established the Legislative Division of Post-Audit (LDPA). The LDPA is independent of the LRD. Its purpose is to hold state agencies accountable for the tax dollars they spend by auditing each state agency every other year. The LDPA also conducts performance audits of state agencies in order to assess the effectiveness of state programs given the cost and the level of services provided.[35] The work of the LDPA assists the legislature's oversight of executive agencies.

The final significant reform occurred in 1989. During the previous eight years Democratic Governor John Carlin would often submit "unbalanced budgets." Republican lawmakers argued that Governor Carlin's budgets were unbalanced because they included new revenues from proposed but unpassed tax increases. Thus, immediately after Carlin left office, the legislature passed and Governor Hayden signed a new law requiring the governor to submit a balanced budget based on existing state revenues (sans proposed tax increases). During tough budget cycles this provision forces the governor's office to make the hard choices prior to presenting the budget to the state legislature.

A good example of this occurred during the 2003 legislative session. Facing a revenue shortfall of several hundred million dollars, newly elected Governor Sebelius was forced to submit a balanced budget. Given her campaign promise to maintain funding for K–12 education, Governor Sebelius proposed cutting most state agency budgets, withholding funding for the state's highway plan, and all but eliminating the statutorily required 7.5 percent ending-balance reserve.[36]

Even though the legislature can change the governor's budget, in most cases legislative committees only make minor adjustments to the governor's recommendations. This acceptance saves legislators from spending their time, energy, and political capital on making these initial tough decisions. One long-time lobbyist confided that the legislature conducts the appropriations process from "30,000 feet." Legislators depend on summary documents from the LRD to decide how to cast their votes. "It is a rare occasion when a legislator digs into the details of an agency's budget, even if he or she serves on an agency's appropriations subcommittee." This reality has led some conservative lawmakers to question the wisdom of short legislative sessions of ninety days. They argue that this process is largely responsible for the state's total budget topping twelve billion dollars for FY 2008, an eighteen percent increase over spending in FY 2006.[37] Thus some from the individualist political culture are calling for longer legislative sessions or for the governor to deliver the budget to legislative committees in December in order to allow legislators to conduct top-to-bottom reviews of state agency budgets and to determine appropriate cuts in spending.

Organization and Leadership

The final and perhaps most important means through which the state legislature has been able to maintain its part-time semi-amateur status is the organization and leadership of both the house and senate. The leadership in both chambers have well-developed formal and informal powers to control the flow of legislation and to regulate the behavior of party members.[38] Against the backdrop of a legislative institution shaped by constitutional restraints and battling the normal tendencies of legislative bodies to drift toward competition, decentralization, and fragmentation, the organization and leadership bring a semblance of order and rationality so that the legislative calendar generally concludes sometime in May of each year.[39]

At one level the organization of both chambers of the Kansas legislature is typical for legislatures in the United States. The three main components of this organization are parties, leadership, and committees.[40] Among these building blocks the most important are political parties. The members of the majority party determine which legislators occupy the leadership positions, the committee structure, the legislative calendar, and the rules for floor debate.[41]

With three minor exceptions Republicans have controlled the legislature since the state's birth in 1861. The Democrats controlled both chambers for two years after the 1912 elections (progressives versus standpatters) but were unable to maintain their majority. Also, Democrats controlled the lower chamber for two years after the 1976 and 1990 elections. Figure 7 in chapter 3 shows the proportion of state house and senate seats controlled by the Democrats. Even though the Democrats were competitive from the 1970s through the early 1990s, since the 1994 election the GOP has maintained large majorities in both chambers.

One of the key debates that has raged on and off since the populist era at the turn of the twentieth century is whether political parties are a nuisance to the operation of legislatures that produce poor public policy and legislators who are unaccountable to their constituencies. Interestingly, this perception appears not to be the case in Kansas. Gerald Wright and Brian Schaffner tested this proposition by comparing the roll-call voting behavior of the Kansas Senate with Nebraska's nonpartisan unicameral legislature.[42] The authors found clear and convincing evidence that parties in the Kansas Senate structure roll-call voting behavior in a predictable manner that corresponded with candidates' stated positions during the election. In Nebraska's nonpartisan legislature a different story emerged. Despite the clearly stated campaign positions, legislators exhibited virtually random roll-call voting behavior. Wright and Schaffner concluded that political parties provide structure to legislatures, facilitate representation, and enhance democratic accountability.

Leadership is another key legislative building block. With 125 members from a variety of urban and rural environments, the house leadership follows the strong speaker model. The majority party caucus nominates the speaker and speaker pro tem, who are elected by the entire house membership. The majority party caucus selects the majority leader and other majority party leadership positions, while the minority party caucus elects its leaders.

The strength of the speaker emanates from his or her power to choose committee members, including committee chairs and vice chairs.[43] Naturally most choice committee assignments go to supporters of the speaker. In the house the minority leader appoints all minority party committee members, including the ranking minority committee members.[44] The seniority system does not play a strong role in influencing leadership decisions for either party.

The president of the senate used to wield power comparable to that of the speaker, but this changed in the wake of Paul R. Wunsch's tenure as president in the 1960s. Wunsch wielded unparallel powers as president. After his tenure the senate changed its rules so as to limit the president's powers.[45] Like the speaker, the president and vice president are nominated by the majority party caucus and elected by the entire senate as its presiding officers. After nominating the president, the majority caucus also chooses the majority leader and the other whip positions. However, unlike the speaker, the president does not directly choose the membership or leadership of senate committees. Rather, the Committee on Organization, Calendar, and Rules (OCR), chaired by the president, makes all assignments to committees and to leadership positions for members from both parties. By senate rules there are no members of the minority party on the OCR, but by tradition the minority party leader is able to make requests to the OCR for committee memberships for Democrats. In most cases the OCR will follow the requests of the minority party leader but not always.[46]

The existence of the OCR means that the president's ability to lead the senate filters through this body. Nonetheless, the president uses the OCR to effectively maintain party discipline. In 1989 the GOP maintained a slight majority (twenty-two Republicans to eighteen Democrats). President Paul "Bud" Burke used the OCR to change the senate rules to require twenty-one votes to compel roll-call votes on amendments, thus protecting Republicans from embarrassing votes on sensitive issues. The OCR also changed the rules to require twenty-seven votes instead of twenty-one in order to pull a bill out of a senate committee.[47] The Democrats were furious, but the new rule helped Burke maintain party discipline by giving him greater control over the content of bills coming out of senate committees.

Compared to the house, the senate's majority leader is a much more important position. The majority leader runs the majority party caucus meetings and through the OCR sets the calendar for the senate. By tradition, but not by rule, the president and the majority leader are strongly tied to one another. The majority party caucus will typically elect the president's hand-picked choice for majority leader. Consequently, the president's will is generally reflected through the actions of the majority leader. Nonetheless, compared to the speaker who can act directly, this indirect rule is another manner in which the power of the president filters through another position.

The leadership of both chambers and parties exert influence and control throughout the legislative session via regularly scheduled party caucus meetings, usually held in the mornings. In these meetings each party's leadership gathers together with members of their respective party from their chamber. The leadership discusses the legislative calendar, the flow of bills through committees, possible rules for floor debate, possible amendments, and roll-call votes. Ultimately all party caucus meetings are about which legislative strategies will be employed to pass, change, or block legislation. These caucus gatherings are key organizing meetings, allowing leaders to receive informal feedback from party members mostly through discussions but sometimes through debates and straw votes. Speaking to a group of college students, Republican Doug Mays, speaker of the house from 2003 to 2006, made it clear that he led the GOP in the house based on a "majority of the majority" of the Republican Party caucus in the house. He noted that if a bill lacked the majority support of his party's caucus, he did everything in his power to kill the legislation.[48]

The final building block of the legislature is the committee system. Like almost all legislatures, committees do most of the work in the Kansas legislature. Since the mid-1960s the number of committees in the senate has ranged from sixteen to nineteen. However, back in 1939 the senate had forty-two committees. Over the years the variation of the number of house committees has ranged from a high of forty-three in 1949 to a low of seventeen in 1993. Since the late 1990s the number of house committees has varied from twenty-eight to thirty-one.[49]

In his studies of the U.S. Congress Joseph Cooper pointed out that the committee system is a convenient and efficient way to divide labor and expertise within each chamber.[50] Perhaps because the Kansas legislature meets for approximately ninety days annually, the committee system is by necessity the center of legislative activities. Legislators in both chambers and on both sides of the aisle say legislation is rarely written on the floor. Rather, legislators and the leadership use the committee system to draft legislation through the process of conducting hearings, obtaining testimony, engaging in debate, and to some extent on most bills, compromising among legislators in order to build a majority to pass the bill out of committee.[51]

Smith and Erickson judge the effectiveness of the committee system by analyzing the ratio of bills introduced by committees versus individual members. In the senate the percentage of committee-introduced bills varied between seventy-seven percent in the 1994 session to eighty-seven in the 2002 session. In the house committee-introduced bills have steadily increased since the early 1990s. In 1993 house committees introduced only fifty-five percent of bills. In 2003 they introduced almost seventy-five percent. Interestingly, many of these committee-sponsored bills are the products of intersession joint committees of the house and senate. Thus much of the work of the legislature is processed first through two layers of the committee structure before it is reported out of committee.[52]

In the house the speaker's powers are closely tied to the committee system. As such, the vast majority of the bills reported out of house committees have the speaker's blessing, which all but insures passage. However, in recent years there have been a couple of notable and significant exceptions. Mostly these exceptions pertain to the issue of K–12 education funding. In the 2004 legislative session a band of moderate Republicans, led by Bill Kassebaum (R-Burdick), worked with house Democrats to push through a substitute education finance bill. The substitute would have increased spending on K–12 education by $155 million and increased sales, income, and property taxes to fund the initiative. Speaker Mays had endorsed the Education Planning Committee's $52 million bill.[53] In the end Kassebaum's alternative passed in the house, but it died in the senate. Toward the end of the session a bill with a smaller price tag, using existing tax revenues and more closely reflecting the speaker's point of view, passed both chambers.[54] But this is not the last chapter of this story. As will be discussed later in this chapter, this coalition of Democrats and moderate Republicans would also emerge in the 2005 special session and again in the 2006 legislative session to pass school finance packages that were significantly different than the bills reported out of committee and supported by the speaker.

In the senate the committee system is tied to a leadership team, which is led by the president and the majority leader and indirectly by the OCR. As one might expect, given this more diffuse power base, senate committees have more leeway in drafting legislation that varies from the desires of the president. Even with this prevailing norm, it is nonetheless unusual for a committee's bill to vary significantly from the president's desires, especially on major spending priorities. Like the blessing of the house's speaker, that of the president greases the wheels for passage on the senate floor.

However, just like the house, sometimes not even the support of the leadership is enough to secure passage. One infamous case of outright rebellion against the senate president occurred in the 2002 session. Senate President Dave Kerr (R-Hutchinson) and his moderate loyalists on the Senate Reapportionment Committee drew a reapportionment plan that would combine into one district in northwest Kansas the constituencies of Senators Janis Lee (D-Kensington) and Stan Clark (R-Oakley). The plan also cobbled together a senate district in Johnson County that was favorably disposed toward the election of a moderate Republican. Ed Pugh (R-Wamego) led an "unholy alliance" of conservative Republicans and some rural Republicans and Democrats to promote a substitute plan.[55] This plan combined Lee's district with that of Larry Salmans (R-Hanston) into a district that included the city of Hays and drew a new Johnson County district inclined toward electing a conservative Republican. Most important, this unholy alliance of eleven Republicans and ten Democrats included the Republican Majority Leader Lana Oleen (R-Manhattan).

Three comments by different parts of the alliance explain this rebellion. Conservative Kay O'Conner (R-Olathe) said that "it was a predictable train wreck, if you disenfranchise a section of your own party [conservative Republicans], they have to go somewhere." Senator Lee echoed this sentiment from the Democrats point of view, noting that "the leadership of the Republican Party thought they could stuff their ideas down the throat of the minority party."[56] Finally, in explaining her support for the alternative, Majority Leader Oleen said that the "Lee-Salmans pairing is fairer than the

Lee-Clark one."[57] Oleen's comments reveal the personal nature of this issue for some senators. Lee was (and remains) widely liked and respected by members on both sides of the aisle, especially by more rural senators. Most felt she had a better chance to beat Salmans than Clark. As a consequence, Oleen was stating a preference, which was shared by rural Republicans, that she preferred Lee over Salmans, even though Lee was a Democrat.

Whither the Citizen Legislature?

Kansas is likely to maintain its citizen-based semiamateur legislature for years to come. As of this writing there is only an initial grumbling from some conservative quarters who want an expansion of legislative sessions beyond their current limits or a start of the budget committees' deliberations prior to January in order to help lawmakers gain a handle on the state's budget.[58] Even though there are occasional cries to increase the base pay of legislators, most of these calls go unheeded because few legislators will vote for a large pay raise for themselves. There may be no great outcry to reform the Kansas legislature because when the final gavel comes down at the sine die (the end of the session), the status quo appears to handle the annual demands for legislation in Kansas. To be sure, there is the typical rush of legislation and appropriations bills at the end of each legislative session, but this is a consistent feature of most legislatures, no matter whether they are full-time or part-time.

POLITICAL CULTURE AND THE POLITICS
OF THE KANSAS LEGISLATURE

Newspapers and pundits often portray the current state of politics in the Kansas legislature as a battle among moderate Republicans, conservative Republicans, and Democrats.[59] Even though these types of shorthand descriptors help newspaper readers navigate through the legislative labyrinth each spring, chapter 1 shows that a more useful manner to conceptualize current politics in Kansas is in terms of interplay between political parties and the dominant political cultures of Kansas. The analysis in this section uses this framework to shed light on legislative politics in the late twentieth and early twenty-first centuries.

As noted in chapter 1 and described in chapter 3, Reagan's New Right partisan realignment swept through Kansas in 1980 and brought together those with a preference toward liberty (lower taxes, smaller government, and less regulation) with those with a preference for order via an opposition to abortion rights. This dynamic led to the emergence of polar alliance Republicans, who are at the extremes of this axis between liberty and order and who rarely compromise these Reagan-inspired core values. Moderate Republicans differ from polar alliance Republicans in that they are willing to compromise their conservative values on the liberty-order axis. Thus moderate Republicans have been known to support tax increases and are not politically driven by an opposition to abortion rights. In the late 1980s and early 1990s polar alliance Republicans began to actively compete with moderate Republicans for control of the GOP state party organization and for nomination to elective office. In the aftermath of the 1994 GOP landslide victory over the Democrats, polar alliance Republicans, led by Tim Shallenberger, gained control of the Kansas State House.

Given this level of factionalism in the Republican Party since 1994, at least two distinct outcomes for the politics of the Kansas legislature may occur. First, the development of systematic outward signs of a factionalized GOP might appear. Signs of factionalization include, but are not limited to, incumbent Republican legislators facing primary challenges, split factional control of the house and senate, and high levels of turnover among the leadership. Second, given the Democrats overtures to moderate Republicans, there may be an increased number of issues in which a moderate coalition forms between Democrats and moderate Republicans.[60]

The first venue in which to examine the emergence of a factionalized GOP is that of primary election challenges of sitting incumbent legislators. These types of challenges are a sign of factionalization because they are a strong indicator of intraparty strife. A primary challenge to an incumbent legislator usually indicates that a faction within the party feels that the incumbent legislator is not adequately reflecting its policy stances. Because incumbents are difficult to unseat and because it may place in jeopardy the party's control of that seat, a primary challenge to an incumbent underscores the depth of the faction's dissatisfaction.[61]

Although there have been a number of instances of this type of challenge in recent years, two examples stand out. In 2002 Bill Kassebaum (R-Burdick), son of former U.S. Senator Nancy Landon Kassebaum (now Nancy Kassebaum Baker), challenged the majority leader of the Kansas House, Shari Weber (R-Herrington). Kassebaum, a moderate Republican, won his primary challenge by 145 votes. Weber, a polar alliance Republican, was upset and dismayed by the "lack of turnout" in the primary election. In the general election she ran an unsuccessful write-in campaign, garnering thirty-one percent of the votes.[62] In 2004 Weber returned the favor, challenging Kassebaum in the GOP primary. As noted earlier in this chapter, Kassebaum

Table 12: Primary Challenges to Republican Incumbents, 1990–2006

Year	# Contested	# Lost
Kansas Senate		
1992	3	0
1996	5	2
2000	7	2
2004	11	2
Kansas House		
1990	11	1
1992	12	2
1994	9	1
1996	7	1
1998	9	1
2000	7	0
2002	24	4
2004	25	5
2006	9	2

Source: Collected by the authors from Kansas Secretary of State.

drew the additional ire of polar alliance Republicans by championing efforts to increase funding for K–12 education. Kassebaum was beaten by Weber (fifty-three percent of the vote to forty-seven) in the GOP primary.[63]

Polar alliance Republican state Senator Susan Wagle (R-Wichita), who made a name for herself in the Kansas House in the 1990s as a polar alliance leader, was elected to the Kansas Senate in 2000 by beating a moderate businesswoman in the GOP primary and then defeating Democratic incumbent Senator Henry Helgerson (D-Wichita). In 2004 Wagle drew a primary challenge from the former mayor of Wichita and 2002 GOP gubernatorial candidate Bob Knight. Knight's campaign specifically focused on Wagle's litmus test conservative views. But Wagle, who was a burr under the saddle of the moderate leadership of the senate, raised more money and easily defeated Knight in the primary.[64]

Table 12 shows a summary of contested Republican incumbent primary elections from 1990 to 2006. Although it is difficult, perhaps impossible, to go back in time and designate GOP legislators as a moderate or polar alliance Republican, given the anecdotal evidence, most of these challenges likely represent a contest between candidates representing these two factions.

Table 12 shows a clear spike in the number of primary challengers to

Republican incumbent legislators in 2002 and 2004. In the 1990s the number of incumbents challenged in the Kansas Senate grew from only three in 1992 to eleven by 2004. In each senate primary since 1996 only two GOP incumbent senators were defeated. In the Kansas House the number of contested GOP incumbents climbs from below twelve in the 1990s to twenty-four in 2002 and twenty-five in 2004. As the number of primary challenges increased, so did the number of GOP incumbent legislators who lost their primary bid. In 2002 four of the twenty-four lost. In 2004 five of the twenty-five lost.[65]

Prior to 2000 moderate Republicans did not have a substantial history of challenging polar alliance Republicans in the primaries. Rather, in the 1990s mostly polar alliance Republicans such as Cedric Boehr (R-Whitewater) challenged moderate Republican incumbents such as Ellen Samuelson (R-Hesston) in the GOP primary.[66]

However, this pattern changed in the wake of the 2000 Kansas State Board of Education primary races. In these elections moderate Republicans challenged and beat three of four polar alliance GOP incumbents in the primaries. This achievement set an important precedent for moderate Republicans to challenge polar alliance Republicans in other electoral arenas, including the state legislature. In the 2002 and 2004 primaries moderates like Cindy Neighbor (R-Shawnee) and Kassebaum challenged polar alliance legislators like Mary Pilcher-Cook (R-Shawnee) and Weber, respectively. The spikes in challenges in 2002 and 2004 represent moderate Republicans striking back against polar alliance Republicans for their challenges in the 1990s.

The decline in contested primaries in 2006 could be interpreted as a slowing of the intraparty rivalry; however, this decline is more likely a product of both factions having sorted out the seats. Those districts that are polar alliance seats and those that are moderate seats are likely to remain so. Both sides realize the general futility of challenging safe incumbents unless they have a overriding reason to do so.

A second venue through which to examine the factionalized GOP is that of battles for leadership within the Republican Party caucus for speaker of the Kansas House and president of the Kansas Senate. As one would expect, there is a high incidence of divided control between the house and senate: polar alliance Republicans tend to control the leadership of the house and moderates control the leadership of the senate. This moderate-polar split of the leadership in the Kansas legislature is shown in table 13, which lists all of the presidents of the senate and speakers of the house since 1993. In some instances these leaders were chosen under competitive conditions.

Table 13: House Speakers and Senate Presidents, 1993–2007

Year	Speaker	Party	President	Party
1993	Robert Miller (38–28)	Moderate	Paul "Bud" Burke	Moderate
1995	Tim Shallenberger (45–38)	Polar	Paul "Bud" Burke	Moderate
1997	Tim Shallenberger	Polar	Dick Bond (15–12)	Moderate
1999	Robin Jenison (41–38)	Rep	Dick Bond	Moderate
2001	Kent Glasscock (40–39)	Moderate	Dave Kerr	Moderate
2003	Doug Mays	Polar	Dave Kerr	Moderate
2005	Doug Mays	Polar	Steve Morrison (17–15)	Moderate
2007	Melvin Neufeld (47–31)	Polar	Steve Morrison	Moderate

When competition was the case, the leader's winning vote totals are in parentheses.

From 1993 to 2007 only two moderate Republicans have held the speakership, Robert Miller (1993–94), who was deposed by Shallenberger in 1995, and Kent Glasscock (2001–2). The 1999 speaker, Robin Jenison, was not in either camp. In his bid for the speaker's position the moderate Republican wing of the House Republicans supported Jenison because he was a more moderate alternative to Wagle, an ardent polar alliance Republican. While the moderates in the senate had some close calls in 1997 and 2005, thus far they have not relinquished control of the senate.

Taken together, there have been two distinctive periods of divided intraparty control of the legislature. The first period was during the Graves administration (1995–98). During this time Shallenberger was the speaker and Burke and Bond were the senate presidents. The second period began in 2003 during the first administration of Governor Sebelius. From 2003 to 2006 Mays was the speaker, and Kerr and Morrison were the presidents of the senate.

The factionalization of the GOP is not limited to battles over the top two leadership posts. It also affects the turnover rate among the party's top legislative leaders. By tradition and chamber rules, the speaker is limited to two two-year terms. This limitation means that leadership turnover is built into the house system. Even taking these rules into account, the leadership turnover among house Republicans has been excessive over the past ten to fourteen years. By the time one takes into account retirements, lost reelection bids, and leadership challenges, the average turnover rate for the top 6 house Republican leadership positions between the 1993–94 sessions and the 2003–04 sessions averaged 5 of 6. By comparison, the average is 3 of 6 for house Democrats. Perhaps because the senate president is not term limited and the fact that the senate membership is more stable, facing voters only once every four years versus every two years, the average leadership turnover rate for the senate's top 5 positions is much lower. For senate Republicans the average was 2.5 of 5 while for senate Democrats, it was 1.5 of 5.[67]

The differences in factional control of the house and senate are important only if they lead to different patterns of conflict that are consistent with the development of a moderate coalition. To examine this issue, we analyzed the content of newspaper stories from the *Wichita Eagle*, the state's largest newspaper. We choose news stories from the *Eagle* for three reasons. First, it is the only major newspaper that has an electronic archive of its articles available from the late 1980s to the present. Second, the *Eagle*'s archives can be searched using Boolean criteria, allowing for a focused search on articles that mention both chambers of the legislature within its text. This criteria is used in the search to concentrate on articles that may uncover instances of cooperation or conflict between the leadership of the house and senate. Third, the *Eagle* has consistently covered the legislature by having a reporter in Topeka during most years.[68]

To make the content analysis manageable, we randomly choose one year from each gubernatorial administration starting with Governor Hayden. The Hayden and Finney administrations are analyzed to establish a base line for understanding interchamber politics before polar alliance Republicans made a big splash in the GOP in 1994. The year is randomly selected to avoid the possibility of "selecting on the dependent variable," thus choosing to analyze legislative years when factionalization may be great and confirming the hypotheses.

We content analyzed news stories from 1988 (Hayden), 1993 (Finney), 1995 (Graves I), 2001 (Graves II), and 2005 (Sebelius).[69] The patterns of conflict are expected to be consistent with classic two-party politics in 1988, 1993, and 2001. Such politics means that when there is partisan conflict reported, the partisan divisions in the newspaper account will be primarily between Democrats and Republicans. In these years there should be only a few instances of moderates splitting away from other Republicans to form coalitions with Democrats. However, this pattern should not be the case in 1995 and 2005. In these two years a pattern of conflict consistent with the factionalization of the GOP is expected. Thus there should be signs of moderate coalitions between moderates and Democrats.

Table 14 shows a simple summary of stories, broken down by year and whether the story entailed some type of partisan conflict.[70] Interestingly, news stories about the legislature tend to be nonpartisan.[71] Most news accounts report the workings of the legislature in terms of testimony on pro-

Table 14: Number and Percentage of Partisan News Stories in *Wichita Eagle*

	1988	1993	1995	2001	2005	All Years
Partisan	7	32	45	15	46	145
% w/in year	10.29	22.22	35.43	17.24	28.22	24.62
Nonpartisan	61	112	82	72	117	444
% w/in year	89.71	77.78	64.57	82.76	71.78	75.38
Total	68	144	127	87	163	589
	100.00	100.00	100.00	100.00	100.00	100.00

posed legislation, bills making their way through the committee process, or the outcome of final action. As numerous legislators report, most of what they do is nonpartisan and uncontroversial. Only about twenty-five percent of the stories reported in the *Eagle* entail some type of partisan conflict.

In 1988 and 2001 two legislative sessions during which moderates controlled all three branches (governor, house, and senate) and during which the legislature was not facing a lean budget, the number of total stories (less than ninety) and the percentage of these stories that are partisan (less than eighteen percent) are comparatively low. The highest percentage of partisan stories occur in 1995 (thirty-five percent) and 2005 (twenty-eight percent).

Table 15 analyzes only those stories that have a partisan tone. In 1988 and 1993 two-party (Democrat versus Republican) politics dominated the content of the partisan stories (over ninety percent of stories in both years combined). This pattern changed in 1995 when Shallenberger and the polar alliance Republicans took control of the Kansas House. Over fifty percent of the partisan stories entailed a conflict between polar alliance Republicans and moderate Republicans-Democrats. A closer examination of these twenty-three stories reveals that the policy domains associated with the type of partisan conflict are abortion, K–12 education, law and order, property taxes, and gaming. Moderate coalition politics in 1995 covered the waterfront of issues on the liberty-order axis.

In 2001 the total number of partisan stories is only fifteen. However, these fifteen stories are evenly split between two-party and moderate coalition politics. It appears that in 2001 the moderate Republican leadership (Graves, Kerr, and Glasscock) was able to keep partisan conflict to a minimum, but when it did erupt, it followed patterns similar to 1995.

Finally, the partisan politics of 2005 are an interesting mix of two-party and moderate coalition politics. In 2005 Democrats controlled the gover-

Table 15: Partisan Stories in *Wichita Eagle*, for Selected Years, 1988–2005

	1988	1993	1995	2001	2005	All Years
Two-Party	7	27	22	8	31	95
% w/in year	100.00	84.38	48.89	53.33	67.39	65.52
Mod Coalition	0	5	23	7	15	50
% w/in year	0.00	15.63	51.11	46.67	32.61	34.48
Total	7	32	45	15	46	145
	100.00	100.00	100.00	100.00	100.00	100.00

norship (Sebelius), moderates controlled the senate (Morrison), and polar alliance Republicans controlled the house (Mays). Unlike 1995, two-party politics is the focus of two-thirds of partisan stories. Also, unlike 1995 when moderate coalition politics is evident across a number of policy domains, most of the moderate coalition stories—nine of the fifteen—addressed school finance. In almost all of these cases Democrats and moderate Republicans are either in the process of forming or have formed a moderate coalition against polar alliance Republicans in order to fund K–12 education. Year in and year out, the school finance question is the most significant topic faced by the legislature. The development of the moderate coalition on this issue is significant, and as such, it represented a major setback for the polar alliance leadership of the Kansas House.

The content analysis suggests that except for the school finance issue, and this is a big exception, two-party politics was the norm for partisan politics in 2005. But, alas, this major exception on an important issue is what makes Kansas legislative politics interesting. There is always the threat of moderate coalition politics emerging on a major issue to throw road blocks in the way of those promoting polar alliance issues. In 2005 the moderate coalition was large enough and strong enough to form a majority in support of increased spending on education funding. Even in 2008 this coalition has remained intact. By contrast, in 1995 the moderate coalition was usually on the losing side of most, if not all, votes.[72] In the wake of the 1994 elections in the house, polar alliance Republicans were strong enough to carry the day.

So what are the lessons from Kansas that can be applied to other states? First, when there are clearly defined ideologically distinct groups within the majority party that persist over time, these factions will compete against one another for leadership positions in the legislature and, second, will recruit candidates to run in primaries against incumbents from the other faction and for open seats. Finally, in legislative sessions one of the factions will seek to form coalitions with the minority party in order to overcome the opposition of the other faction on key issues.

One may be tempted to look at the longevity of the Conservative Coalition in Congress, a coalition that formed and functioned for almost fifty years at the national level, to conclude that the moderate coalition in Kansas can thrive for many years to come. However, this comparison may not be appropriate. Because moderate Republicans and polar alliance Republicans challenge each other's incumbents and continue to split control between the house and senate leadership, there are more political venues for friction between these factions in Kansas. Simply put, there are simply too many opportunities for intraparty strife, and there is only so much dissension that one party can take.

The part-time orientation of the Kansas legislature seems to fit the desires of the dominant political cultures in Kansas, particularly that with a preference for liberty. To maintain its part-time status in the modern era when the demands for a full-time legislative body have increased, the Kansas legislature has adopted several institutional reforms that enable it to continue to serve the representational needs of Kansans. These reforms encompass the Legislative Research Department, which conducts nonpartisan policy evaluation research for all legislators; a unified appropriations process in which the governor is charged with the responsibility of generating a balanced budget proposal based on existing tax revenues; and an interim committee process in which legislators meet between sessions to hear testimony and to generate new legislation to be ready for consideration at the beginning of a session. All of these reforms save time and enable the Kansas legislature to remain a part-time body for most of its members.

The organizational patterns and leadership responsibilities in the Kansas state house and senate are consistent with other state legislatures. Committees perform the work of the state legislature. The leadership of the committees are assigned to those members who are loyal supporters of the speaker or the OCR. The leadership of both chambers set their legislative calendar and rules of debate. In recent years the leadership of the house has experienced a high degree of turnover reflecting both the part-time nature of the legislature and the topsy-turvy nature of politics within the Kansas Republican Party.

Finally, there is much evidence that Kansas Republicans are factionalized and that moderate Republicans split off to join Democrats in a moderate coalition on key issues during the 1990s and 2000s. Although traditional two-party politics is the norm, there is an undercurrent of moderate coalition politics that emerges in primary challenges to sitting incumbents, divided control of the senate and house between GOP factions, and the formation of moderate coalitions to support or oppose legislation particularly in 1995 and 2005 when the leadership of the chambers was divided between the factions.

The Kansas legislature has always been dominated by part-time legislators and Republicans. Even though this political reality is unlikely to change, partisan change is not improbable. If the Kansas Republicans are unable to bridge the ideological divide separating moderates from polar alliance Republicans, Kansas Democrats may be able to translate intermittent moderate coalitions with moderate Republicans into a Democratic majority, overturning almost a century and a half of GOP domination. Unlikely—yes. Impossible—no.

CHAPTER FIVE

The Governor

The elected chief executive represents a uniquely American invention that provides an independent source of energy and initiative in democratic governance. State governors occupy a preeminent position in state government that parallels the U.S. president at the national level. The powers of governorship offer those who occupy the office the potential for state leadership.

From the beginning the Kansas governorship, like many governorships that took shape in the nineteenth century, reflected a political culture of individualism that distrusted government. The framers of the Kansas Constitution and later state lawmakers in the early decades of statehood sought to limit political powers, including those of the governor. Progressive era governors broke loose from these early restraints to elevate the office and to demonstrate leadership in political, economic, and moral reforms during the early part of the twentieth century. The powers of the office slowly evolved until the 1970s when the executive, along with legislative and judicial branches, underwent a fundamental transformation from which the modern Kansas governorship emerged.

Today most Kansans see their governor as the face of state government. Kansas governors are expected to exercise leadership in state policy making and in the management of state government. The governor represents all Kansans as chief of state, and Kansans hold the governor accountable when things go wrong.

In this chapter the Kansas governorship is examined in historical context with emphasis on the modern governorship and those governors serving after the transformation of the office in the early 1970s. The governorship is also viewed historically in cultural context as a negotiator of the cultural dilemmas that confront individual governors.

KANSAS GOVERNORS

Forty-one Kansans have been elected to the office of governor (see table 16); another three individuals served as governor after being elevated to the office from the position of lieutenant governor in transition periods of less than three months.[1] Ten other individuals appointed by presidents Franklin Pierce and James Buchanan served as territorial governors of Kansas in the period prior to statehood, 1854 to 1861.[2]

The late Kansas historian Homer Socolofsky observed in 1990 that Kansans had provided "an informal profile of their governors" as "male, white, native-born Americans of a dominant northwestern European stock, solidly middle-class and Protestant."[3] After he made this observation, Kansans elected two women of Catholic religious affiliation as governor. As a result the profile of Kansas governors may now be revised as white native-born Americans of a dominant northwestern European stock, solidly middle-class, Christian, and until recently mostly male.

Business and professional occupations characterize those who have been elected governor in Kansas. Nineteen governors had business backgrounds—seven as bankers, six as newspaper publishers, three as merchants, and three others with ties to construction, oil, and insurance. Twelve practiced law; and seven were farmers. The occupations of the last three governors, Finney, Graves, and Sebelius, may best be described as politics. Finney worked in political offices and was then elected state treasurer, serving four consecutive terms for a total of sixteen years. Graves left the family business once elected secretary of state and served in that office for eight years. Sebelius worked as a lobbyist and then served as a state legislator before her election for two terms as insurance commissioner.

With few exceptions Kansas governors have had prior elective experience.[4] Twenty-seven of the forty-one governors served in the Kansas legislature prior to their election. Indeed, seventeen of the first eighteen governors had prior legislative experience. Nine were elected governor after election to other statewide offices—four as lieutenant governor, two as attorney general, and one each as secretary of state, state treasurer, and insurance commissioner. Arthur Capper and George Docking succeeded in election to the governor's office after an earlier defeat for the office. Thirteen governors had elective experience in local government, six as local prosecutors.

The last six governors provide a contrast in prior political experience to those who went before. Those governors serving from 1975 through 1991—Bennett, Carlin, and Hayden—served as legislative leaders immediately prior to their elections as governor. Their successors serving from

Table 16: Kansas Governors, 1859–2008

Name (term of office)	Party	Residence	Occupation	Prior Elective Experience		
				Ks Leg	Ks Exec	Local
Charles Robinson (1861–63)	R	Lawrence	farmer	x		
Thomas Carney (1863–65)	R	Leavenworth	merchant	x		
Samuel Crawford (1865–68)	R	Garnett	law	x		
Nehemiah Green (1868–69)	R	Manhattan	minister	x	x	
James Harvey (1869–73)	R	Vinton	farmer	x		
Thomas Osborn (1873–77)	R	Leavenworth	law	x	x	
George Anthony (1877–79)	R	Leavenworth	publisher	x		
John St. John (1879–83)	R	Olathe	law	x		
George Glick (1883–85)	D	Atchison	law	x		x
John Martin (1885–89)	R	Atchison	publisher	x	x	x
Lyman Humphrey (1889–93)	R	Independence	banker	x		
Lorenzo Lewelling (1893–95)	P	Wichita	merchant	x		
Edmund Morrill (1895–97)	R	Hiawatha	banker	x		x
John Leedy (1897–99)	P	LeRoy	farmer	x		
William Stanley (1899–03)	R	Wichita	law	x		x
Willis Bailey (1903–05)	R	Baileyville	banker	x		
Edward Hoch (1905–09)	R	Marion	publisher	x		
Walter Stubbs (1909–13)	R	Lawrence	contractor	x		
George Hodges (1913–15)	D	Olathe	merchant	x		
Arthur Capper (1915–19)	R	Topeka	publisher	x		
Henry Allen (1919–23)	R	Wichita	publisher			
Jonathan Davis (1923–25)	D	Bronson	farmer	x		

1991 to 2009—Finney, Graves, and Sebelius—each served two or more terms in statewide executive offices.

All but three of the forty-one Kansas governors resided in the eastern half of Kansas when elected, and most of this number hailed from mid-sized urban communities. Seventeen came from the northeast quadrant; twelve from central Kansas; and nine from the southeast quadrant. No resident of Kansas City, the state's largest city from 1890 to 1940, has been elected governor. Wichita, the state's largest city since 1950, has seen four of its residents elected, although none since 1952, and Topeka, which has ranked second or third in population since 1880, has had three residents elected governor, two since 1990.

The governor of Kansas is currently paid an annual salary of $110,707

Name (term of office)	Party	Residence	Occupation	Prior Elective Experience		
				Ks Leg	Ks Exec	Local
Benjamin Paulen (1925–29)	R	Fredonia	banker	x	x	x
Clyde Reed (1929–31)	R	Parsons	publisher			
Harry Woodring (1931–33)	D	Neodesha	banker			
Alf Landon (1933–37)	R	Independence	oil			
Walter Huxman (1937–39)	D	Hutchinson	law			x
Payne Ratner (1939–43)	R	Parsons	law	x		x
Andrew Schoeppel (1943–47)	R	Ness City	law			x
Frank Carlson (1947–50)	R	Concordia	farmer	x		
Edward Arn (1951–55)	R	Wichita	law		x	
Fredrick Hall (1955–57)	R	Dodge City	law		x	x
George Docking (1957–61)	D	Lawrence	banker			
John Anderson (1961–65)	R	Olathe	law	x		x
William Avery (1965–67)	R	Wakefield	farmer	x		
Robert Docking (1967–75)	D	Arkansas City	banker			x
Robert Bennett (1975–79)	R	Prairie Village	law	x		x
John Carlin (1979–87)	D	Smolan	farmer	x		
Mike Hayden (1987–91)	R	Atwood	insurance agent	x		
Joan Finney (1991–95)	D	Topeka	state executive		x	
Bill Graves (1995–03)	R	Salina	state executive		x	
Kathleen Sebelius (2003–09)	D	Topeka	state executive	x	x	

Note: On party, P represents the Populist Party. On prior elective experience, *Ks Leg* represents Kansas legislative experience; *Ks Exec* represents Kansas executive experience; and *Local* represents local experience.

and is provided an official residence at Cedar Crest in Topeka for family living and official entertainment.[5] The governor is provided a car and driver, personal security around the clock, and first call on the state's executive aircraft for official travel. The governor has a personal staff of twenty-four, four additional staff to assist with the governor's residence, and a budget staff of twenty, along with having the ability to draw upon two dozen agency heads, who serve at the pleasure of the governor, as well as their staffs. The governor's budget provides generous support for travel and flexibility in entertaining friends and political supporters at the official residence.[6]

Most of the accoutrements to gubernatorial office evolved in the latter half of the twentieth century. In 1900 the annual salary was $3,000 and authorized staff was a personal secretary at $2,000 plus $2,000 more for a chief clerk, a stenographer, and a messenger. In 1950 the governor's annual salary was $8,000, and the governor was authorized a private secretary and a pardon attorney at $4,000 each plus $19,000 for any additional staff. Cedar Crest was given to the state as a residence for the governor in 1955, but George Docking, allegedly acting out of fiscal restraint, refused to live there. John Anderson and his family became the first official occupants in 1962; all governors have lived there since.[7] An executive aircraft was purchased in 1969 primarily for the governor's use.

BECOMING GOVERNOR AND HOLDING ONTO THE OFFICE

Becoming governor requires winning the nomination of a political party, and except for the populist incursions of 1892 and 1896, Kansas governors have been nominated by either the Republican or Democratic parties. Before the enactment of primary elections candidates for governor were nominated at party conventions, and in twenty-one of twenty-four gubernatorial elections prior to 1908 that meant mostly Republican Party conventions. In that era of individualism control of the Republican Party convention and the nomination for governor gravitated toward dominant economic interests, particularly a few railroads and the party oligarchy at the time.[8]

Although Republicans have dominated the office of governor historically, table 17 shows how their control of the office has shifted with time.

Democrats failed to field candidates under their party's label in five of the first eight contests and won the governorship in their own right on only three occasions in the state's first seventy years. As explained in chapter 3, the New Deal realignment fundamentally changed party voting in Kansas, and as a result Democratic gubernatorial candidates became more competitive. Democratic candidates won only one of the first twelve elections during this New Deal era but would win seven of the next eleven elections, 1956–78. In 1958 George Docking became the first Democrat to win reelection in Kansas. Since then Bob Docking won reelection on three occasions, and both Carlin and Sebelius had successful reelection bids. In contrast, four of the last six Republican governors have been turned out of office in reelection contests. Democratic successes as well as Republican losses may be explained in part by Republicans' inability in sustaining a unified cultural coalition, as noted in chapter 1. The breakup of the party into moderate and polar alliance camps has helped defeat incumbent Republican governors and aided in the election and reelection of Democrats to the office of governor.

Except for Finney in 1994, every Kansas governor elected to the office

Table 17: Election Victories in Kansas Gubernatorial Contests,
by Party, 1861–2006

Period	Republican	Democrat	Populist
Republican era, 1859–1902	19	1	2
Progressive era, 1904–1930	11	3	—
New Deal, 1932–1978	15	8	—
New Right, 1982–2006	3	4	—
Total	48	16	2

sought to stay in the office by seeking the traditional second term. However, nineteen of forty-one Kansas governors left office in defeat—eleven Republicans, six Democrats, and two populists.[9] Six Republicans were denied a second term by their party, four at party conventions, and two in primary elections. The other thirteen governors, Republicans and Democrats, were defeated in general elections, two (St. John and George Docking) in bids for a third term. Robert Docking became the first and only governor to win a third term as well as a fourth term. After leaving office, seven former governors sought to retake the office; all failed.

Kansans have experienced some unusual campaigns for governor. The most unique was the campaign of Allen who was out of the country during the entire campaign of 1918. Allen volunteered for the Red Cross in Europe during WWI, missing but still winning both the primary and general elections. The state's infamous goat-gland doctor, John Brinkley, made effective use of radio and billboards in campaigning for governor as a write-in candidate in 1930 and on the ballot in 1932. In contrast to more sedate gubernatorial campaigns, Brinkley toured the state in his airplane or in his "$20,000, silver mounted, sixteen-cylinder limousine" and staged campaign performances with an "entertainment troupe and minister of the gospel to introduce him."[10] He lost both elections but only narrowly in 1930.

Most campaigns for governor in the first half of the twentieth century were more mundane, as described by Rhoten Smith and Clarence Hein:

you drive from town to town, often alone and nearly always tired. When you reach the next town you meet the county chairman (some will be on your side, some will not) or your principal supporter, and you begin to "do" the town. First, perhaps, you stop at a bank and go in to meet the president; the next stop may be a grain elevator where you see the manager and some of the important local farmers. The manager of the chamber of commerce, real-estate dealers, insurance men, the bigger merchants, the boys in the backs of the shops—you see all of these and other important people as time allows. You contact people who might contribute to the campaign. And along the street you stop and shake hands and smile and chat with anyone who comes along, for each has one vote.[11]

Change came with new campaign technologies. Hall first used television in his campaign of 1954 with significant impact. In campaigning for reelection in 1956, he flew around the state "from one regional center to another, televising a new speech on the problems of the state." Robert Docking made extensive use of polling, political consultants, and media professionals in his four winning campaigns, 1966 though 1972. Campaign funds were increasingly diverted to these new technologies rather than newspaper ads, posters, and other literature, and the costs of campaigning began to escalate. In the 2002 campaign for governor expenditures on consultants and TV and radio advertising was ten times that for printing, yard signs, and newspaper ads.[12]

The cost of becoming governor has escalated. Campaign expenditures for gubernatorial aspirants jumped from less than $1 million in 1970 to over $3 million in 1982 and to over $9 million in 2002. Sebelius topped all prior campaign spending by raising and spending $4.5 million on her successful bid for the governorship in 2002; this price tag included expenditures of over $3 million for political consultants and on TV and radio broadcasting.[13] In the last three gubernatorial campaigns the top spenders, Graves in 1994 and 1998 and Sebelius in 2002, were the winners. However, money helps but does not assure a winning campaign. In 1990 Hayden outspent Finney but still lost the general election. Four years earlier, Hayden was outspent in the Republican primary by three other candidates, including two million-dollar campaigns; he won by only spending just over $200,000.

FORMAL POWERS

The governor's formal powers derive from the state constitution, from state statutes, and through precedents established by previous governors. Scholars point to five primary powers that determine whether a governorship may be characterized as strong or weak. These powers are executive structure, tenure of office, veto powers, powers of appointment, and fiscal powers. To these primary formal powers may be added two key administrative powers: the power of organization and the power of command, which emanate from a governor's powers of appointment.[14] The Kansas governorship has evolved and been fundamentally transformed over the course of state history, and an examination of this history gives insight into the formal powers of the modern Kansas governorship.

The Wyandotte Constitution of 1859 was drafted in a prevailing culture of individualism that distrusted political power and sought to restrain state government. Certain powers assigned to the governor, however, followed a standard pattern adopted in the U.S. Constitution for the president as well as for governors of most other states. For example, the executive article of the state constitution provides that the governor "shall see that the laws are faithfully executed" and "may require information in writing from the officers of the executive department, upon any subject relating to their specific duties." Additionally, the governor "may, on extraordinary occasions, convene the Legislature by proclamation, and shall, at the commencement of every session, communicate in writing such information as he may possess in reference to the condition of the State, and recommend such measures as he may deem expedient." The governor is also assigned "pardoning powers" and charged to be "commander in chief" of the state militia. These powers with minor changes in wording and gender neutrality remain intact today.

Cultural restraints were reflected in the executive structure designed by the framers of the 1859 constitution. In the executive article, for example, the "supreme executive power" was vested in a governor, but at the same time the framers determined that Kansas voters would elect six additional executives independently of the governor—a lieutenant governor, secretary of state, auditor, treasurer, attorney general, and superintendent of public instruction. An elected state printer was added to the constitution in 1904. These constitutional executives were limited to two-year terms. The framers, and voters as well, preferred diffusion of executive powers and competing power sources rather than a unified executive.[15]

In response to new demands state lawmakers began diffusing executive authority further by adding executive agencies independent of gubernatorial control. These new agencies were often placed under the control of a separate board or commission. By 1905 the organization chart of Kansas state government showed seventy-six offices, agencies, boards, and institutions in addition to the seven constitutional executives established in 1859. Initial steps taken during the progressive era to establish management and financial controls of state agencies and institutions slowed the growth slightly, but by 1950 142 separate boxes appeared on the state organization chart.[16] Major functions of state government—highways, education, public health, social welfare, and state institutions—were headed by boards and commissions. State administration was fragmented, and the "supreme" executive power of the governor was steadily diluted.

The disorder in state administration prompted numerous studies beginning in the progressive era, but the issue of gubernatorial powers was not fully addressed until done so by the Kansas Commission on Executive Organization, a statutory study commission jointly appointed by Robert Docking and legislative leaders in 1970. In its final report the commission declared that "the executive branch of state government is an organizational jungle. . . . Kansas has nearly 200 agencies, boards, commissions, committees, councils and other groups for whose actions the governor is at least theoretically responsible. It is obviously impossible for anyone to properly govern the state as long as this inadequately structured organization exists. The governor of Kansas should be the chief executive . . . [and so] give him powers commensurate with his responsibilities." The commission recommended the establishment of a cabinet structure, the consolidation of agencies into "a few departments, each directed by a secretary chosen by and responsible to the governor."[17]

The work of the commission triggered a series of constitutional amendments, reorganizations, and statutory changes designed to strengthen the governorship. In 1972 state lawmakers began reorganization by creating the Department of Administration and the Department of Revenue, each headed by a secretary who was appointed by the governor with the consent of the senate and who served at the pleasure of the governor. Later in 1972 voters approved a fundamental overhaul of the executive article that changed the governor's term from two to four years, provided for the governor and lieutenant governor to run as a team instead of independently, gave the governor new powers of executive reorganization, removed the state auditor and treasurer from their status as constitutional officers, and limited the governor to two successive four-year terms.

In 1973 Robert Docking exercised his newly acquired powers of executive reorganization and established the Department of Social and Rehabilitation Services and the Department of Health and Environment, each with department heads subject to the governor's removal powers. State lawmakers also eliminated the elective office of state auditor and implemented changes in the governor's term to be effective in the 1974 election. In 1974 voters adopted a constitutional amendment removing the state printer from the constitution as an elective office, with that office being abolished by lawmakers the following year. Lawmakers established the Department of Transportation as a cabinet agency in 1975, and Bennett used executive reorganization orders to establish the Department of Economic Development in 1975 and the Department of Human Resources in 1976. In 1977 state lawmakers established the Department on Aging as a cabinet agency and made the secretary of the Department of Corrections subject to removal by the governor. Hayden established the Department of Wildlife and Parks through executive reorganization order in 1987. Finally, in 1995 lawmakers organized the Department of Agriculture into a cabinet agency.

The transformation enhanced the formal powers of the Kansas governorship. First, the plural executive established by the framers and augmented by lawmakers was substantially unified. The number of executives running for statewide office independently of the governor was reduced from eight to four. The lieutenant governor would be chosen by and run on the ticket with the governor. The offices of elected auditor and printer were abolished. Only the attorney general and the secretary of state remained as independent constitutional executives. The elected state treasurer had been removed from constitutional status and was now susceptible along with the insurance commissioner to being abolished at any legislative session. In sum, the number of state executives who could lay claim to a statewide constituency and who could develop his or her own political base independent of the governor had been cut in half. Figure 13 depicts the current organization structure of state government.

Second, the tenure potential of Kansas governors was enhanced by the transformation. Beginning with the 1974 election, the governor has been elected to a four-year term and may run for one additional successive term. This change removes the constraints of the two-year term and gives a governor more time to master the duties of the office and to exercise leadership. The impact of this change has been immediate. The six governors elected since 1974 have served an average of 5.3 years, compared to an average tenure of 3.3 years for their thirty-five predecessors.

Third, the governor's veto powers were not directly affected by the changes of the early 1970s. The Wyandotte Constitution granted the governor the power to veto bills subject to being overridden by a vote of two-thirds of both houses of the legislature. In 1904 Kansans adopted a constitutional amendment giving the governor the additional power of a line-item veto of appropriation bills. This power allows the governor to approve an appropriation bill but at the same time reject, or veto, one or more line items in that appropriation bill. A two-thirds majority in both legislative houses is also required to override a line-item veto.

Fourth, the governor's powers of appointment, that is, the power to hire and fire executive officials, was dramatically strengthened in the transformation. Except for education, the heads of eleven cabinet agencies representing the major line departments of state government are now chosen by and serve at the pleasure of the governor. The heads of another two dozen smaller state agencies are also appointed by and subject to the governor's power of removal. Another fifty second-level positions in these executive

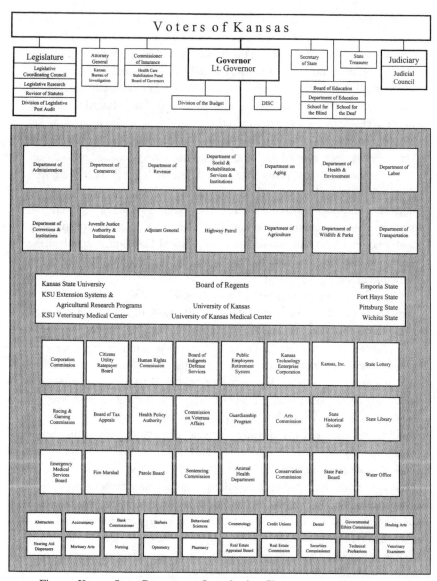

Fig. 13. Kansas State Government Organization Chart

agencies are subject to the governor's reach through appointment or control of salaries.

Fifth, the fiscal powers of the governor, that is, the power to direct or substantially influence levels of state taxing and spending, has evolved since the progressive era and been enhanced through a more unified executive structure and broader gubernatorial control of appointments. Kansans had overwhelmingly supported giving the governor the power of line-item veto in 1904. Further, in 1925 state lawmakers officially granted the governor the initiative in state budgeting. This budget authority charged the governor with budgetary powers, to prepare and recommend an executive budget, and to established a budget office headed by a gubernatorial appointee to assist and support the governor's budget.[18] Since that time Kansas governors have annually recommended a plan for expenditures, revenues, and year-end balances and have the authority to enforce their fiscal recommendations through the use of veto powers, the outright veto of appropriation bills, line-item vetoes of appropriation bills, and the threat of vetoes. Further, enhanced appointment powers assure that most executive officials will be defending the governor's budget before legislative committees.

Sixth, the constitutional power of executive reorganization coupled with organizational discretion resulting from expanded powers of appointment has shifted initiative for organizational change to the chief executive. The constitutional power of executive reorganization grants Kansas governors the power to initiate executive reorganization orders "transferring, abolishing, consolidating or coordinating the whole or any part of any state agency, or the functions thereof, within the executive branch of state government." A governor must submit an order within the first thirty days of a regular legislative session, and that order will become effective unless disapproved within sixty calendar days by a majority vote of either house of the legislature.

Governors have applied these expanded organizational powers to accomplish diverse purposes such as unifying gubernatorial control, formulating public policy, coordinating internal administration, and conferring organizational status by giving certain public purposes, programs, and constituencies higher priority and visibility than others. Since authorized in 1972, governors have issued executive reorganization orders successfully on nineteen occasions that have created and abolished offices and that have assigned purposes, authority, and duties to these offices, including the establishment of five cabinet-level departments within the governor's span of control. Expanded powers of appointment have been used by governors to formulate policy recommendations through blue-ribbon commissions or to manage state government through subcabinet task forces.

Seventh, expanded powers of appointment also gives Kansas governors the authority to direct the actions of executive officials. The span of the governor's power of command extends to the statutory discretion lodged with agency heads who serve at the pleasure of the governor. Since most state statutes grant broad discretion to agency heads, gubernatorial command encompasses individual acts of agency officials as well as their authority to issue rules and regulations. Gubernatorial orders may take the form of verbal instructions, executive orders, proclamations, memoranda, and various other policy directives. The legislature may restrict this power only by limiting appointment powers or by narrowing the scope of agency authority.

Over the span of twenty-five years the Kansas governorship has been modernized, and the executive branch profoundly transformed. Fragmentation and diffusion of authority has given ground to a more ordered, hierarchical structure within the executive branch of state government. The executive branch is not a pure hierarchy, but scholars who had ranked the Kansas governorship in the bottom third among the fifty states in terms of formal powers of the governor prior to transformation of the early 1970s now place the governorship in the top two-fifths.[19]

Governors apply the formal powers of governorship in a variety of roles, but the two primary roles of the modern governorship are those of chief policy maker in state government and chief manager of state administration. Formal powers create the potential for gubernatorial leadership in these roles but do not assure leadership nor success in attempts at such leadership. At the same time no Kansas governor may today avoid these roles.

Governor as Chief Policy Maker

Every Kansas governor has exercised his or her constitutional obligation to report at "every legislative session" on "the condition of the State" and to "recommend such measures as he deems expedient." This assignment clearly grants the governor the opportunity to set an agenda for legislative action, or in other words, to be chief policy maker, and most all of the forty-one governors have undertaken this assignment with utmost seriousness.

The Kansas governors of the nineteenth century were greatly handicapped in their performance of the role of chief policy maker. The first three were consumed in the turmoil of the Civil War. Seven of the first thirteen served only one two-year term; four of this number served when the legislature met every other year and would have been delivering their only legislative message a few weeks after their election and days after being sworn into office. Most important, the politics of an individualistic era gave political parties a primary role in formulating party platforms that their elected representatives—governor and legislators alike—were expected to carry forward. The tumult of the populist era further undermined the possibilities for gubernatorial leadership in state policy.

Even with these handicaps St. John demonstrated that a nineteenth-century governor could exercise independent leadership in state policy. First, he championed constitutional prohibition and helped gain legislative support in placing the measure on the ballot. He then campaigned for the measure while running for reelection, winning both contests handily. Second, he proclaimed in his biennial message to the 1881 legislature that "we are creating no new debts, but pay as we go." His forceful proclamation became a leading precept of public finance in Kansas well into the twentieth century and led to a debt-free state by 1916. Both actions left indelible imprints on state policy for the next one hundred years.[20]

The potential for independent gubernatorial leadership in public policy emerged dramatically after the turn of the century through a series of progressive Republican governors. Hoch, Stubbs, Capper, and Allen initiated a broad agenda of economic and political change that reformed state politics, regulated the economy, augmented state authority, and improved the management of state agencies.[21] The precedents in leadership demonstrated by these progressive chief executives at the beginning of the twentieth century charted paths in executive initiative that would be tread by governors throughout the balance of the century.

While Kansas governors have no direct authority in amending the state constitution, they have been in the forefront of constitutional change. Progressive era governors helped set the stage for Kansans to embrace in 1932 a constitutional amendment authorizing the first state income tax. Democrat Robert Docking cooperated with Republican legislative leaders to produce a flood of successful amendments implementing executive and judicial reforms in the early 1970s. Democrat Carlin, again in cooperation with Republican legislative leaders, led in securing a series of constitutional amendments reforming the property tax, bringing the century-long struggle with prohibition to a close, neutering the long-standing internal improvements prohibition, and authorizing state-sponsored gaming.

Kansas governors have with rare exception been in the forefront of any change in general taxes, in some instances suffering politically as a result.[22] Landon campaigned for a constitutional amendment authorizing a state income tax in 1932 and as governor called for its enactment in 1933. Recommendations by Huxman led to enactment of the first state sales tax in 1937. Avery became the first Kansas governor to recommend and achieve

Table 18: Gubernatorial Vetoes and Veto Overrides, by Governor, 1967 to present

Governor	legislative sessions	bill vetoes	overridden	line-item vetoes	overridden
R. Docking	1967–1974	130	33	28	3
Bennett	1975–1978	45	0	8	1
Carlin	1979–1986	103	0	24	0
Hayden	1987–1990	11	0	20	0
Finney	1991–1994	70	19	78	13
Graves	1995–2002	17	0	91	0
Sebelius	2003–2008	32	2	43	0

rate increases in both income and sales taxes as well as cigarette taxes. Income-tax rate increases were enacted at the initiative of George Docking and Robert Docking. Increases in sales tax rates were led by George Docking, Carlin, and Finney. Carlin helped initiate property tax reappraisal and classification, and Hayden implemented the reforms. Avery's reelection defeat in 1966 is attributed by most observers to his tax initiatives. Carlin and Hayden trace their losses in the gubernatorial contests of 1990 to voter retaliation on property tax reform. Finney became the first Kansas governor not to run for a second term after supporting rate increases on sales and upper-bracket income taxpayers.

Gubernatorial initiative in policy making operates in a partisan manner. Kansas voters have elected a divided state government, that is, divided party control between legislative and executive branches, for twenty-eight of the last forty years, 1967–2007. Except for a brief two-year term, the four Democratic governors serving in this period faced a Republican-controlled legislature.[23] Partisan conflicts are reflected in both the number of vetoes and veto overrides, which are summarized in table 18.

Democratic governors exercised bill vetoes more frequently than Republicans in this period and, except for Carlin, were more likely to have their vetoes overridden. The high number of line-item vetoes in the Finney and Graves administration reveals these two governors fending off the legislature's growing propensity to attach riders to appropriation bills, which the legislators also used to mandate some executive actions. Even with partisan divisions, however, both Robert Docking and Carlin demonstrated success in building the bipartisan coalitions necessary for constitutional revision as well as for other substantive legislation. Finney also succeeded in building bipartisan support for a major overhaul of school finance in 1992. On the other hand, Sebelius's legislative initiatives in educational finance and organization of health care services have been blocked or delayed by a solidly Republican legislature.

Unified party control between the governor and the legislature does not assure a governor legislative success. Republican legislators helped defeat Bennett's reorganization orders abolishing the elected offices of state treasurer and insurance commissioner. A Republican-controlled legislature failed to reinstate the death penalty, a major campaign commitment of Hayden. A Republican-controlled house slammed the door on Grave's debt-laden highway program by a unanimous vote of 125 members in opposition. Still, unified party control does allow executive and legislative leaders to reduce the necessity of vetoes and to minimize overrides.

Governors who have come to office from positions of legislative leadership have been the most aggressive in the role of chief policy maker. Bennett issued eleven executive reorganization orders, securing approval for all but three, and obtained substantial expansions in educational funding. Carlin demonstrated dramatic success in tax policy, constitutional change, and initiatives in economic development. Hayden, labeled by one scholar as a policy entrepreneur, secured major initiatives in tax reform, highway finance, water plan finance, and executive reorganization.[24] After the gubernatorial activism of the 1970s and 1980s, the three most recent governors coming from positions as elected state executives—state treasurer, secretary of state, and insurance commissioner—have been more cautious in exercising policy leadership.

Governor as Chief Manager

The executive transformation of the early 1970s solidified key administrative powers of the Kansas governor—the power of appointment, fiscal powers, power of command, and power of organization—and gives each new governor an opportunity to perform the role of chief manager in state administration. No Kansas governor today can avoid the exercise of administrative powers but must do so with an awareness of the political context and consequences.

The governor's administrative powers are shared powers, shared primarily with the state legislature, and therefore have a political context. For example, the legislature may restrict through statute the governor's powers of appointment by placing an executive position under a board or commission or under civil service protection independent of the governor's authority or by requiring legislative confirmation or by establishing statutory criteria for appointments to certain positions. The Kansas legislature has over the past thirty-five years shown a propensity to expand rather than restrict guber-natorial appointment powers, but at the same time legislators cannot resist leaving their own mark on executive appointments.

Legislative intrusion into executive appointments ranges from mild to the ridiculous. On the mild side lawmakers have required that gubernatorial ap-pointments to certain boards show geographic and party balance. In recent years, however, legislators have more frequently restricted gubernatorial ap-pointment powers by imposing legislative appointments, most commonly the appointment of legislators by legislative leaders, onto boards conducting executive functions. For example, in 1986 in establishing key economic de-velopment agencies, Kansas Inc. and Kansas Technology Enterprise Corpo-ration, lawmakers mandated legislative appointments for both agencies. In an extreme example the Bioscience Authority established by lawmakers in 2004 gives legislative leaders six appointments on an eleven-member board, with the governor only having two appointments.[25] This practice of legisla-tive appointments violates the democratic ideal of separating legislative and executive powers and creates an encroachment that would be prohibited at the national level by the U.S. Constitution.

Lawmakers have on occasion succumbed to special interest politics and diminished the governor's role in appointment through narrow statutory criteria for making appointments to state boards. For example, lawmakers enacted statutes requiring that eight of ten gubernatorial appointments to the twenty-four-member Water Resources Authority be made from nominees of specific interest groups and associations. In extreme cases lawmakers have completely turned state administration over to an industrial group, for example by requiring that the boards of two small agricultural marketing agencies, the Dairy Commission and the Sheep Council, be elected by their respective constituencies without any gubernatorial involvement.[26]

These legislative intrusions into the power of appointment will likely ac-cumulate in time, create new disorder in state administration, and likely undermine the effectiveness of executive agencies. In most cases, however, they represent minor meddling given the broad appointive powers of the governor and simply serve as political distractions to the governor's role as chief manager. Still, the statutes establishing the Bioscience Authority grant legislative appointees majority control of an executive agency, potentially putting legislators in charge of the execution of public policy in addition to holding powers of authorization and appropriation. This meshing of execu-tive with legislative powers may eventually lead to mischief.

The exercise of administrative powers such as the hiring and firing of executive officials may incur political liabilities for a governor. Bennett sought to establish the highest professional standards in appointing the first cabinet secretary of a newly reorganized Department of Transportation, whose duties were historically supervised by a highly politicized highway commission.[27] The new secretary performed as Bennett desired but often put the governor on the defensive in supporting the secretary's allocation of funds based on technical assessments of need and personnel decisions based on merit. Parochial highway boosters and local partisans hotly disputed the governor, and the conflict cost him politically in his bid for reelection. Hayden incurred the wrath of partisan legislative leaders when he continued the appointment of a talented secretary of revenue of the opposing party from the prior administration. The political fallout of appointment snafus by Finney, including three different secretaries of administration in one week, likely reinforced her decision not to run for reelection.

The power of the purse—the ultimate power to determine state taxing and spending—resides with the state legislature, but as noted above, Kansas governors often lead in exercising fiscal powers. The Kansas legislature does not accept the governor's spending priorities without alteration, but legislative changes normally work on the margins of the governor's budget recommendations. The legislature relied upon the governor's budget office for fiscal advice up until 1974 when a fiscal staff serving only the legislature was put in place. Even with its own independent staff, the legislature takes the governor's budget as a starting point that is vigorously defended by the governor's budget staff as well as agency officials who serve at the pleasure of the governor.

One more recent legislative response to executive domination of the budget process has been to attach detailed provisos, or riders, to agency appropriation bills. These provisos have been increasingly used by the legislature to prescribe that certain actions be taken by agency officials, essentially preempting executive discretion. On occasion a governor has negated a proviso by striking through it as an exercise of gubernatorial authority of line-item veto. This use of the line-item veto has never been challenged or judged constitutional by the courts.

Governors also share powers of organization with the legislature. Since 1974 Kansas governors have issued thirty-four executive reorganization orders, with fifteen orders having been disapproved by legislative action, as shown in table 19.

Robert Docking and Bennett issued sixteen reorganization orders in a four-year period, 1974–77, and only six were disapproved. In the twenty-eight years since 1977, Republican-controlled legislative bodies have disapproved nine of eighteen reorganization orders, three of which were issued

Table 19: Executive Reorganization Orders, Proposed and Disapproved,
       by Governor, 1974–2008

Governor	legislative sessions	proposed	disapproved
R. Docking	1973–1974	5	3
Bennett	1975–1978	11	3
Carlin	1979–1986	5	3
Hayden	1987–1990	1	0
Finney	1991–1994	3	1
Graves	1995–2002	4	3
Sebelius	2003–2008	5	2

by Republican Graves and six by Democrats Carlin, Finney, and Sebelius. More recently, legislative leaders have discouraged governors from using executive reorganization orders as reflected in both the reduced use of such orders by governors as well as the increase in disapprovals by legislative bodies.

Legislative leaders have apparently concluded that the governor's constitutional power of executive reorganization preempts legislative prerogatives with respect to state organization. The configuration of executive branch agencies is allied with a complex mosaic of special interests throughout the state, and reorganization disrupts these "iron triangles" of state administration, that is, the comfortable three-way alliances of entrenched bureaucracies, special interest groups, and legislative committees. Such alliances were at work, for example, in defeating Bennett's order abolishing an elected insurance commissioner in 1975 and Carlin's order attempting to bring the Department of Agriculture under gubernatorial control in 1986. Gubernatorial initiative in reorganization unsettles these triangles and puts legislators on the defensive with special interests and resistant administrators who feel their influence diminished by organizational change. Legislators prefer to negotiate those organizational alliances with as much freedom from gubernatorial intervention as possible.

Kansas governors have exercised their constitutional power of reorganization successfully on matters large and small. Robert Docking, Bennett, and Hayden established five major cabinet departments through reorganization orders in 1974, 1975, 1976, and 1987. Both Docking and Bennett had their proposal to make the state treasurer an appointive office rejected. On three occasions legislators have blocked gubernatorial orders only to turn around and approve by statute a similar reorganization shaped more to their liking. This reaction occurred on two substantial reorganizations proposed by Carlin, one related to water resources and another to agriculture, and a major reorganization of health care services proposed by Sebelius. Other reorganization orders have been more modest in their political impacts.

Organizational change has political consequences as well as institutional constraints. Bennett articulated these consequences as follows:

> During the election campaign there wasn't a candidate of either party . . . that didn't proclaim loud and clear that he was for reorganization, he was going to abolish unneeded activity, he was going to merge . . . duplicating departments, he in fact was going to streamline government. In the abstract, it is without a doubt one of the finest and one of the most palatable theories ever espoused by a modern day politician. But in practice, however, it becomes the loss of a job for your brother or your sister, your uncle or your aunt. It becomes the closing of an office on which you have learned to depend for a small portion of your municipal economic sustenance. It becomes the doing away with an activity that is of personal economic benefit to you although it may be of little benefit to others. So there may in many instances be more agony than anything else in this reorganization process.[28]

Beyond the constitutional power of organization, Kansas governors frequently use their inherent powers of organization to manage the process of policy formulation. Governors freely establish task forces, blue-ribbon commissions, and other such mechanisms in order to highlight gubernatorial priorities, address complex state issues, and formulate policy options. Hayden and Graves used task forces on highways and transportation, respectively, that formulated recommendations and eventually led to fundamental policy commitments. Finney used a task force to develop recommendations on school finance. Sebelius convened a health care roundtable to build consensus on the reorganization of health care services. On occasion a task force fashions recommendations that make a governor run for cover, as did Grave's committee on visioning economic development. In such cases task force members receive a thank you, possibly a plaque, and their report is quickly shelved to gather dust.

Governors often exercise the power of command through executive orders that direct and coordinate the actions of executive officials. Bennett issued an executive order to establish standards of conduct on conflicts of interest for his appointees. Recent governors have used executive orders to organize a cabinet and to establish cabinet status for executive officials. Every recent governor has used executive orders to coordinate executive agencies on a particular subject, for example as Hayden did on water conservation and Finney did on workforce programs. Governors also use executive orders to carry out their discretionary authority under state statutes, for example to issue rewards for incidents of crime or to implement certain personnel actions.

The power of Kansas governors to command the actions of executive officials ultimately relies on the scope of the governor's appointment powers, that is, the ability to enforce commands if necessary through removal of reluctant officials. Executive officials who serve at the pleasure of the governor rarely have to be informed of this relationship. Such cases, however, do occur for various reasons. Carlin ordered his budget director to hire a specific individual as analyst. When the director refused, Carlin sacked him and found someone more amenable to the governor's commands, explaining that "everybody has to know who is in charge."[29]

Gubernatorial directives of course may have political consequences. Out of a desire to avoid requests for supplemental appropriations, Hayden ordered his welfare agency head to limit eligibility for certain beneficiaries. The action came just before the holiday season and cast the governor as a hard-hearted Scrooge. On the other hand, Finney ordered correction officials to buy electric fans for prisoners during the peak of a summer heat wave and was viewed as a compassionate soul.

GOVERNORS IN CULTURAL CONTEXT

Observers of Kansas politics often compare the performance of the state's governors, but such comparisons are often subjective. One governor maintained a high level of popularity but fell short in results, while another led the state to major accomplishments in public policy but failed to be reelected. U.S. presidents are often compared by surveying "experts" on presidential performance and polling citizens on their "approval" of a president's performance. No expert assessment of gubernatorial performance by Kansas governors exists, nor is systematic polling data on approval ratings readily available.

Viewing governors in cultural context can provide insights into gubernatorial performance.[30] From a cultural perspective leadership by the chief executive comprises "the art of building or sustaining cultural coalitions."[31] A full examination of Kansas' forty-one governors in cultural context is beyond the scope of this volume, but a few historical sketches illustrate governors as they grapple with cultural dilemmas and provide a lens for observing and assessing the performance of contemporary governors.

Governor as Egalitarian: Populist Lewelling

The political cultures of individualism, hierarchy, and egalitarianism have all had moments of ascendancy in Kansas, as shown in chapter 1, and cultural theory suggests what form leadership might take in varying political cultures. For example, an egalitarian culture seeks to diminish differences in authority and among people: "Would-be egalitarian leaders are thus in trouble before they start, for authority makes a prima-facie instance of inequality. . . . Leaders who push themselves forward, attempting to lead rather than merely convene or facilitate discussion, will be attacked for attempting to lord it over others. . . . Leadership may, however, be justified in the name of redressing inequalities."[32]

Of all Kansas governors Populist Lewelling (1893–95) may best personify the governor as egalitarian. He roomed at a dollar-a-day hotel, not the up-scale hotel used by his predecessors, and spoke eloquently in his inaugural address of the inequities resulting from markets: "The 'survival of the fittest' (or strongest) is the government of brutes and reptiles. . . . I have a dream of the future. . . . I behold the abolition of poverty. A time is coming when . . . equality and justice shall have permanent abiding places in this republic."[33] According to Socolofsky, Lewelling "favored state action on behalf of the oppressed" and gained national notoriety with his issuance of a "tramp circular" condemning police enforcement of vagrancy laws, stating, "thousands of men, guilty of no crime but that of seeking employment, have languished in the city prisons of Kansas or performed unrequited toil in 'rock piles' as municipal slaves, because ignorance of economic conditions has made us cruel."[34] Lewelling also ordered out state troops to protect miners from strikebreakers and to prevent a lynching.

Lewelling's actions on behalf of the oppressed failed to build an egalitarian base or to attract cultural allies. Populist leaders distrusted anyone in authority, including one of their own, and turned on the governor. According to historian James Malin, "no one outside of the Populist party said any harsher things about Populist leadership than Populists themselves."[35] As a result Lewelling's governorship accomplished little, and populist control of state offices was short-lived. Lewelling lost his bid for reelection, dropping forty-five thousand votes below his tally of two years earlier. The other four populists holding statewide executive offices—lieutenant governor, attorney general, secretary of state, and treasurer—were also defeated. Populists further lost four of eight congressional seats and dropped twenty seats in the state house.

Building a Cultural Alliance:
Republicans Stubbs, Capper, and Landon

Republican governors have grappled with the dilemmas posed by a cultural alliance of liberty and order. In an individualistic political culture leaders avoid coercive authority, support limits on the scope of government, and seek agreement through negotiation and accommodation among competing powers. Such leaders want to be viewed as responding to external pressures rather than acting on their own intentions. With three possible exceptions—Lewelling and Leedy, the populist governors of the 1890s, and St. John, the champion of constitutional prohibition—most Kansas governors of the nineteenth century were likely characterized by the era of individualism in which they served. These early Kansas governors were willing to preside on behalf of a minimalist state government that encouraged individual liberty, provided incentives to business, and allowed local governments to shoulder the primary burden of delivering public services.

With the emergence of the progressive era Republican politics began to take shape on a liberty-order axis. Progressive era Republican governors gravitated away from a purely individualistic view toward one that saw the governorship as an instrument of moral, economic, and political order. The cultural dilemma presented by this realignment defined many intraparty conflicts as party faithful split into factions, with individualists labeled "standpatters" and hierarchs tagged as "progressives."[36] The performance of governors in negotiating these cultural conflicts left some governors vulnerable and their party in a state of disorder; others were more successful. The governorships of Stubbs, Capper, and Landon illustrate how three Republican governors uniquely negotiated their party's cultural dilemma.

In a hierarchic culture "leaders are expected to lead; authority inheres in the position. . . . [L]eadership is necessary and should be supported."[37] Republican Stubbs (1909–13) embraced this view and may best personify governor as hierarch. William Allen White described Stubbs as the best governor in Kansas history for his performance in deploying the powers of state government to boost and enforce moral, political, and economic order. According to historian Robert La Forte, Stubbs took order and hierarchy to excess, expecting other players to follow his directives. As governor Stubbs was stubborn, impolitic, and incapable of comradery. He shunned legislators, coerced reluctant legislators, vetoed unimportant local bills carried by legislators, and eliminated sinecures valued by legislators. He "tried to keep men who smoked and drank off the state payroll," promised to run "roughshod" over violators of prohibition laws, and threatened to use military force in a state takeover of mines and railroads.[38]

With Stubbs as governor the Republican cultural alliance of liberty and order came undone, at least temporarily. Stubbs drew primary opposition in 1910 and prevailed but tallied thirty-five thousand fewer votes in the general election than two years earlier. In 1912 he challenged and unseated the standpat incumbent U.S. Senator Charles Curtis in the Republican primary election but in doing so ruptured the party and lost the general election. Republicans lost the senate seat, the governor's office, and both houses of the Kansas legislature, electoral losses that were unprecedented in state history. After his two terms as best governor, Stubbs was defeated in his bids to return to statewide office in 1918 and 1922. Stubbs could point to substantial accomplishments in securing economic, political, and moral order, but he left the Republican cultural alliance in disarray and departed state politics in defeat.

After the Republican debacle of 1912 Capper masterfully repaired factional divisions in the party with a harmony movement, won the governorship in 1914, and mastered the party's cultural divide as few Republican governors have done. For those Kansans preferring liberty and restraint of government, he promised a "business-like" government that would use "modern scientific business methods, in the elimination of useless positions and in requiring the highest efficiency on the part of every public servant."[39] He spoke eloquently of individual liberty: "the first steps toward depriving the individual of his liberty are taken when he is cajoled, or purchased or coerced into the position where he depends upon his government, instead of upon himself, to take care of his needs and provide for his wants."[40]

For Kansans preferring moral order Capper in his first inaugural address expressed his aspiration for "making our beloved state a little cleaner, a little more decent, happier, and more God-like." He wanted tougher enforcement of prohibition and envisioned "universal prohibition for nations." He advocated and signed the "bone-dry law" that made possession of intoxicating liquor a crime, legislation characterized by the *New York Times* as the "most drastic prohibition measure ever enacted." In advancing political order, Capper called for enacting an executive budget and expanding civil service in state government, for authorizing cities to replace political administration with professional managers, and for fine tuning the state's regulatory laws.[41]

Capper negotiated his cultural footing with extraordinary finesse. Contemporaries described him as "modest and self-effacing" and "never arbitrary nor dictatorial." William Allen White described Capper as a "gentle and kind" person who "said nothing to offend anyone." Capper was raised and identified himself as a Quaker with definite pacifist and isolationist leanings, but once World War I was declared, he crisscrossed the state making patriotic speeches and calling for Kansans to endure personal sacrifice in order to win the war. Capper became the only Republican governor to face no primary opposition in two consecutive elections. After completing his second term as governor, Capper ran for the U.S. Senate, winning a four-person primary with sixty percent of the vote and the general election with sixty-four percent of the vote. He won four additional terms to the senate and stepped down in 1949 at the age of eighty-four after serving five consecutive terms.[42] Capper repaired the Republican cultural alliance, and both he and his party benefited as a result.

After the progressive era had run its course, Landon who had been closely aligned with the progressive wing of the Republican Party throughout his adult life, again repositioned the party's cultural balance. His business experience as an independent oilman gave him an individualistic outlook. He had succeeded in the highly competitive and volatile oil business of the 1920s, taking risks and hitting dry holes but also prospering. Landon biographer Donald McCoy characterized Landon's political philosophy as the "balancing of group interests—not only for the general good but so that individual liberty would not be smothered and so that democratic channels for change would be kept open."[43]

Landon governed from an individualist perspective in both form and substance. He avoided dictatorial commands and pointed to public necessity rather than a personal agenda to justify legislative action. He proposed reducing property taxes through enactment of an income tax as follows: "The voters of the state laid down a definite mandate in the November election, demanding passage of a graduated income tax by the Kansas legislature. This duty must be performed." According to Landon, the emergency of the depression necessitated that "we must not spend that which we do not have," and in his first message to the legislature stated that "this is an emergency period. Employers and employees in private business, in many cases, have taken voluntary cuts in pay and time, to keep business on its feet. We . . . need to do likewise." He then outlined steps to reduce a minimal state government even further by paring salaries, including his own; by eliminating jobs; and by persuading "agency heads to cut their expenditures by 25 percent." He advocated relief for those in distress but turned to others—federal officials, local governments, the private sector, and self-help—to ease the crisis and worked to keep the state's contribution for relief to an absolute minimum. He cajoled railroads, oil companies, and public utilities to lighten the burdens placed on state residents.[44]

Landon's minimalist approach to state government propelled his meteoric rise to the Republican presidential nomination in 1936 but also drew fire as he became a national candidate. He gained fame as the extraordinary "budget balancer" during an economic crisis but was criticized for his neglect of public education and the state's meager participation in aiding those in distress. After his landslide loss to Franklin Roosevelt, Landon had no difficulty departing the field as a candidate. He had earlier written: "I have had a lot of fun in politics by not giving a darn. . . . [P]olitics becomes a burden when you commence to worry about your political future."[45]

Every Republican governor since Landon has lineage traceable to the progressive era governors and to the cultural alliances of liberty and order negotiated in that period. Progressive Republican governors tested the bounds of the alliance in various ways, shifted its center of gravity in response to the times, but on the whole established a tradition in Republican governorship of moderation in sustaining a cultural coalition founded on liberty and order. Schoeppel, Carlson, and Arn, the immediate successors to the progressive era trailblazers, served successfully over two terms and further defined the traditional Republican governorship. Two of the next three Republican governors, Hall and Avery, continued the tradition but were unseated respectively by the Dockings whose governing philosophy mimicked Republican cultural turf (see below); in contrast, Anderson succeeded over two terms.

The most recent Republican governors, Bennett, Hayden, and Graves, sought to sustain the cultural foundation set by their progressive predecessors by seeking a moderate balance of liberty and order. Bennett and Hayden had both served as legislative leaders and had frequently negotiated issues across the party's cultural divide. Both believed that government could be made to serve the common good, and their political ancestry was in alignment with the progressive Republican governors of the early twentieth century. Their administrations were associated with professional management, structural modernization, enhancement of public services, and tax reform. However, their progressive inclinations as governors, particularly on tax policies that resulted in higher taxes for some, eroded their political support from the liberty-loving wing of the Republican Party and helped defeat them in their reelection bids. Neither was able to master completely their party's cultural dilemma.

As a pro-choice Republican Hayden faced a particularly formidable challenge in sustaining a cultural coalition of liberty and order. His tax policies inflamed the individualistic wing of the party, and his abortion stand broke with the hierarchic wing. At the same time an alliance of the party's fringe elements was emerging. In his reelection bid he was hammered in the primary on taxes, weakened, and barely survived the challenge. In the general election, a pro-life Democrat won support from Republicans who defected from both of the party's fringes and dealt Hayden defeat.

Moderate Republican Graves faced the polar Republican alliance in full bloom. As he assumed office in 1995, the bipolar faction had elected a majority of the party caucus in the Kansas House and taken control of the state party organization. These factional partisans quickly ousted the incumbent speaker and named one of their own as party chair. As a result Graves spent a good part of his administration dealing with factional disputes. He addressed this cultural dilemma by shifting toward the individualistic wing of the party and embracing a series of tax cuts, deferrals of spending obligations, and expanded issuance of state debt. His fiscal moves served him well in reelection as he trounced the state party chair who challenged him, but he left state government on vulnerable financial footing, particularly in the aftermath of 9/11.[46]

Searching for a Cultural Foundation:
Democrats Docking, Carlin, Finney, and Sebelius

As noted in chapter 1, Kansas Democrats, unlike their national party, have failed to find footing on the cultural alliance of liberty and equality. An examination of the governorship of Robert Docking in cultural context suggests why. Docking enjoys a reputation as one of Kansas' most successful governors, being elected governor for an unprecedented four terms in succession and laying claim to major accomplishments in constitutional reform and executive reorganization, among other achievements, during a time when Republicans dominated the legislature. As a cultural type Docking succeeded in besting Republicans on the Republican cultural axis of liberty and order. As a campaigner and as governor he claimed issues advancing liberty as his own and became known for fiscal conservatism, tax cuts and tax lids, tight-fisted budgeting, and budget freezes. At the same time he aligned with President Nixon on law and order and cracked down on campus unrest at the University of Kansas during the Vietnam conflict.[47] He championed political order through executive reorganization.

While mimicking and besting his opponents on their own cultural grounds, Docking studiously avoided any connection with the egalitarian leanings of the national Democratic Party and its leaders and discouraged any movement in this direction on the part of the Kansas Democrats.[48] In preparing his legislative messages in 1968 and 1970, Docking and his political advisers set aside items of an egalitarian bent in Democratic Party platforms. Proposals for ethnic, minority, or disabled persons, minimum wage, equal pay for women, equal employment, migrant housing, public defenders, gender discrimination in employment, consumer protection, worker safety, and civil rights, were discarded.[49] In running for reelection in 1972, he distanced himself from McGovern on the national ticket, encouraged the formation of a Republicans for Docking organization, and tacitly approved of Nixon-Docking bumper stickers.[50]

In sum, Docking ran for governor and governed on Republican cultural turf.[51] His positions on issues of liberty and order were more extreme and definitive than those of either his general election opponents or more moderate Republican legislative leaders. Egalitarian identification was squashed. He was famously successful in politics and in governing but left his party without its own cultural foundation. Future Democratic gubernatorial aspirants would have to find their own paths to success in building cultural alliances.

Since the Docking administration Democrats holding gubernatorial office—Carlin, Finney, and Sebelius—have cautiously edged their party toward a cultural coalition fashioned after the national party, allying liberty and equality. In campaigning for reelection, Carlin spoke up for those less well represented in the state capital and secured educational funding through new taxes on the oil and gas industry over the vehement objections of one of the state's most powerful political interests. He also advocated serving "the needs of the less fortunate" and supported initiatives for disabled persons.[52]

Finney "viewed herself . . . as a direct descendant of the Kansas Populist tradition" and often championed causes of those without political power.[53] In the tradition of her populist predecessor Lewelling, she ordered state corrections officials to provide electric fans for prisoners suffering through the summer heat. In a more substantive vein she also led an uphill battle in equalizing the financing of schools by mandating uniform property tax levies that targeted wealthy districts while at the same time shifting the financial burden for schools from local property taxpayers toward state income taxpayers, particularly those with higher incomes.

Sebelius has moved even further in seeking to build and sustain a cultural alliance of individualists and egalitarians in Kansas. While in most arenas of state policy she has proceeded cautiously—an admirable quality to those favoring limited government—she has also initiated aggressive tax cuts for business, including substantial property tax exemptions and complete elimination of a business franchise tax. Yet she has also called for universal health care and pushed measures to extend health coverage for all children. Her early endorsement of Barack Obama during the 2008 presidential primary contest also reflects her willingness to embrace a national candidate with egalitarian leanings.

On the political front Sebelius has outflanked polar alliance Republicans by successfully persuading high-profile moderate Republicans to defect and join her on the Democratic ticket and by appointing top Republican officials to key posts in her administration. Her bold moves have demonstrated electoral success by attracting support from moderate Republicans, and a cultural coalition based on preferences for liberty and equality, somewhat patterned after her national party, appears to be emerging for the first time in Kansas history. Whether Sebelius will fundamentally transform the cultural footings of party politics in Kansas in the long term, however, is yet to be seen.

The Kansas governorship has evolved throughout the twentieth century. In the first two decades progressive Republican governors used the office to advance an array of economic, political, and moral reforms. Their initiative in office shifted attention toward the chief executive as a source for political change in the state and also set precedents in activism for those who would follow in office for the balance of the century.

Change in the office of governor has paralleled the expanding scope of state government. The augmentation of state authority through national initiatives, legislative actions, and constitutional revision has placed steadily increasing demands on the governorship. The accretion of state agencies, boards, and commissions challenged governors with a bewildering array of obligations for overseeing the executive branch of state government, and this growing reality ultimately led to transformation of the office.

The Kansas governorship was transformed in the latter third of the twentieth century. Through constitutional change coupled with legislative and executive actions, the number of elected state executives running independently of the governor was cut in half. Eleven major cabinet departments were established under the governor's control. The governor was granted powers of executive reorganization, and the tenure of gubernatorial office was extended. The modern Kansas governorship emerged from these changes, and its ranking among the states in terms of formal gubernatorial powers was substantially elevated.

The modern Kansas governorship now holds the tools and the potential for political leadership. Governors deploy these powers to accomplish their goals and to view their roles as chief policy maker in and chief manager of state government as preeminent among gubernatorial obligations. The governor is now politically accountable for performance in office. When something goes wrong in state government, Kansans quickly look to the governor for answers.

From a cultural perspective gubernatorial performance may be viewed as "the art of building or sustaining cultural coalitions." For most of state history Republican governors have grappled with the cultural dilemmas presented by their party's tenuous coalition that values both liberty and order. Sustaining these conflicting cultures presents a formidable political challenge. Some governors have risen to the challenge, but eleven of twenty-nine Republican governors left office in defeat, traceable in some measure to cultural conflicts. A few Republican governors even left their party in disarray.

In contrast, Kansas Democrats have not historically developed a sustaining cultural foundation as their national party has, and as a result have been more opportunistic in gubernatorial behavior and performance. Some have mimicked the Republican cultural alliance and preempted their Republican opponents. More recent Democratic governors, however, have sought to build a cultural alliance patterned after the national party. Their success is demonstrated by the winning of eleven of the last eighteen gubernatorial contests and the holding onto the office of governor for twenty-eight of the last fifty years.

CHAPTER SIX

Interest Groups and Lobbying

On any given day when the legislature is in session, various groups of Kansans can be found milling about the capitol rotunda. Every fifteen to thirty minutes cavalcades of students with their teachers invade and retreat from the capitol's historic hallways as they learn about its construction, renovations, murals, statuary, and of course, its dome. On their way out they typically schedule a visit with their home legislator in order to take photographs with "their" representative.

Intermingled among the students are bands of semiorganized citizen lobbyists. These citizens, who represent a multitude of causes, interests, communities, programs, and regions, flock to Topeka once or twice each session to press the flesh with "their" representatives and to have their demands heard. Thus each third week in February is Education Week when college students from all of the Regents schools descend on Topeka to lobby for lower tuition and for greater funding for universities. Each Valentine's Day, members of WKREDA (Western Kansas Rural Economic Development Association, with the "w" silent) arrive at the capitol sporting a political button with a Valentine's Day pun ("I ♥ Western KS") to lobby for their regional interests. On Martin Luther King, Jr., Day civil rights advocates rally to celebrate and lobby for the cause of equal rights. And, of course, each January 22, on the anniversary of *Roe v. Wade* (1973), pro-life and pro-choice groups protest at the capitol's steps to decry or to celebrate this landmark decision.

Scattered among the visiting students and citizens are the professional lobbyists. By law the professionals must register as lobbyists and wear name tags identifying who they are. In reality, however, their name tags are unnecessary. They are easily identifiable because they walk the capitol's corridors with confidence, knowing the locations of hearing rooms and the nearest bathroom. These professionals are usually smiling and always talking; they know all the legislators by name (including their committee assignments) and stand ready to provide directions to citizen lobbyists as long as doing so will not interfere with talking to a nearby legislator.

This chapter focuses on interest groups and lobbying in Kansas by analyzing the historical antecedents of interest group politics and by charting the growth of organized interests and the rise of professional lobbyists. Embedded is a profile of Kansas' first professional lobbyist, Pete McGill, who was important because he was the first "hired gun" and his activities were illustrative of the methods by which various interests are represented via professional lobbyists.

Significantly the political culture of individualism tends to dominate interest group politics in the legislative process. Even though there are a few interest groups promoting the culture of equality (the NAACP for example) or moral order (Kansans for Life), most groups still typically lobby legislators to secure favorable government programs or regulations. Pluralist-based models of this process envision it as an excessively competitive process that is focused on maximizing benefits for one's group while minimizing its costs.

The data for this chapter come from public documents and summaries of academic surveys. The most common public document used is the *Kansas Lobbyist Directory*, which has been published annually since 1977 and which is available from the Kansas State Library and the Kansas Secretary of State's Elections and Legislative Division. Over the years three surveys have been conducted of Kansas lobbyists. In 1986 Allan J. Cigler and Dwight C. Kiel surveyed lobbyists and legislators. In 1997 Mandi Serrone, under the direction of Burdett Loomis, conducted a survey of lobbyists and legislators that focused on the growth of contract lobbying in Kansas. Finally, in 2003 Jeremy Stohs, under the direction of Loomis and Joseph Aistrup, conducted a study of lobbyists that also focused on contract lobbying. Stohs is a coauthor of this chapter.[1]

THE RISE OF INTEREST GROUP POLITICS IN KANSAS

Reading through the *Autobiography of William Allen White*, the nationally regarded editor of the *Emporia Gazette*, reveals much about the nature of interest group politics in Kansas prior to World War II.[2] His editorials, spanning more than six decades, address almost every issue of national, state, and local import. In the late 1800s and early 1900s his writings reflected the extensive overlap between interest groups and the political party system. Scholars refer to this period before the progressive movement as the party politics era because the parties were dominated by large business interests. In Kansas this dominance meant primarily railroad corporations.[3] Reflecting the political culture of individualism, these large and powerful interests used the parties as vehicles to exclusively promote their agendas. White, an ardent Republican whose loan to buy the *Gazette* was arranged by Cyrus Leland, the Republican National committeeman with strong ties to the Santa Fe Railroad, stoutly defended these dominant interests against the onslaught of the populist Farmers' Alliance, an alliance that pursued equality at the expense of individualism. In the 1890s White ridiculed the populists' reform agendas designed to weaken the parties' and dominant interests' control on government policies.[4]

White, however, changed his stripes during the progressive era, falling in line with his friend and confidant President Teddy Roosevelt. Following Roosevelt's lead, White promoted a long list of party reforms (direct election primaries, voter registration, the Australian ballot, the direct election of U.S. senators, nonpartisan local elections, and a civil service), many of which were first suggested by the populists and all of which were designed to weaken the hold of the dominant interest groups on political parties.[5] White's support for the progressives' political reform agenda reflected its roots among the growing middle class, especially middle class entrepreneurs, who desired to establish a stronger moral order by ridding government of corruption.

The ultimate success of Theodore Roosevelt, White, and the progressive movement (an interesting topic that is beyond the scope of this book) ushered in the modern eras of interest group politics in the United States and Kansas. The first of these modern eras is that of interest group pluralism.[6] The central characteristic of this era is that the political parties and legislators tended to be influenced by several powerful interests. These powerful interests controlled access within each of the major policy domains, but unlike the party politics era, no single interest group maintained a majority and thus control of the policy-making process. Rather, compromise among interest groups was necessary in order to form a majority and to pass policies.[7] In Kansas the list of the interest groups that dominated in this era was not long; it included farmers and ranchers, chambers of commerce (businesses and bankers) and industry (aviation), railroads, mineral and extraction companies, and the forces for moral order who were seeking to keep Kansas free of alcohol.

Over the course of several decades federal, state, and local governments became more active in new policy domains such as civil rights, socioeconomic welfare issues, and environmental regulations. This diversity helped ignite an explosion in the number and types of interest groups and ushered in a new era of interest group politics dubbed the hyper-pluralism era. Hyper-pluralism first emerged at the federal level in the 1950s and 1960s and trickled down to the state and local arenas in the 1960s and 1970s.

As governmental policy domains and competition among interest groups within the domains proliferated, increased competition among interest groups also led to the emergence of new interest group lobbying tactics to facilitate representation.[8] During this era two types of professional lobbyists emerged in state politics. Contract lobbyists, or "hired guns," are employed by interests to represent their policy positions in the legislature. They typically represent multiple clients, each of whom have different policy priorities. Association, or "in-house," lobbyists represent the same organization that employs them. Their lobbying activities typically cover only a portion of their job description. In this sense they are often part-time lobbyists.[9]

PETE MCGILL AND THE RISE OF CONTRACT LOBBYISTS

Duane S. McGill (1922–2005), known as Pete, and the modern era of interest groups and lobbying in Kansas are synonymous. In the 1960s and 1970s McGill was a state house representative from Winfield who rose to become speaker of the house. After leaving the house in the late 1970s, he became a founder of professional contract lobbying in Kansas, forming the state's largest lobbying firm and becoming a mentor for several prominent lobbyists. His life and times parallel the evolution of modern interest group politics in Topeka.[10] As such, his story, as told through extensive interviews with him in 2003 (two years before his death), is significant because he was at the vanguard of historical trends.[11]

McGill was a native of Iowa and a World War II veteran who saw considerable combat action in the Pacific theater. In 1951 he moved to Winfield to finish his bachelor's degree in political science at Southwestern College. McGill successfully ran for the state house seat in 1960, serving the Winfield area from 1961 through 1965. After reapportionment he was paired in a district with a strong opponent and lost. However, in the 1966 elections McGill mounted a successful comeback. He served in various capacities in the state legislature until 1973 when he was elected speaker, serving in this post until his retirement in 1977.

During McGill's time in office interest group representation in Kansas made the transition from the interest group pluralism era to the hyper-pluralism era. McGill noted that in the 1960s the number of interest groups and the ways they represented their clients were very different from current practices. Back in his early years a smaller number of business and association interests—such as the Kansas Bankers Association, Kansas Farm Bureau, Santa Fe Railroad, and the state chamber of commerce—dominated the legislative process. Since most committees lacked staff to provide information on issues, legislators had few options but to trust the lobbyists' testimony.[12]

Smoke-filled rooms, formally called hospitality suites, dominated the lobbying process. McGill remembers thirteen hospitality rooms that operated in the Jayhawk Hotel at one point and several more that operated out of the Kansas Hotel, both located about a block from the capitol. Most interaction among lobbyists and legislators took place in these hotel suites. While the hospitality rooms provided a more relaxed atmosphere for legislators and lobbyists to get to know each other and to share information, McGill and then Senate President Bob Bennett found these watering holes to be more of a nuisance than a benefit. According to McGill, "at 3 o'clock in the afternoon trying to have a committee hearing, there wouldn't be enough legislators to have a quorum. They'd be over at the hospitality rooms wining and dining." In 1973 both McGill and Bennett recommended a voluntary closing of the hospitality rooms. What was a voluntary reform in 1973 became enshrined in statutes in the mid-1970s. In the wake of the Watergate scandal, which rocked the Nixon White House, several ethics laws were passed in Kansas governing lobbying in 1976. Appendix 2 details the history of ethics laws passed in Kansas that govern lobbying practices.

During McGill's years in the Kansas House the nature of interest group politics in Kansas evolved to more of a hyper-pluralistic model. The main characteristic defining the hyper-pluralism era is the explosion of interest groups, many of which had been formerly excluded. For example, in the late 1960s and the early 1970s the Kansas National Education Association (KNEA) organized in school districts across the state and became a force for collective bargaining. As it did so, it also pursued aggressive lobbying efforts to increase state aid for K–12 education. Other interest groups formed around Great Society federal grant-in-aid or block grant programs. State agencies administered these new federal programs (health, social welfare, and age), many of which required state matching funds.[13] As the federal and state governments expanded their regulatory arms, interest groups formed to combat or encourage these regulations. By the time McGill retired from the house, hyper-pluralism was in hyperdrive in Kansas.

Table 20 reinforces this point. It shows the explosion of lobbying registrations since 1977, the year McGill retired and the first year that registrations were required as the result of ethics reforms.[14] A registration is defined

Table 20: Number of Registrations and Number of Lobbyists, 1977–2006

Year	number of registrations	number of lobbyists
1977	572	490
1979	610	521
1981	725	556
1983	688	545
1985	720	608
1987	915	662
1989	988	692
1991	1039	640
1993	978	613
1995	1029	627
1997	1247	590
1999	1300	595
2001	1378	583
2003	1367	571
2006	1268	476

Source: Kansas Lobbyists Directory (Topeka KS: Kansas Secretary of State, 1977–2006).

as any company, organization, industry, or association represented by a lobbyist in the statehouse. It is the lobbyist's responsibility to register for each client he or she represents. If two lobbyists represent the same client, two registrations must be recorded. From 1977 to 2001 registrations increased by 140 percent. Since 2001 the number of registrations has decreased by about one hundred.

When he left office in 1977, McGill said that he "wasn't going to lobby and wasn't going to run for anything else." But with the explosion of interest groups in Kansas and the increased competition for legislators' attention among them, organized interests with resources soon concluded they needed to hire people like McGill who knew the legislature and knew legislators personally in order to effectively push their agendas through the legislature.[15] After an unsuccessful GOP primary campaign for the 4th congressional seat in 1978, McGill would serendipitously find a new career as a professional lobbyist. This career would span more than twenty years, and McGill would develop the reputation as Kansas' most accomplished professional contract lobbyist.[16]

Bill Farmer, a lawyer in Wichita who was director of the Kansas Bar Association, contacted McGill to do some consulting work for Energy Transportation Systems, Inc., out of San Francisco. This company sought to run a coal slurry pipeline beneath railroad tracks from Wyoming to Louisiana, thus undercutting the railroad companies by transporting coal for half the price. Farmer hired McGill to obtain the right-of-way for several pieces of property in the western part of Kansas and then hired McGill to see that legislation passed that would permit the placement of the pipeline under the publicly acquired railroad track property.

At first McGill refused to be hired as a lobbyist, wanting to focus on his businesses back in Winfield. But as he says, "they paid me more money than I'd ever heard of before." Within six weeks of lobbying the bill passed. That same year, a group of bankers came to McGill to request his lobbying services. They desired more relaxed state standards for branch banking regulations. By the end of the year McGill had a total of four clients. He reflected on his first year with great regard: "That year, I made more money than I had ever made in Winfield. I realized I liked this lobbying business." Sensing an opportunity, McGill returned to Winfield, sold his businesses, and took on contract lobbying full-time. He soon established an office in the Jayhawk Hotel about a block from the statehouse and moved into the former personal residence of Governor Robert Docking.

In 1979 McGill created his contract lobbying firm, calling it Pete McGill & Associates. He started with one lobbyist, himself. As his client list grew, he quickly found the need to hire a group of capable lobbyists to assist him. With each hire McGill schooled them, making certain that they understood how he wanted them to communicate appropriately with legislators and administrators. This careful communication was important because some of these legislators had personalities that were difficult to work with. McGill observed that "you have to be very careful on how you address [public officials], how you treat them, how you approach them." In the 1980s and 1990s McGill & Associates employed four to five lobbyists.

The lobbyists in McGill's firm held meetings at least once a week to review the previous week's activities and to survey the coming week. As needed, the full manpower of the firm was used to pass or block legislation important to major clients. But day in and day out each client in McGill's firm was assigned to a particular lobbyist, with each lobbyist in charge of several clients, depending on the lobbyist's experience and capabilities. The pairing of lobbyists to clients was based on which lobbyist was best qualified to represent the client. Qualification could include knowledge of the client's issues or personal connections to government officials controlling the client's interests.

Lobbyists were largely responsible for managing the lobbying activities for their specified clients as well as for communicating with their clients

Table 21: Growth of Lobbying and Contract Lobbying in Kansas, 1967–2006

Year	total number registrations	total number lobbyists	total number contract lobbyists	percent of registrations by contract lobbyists
1967	not available	266	10	not available
1977	512	490	22	not available
1987	915	662	49	40%*
1997	1,247	590	65	50%
2003	1,367	571	67	62%
2006	1,268	551	75	64%

Sources: Mandi Serrone, "Hired Guns: The Growth of Contract Lobbyists in KS"
(unpublished honors thesis, University of Kansas, 1997) p. 24; and authors.
* Based on data for 1993.

by filing weekly reports and making phone calls to keep clients posted on activities in the capitol. According to McGill, this division of labor helped to guarantee that "not a single client was left unattended. Not a single client didn't [sic] know what was going on in the legislature or about a bill they were interested in."

McGill's firm effectively became a School of Lobbying. About a dozen of Kansas' most successful professional lobbyists earned their wings as associates in McGill's firm. Some of them left abruptly, taking McGill's clients with them, while others left with McGill's blessing and some help in landing their first clients. In 2003 six of McGill's former "students" represented over ten clients a piece. None of them work for the same lobbying firm.

CONTRACT AND ASSOCIATION LOBBYISTS IN KANSAS

One of the byproducts of hyper-pluralism is the emergence of contract lobbyists like McGill. Table 20 and 21 show that contract lobbyists have taken on an ever-increasing percentage of the lobbying work load. The second column of table 20 shows the number of registered lobbyists in Kansas from 1977 to 2006. In the first ten years the number of registered lobbyists climbed to 692. Since 1989, however, the number has trended downward, and by 2006 there were only 476 registered lobbyists, 14 fewer than in 1977 when reporting began.

The total number of lobbyists may have declined, but as table 21 shows, the number of contract lobbyists has continued to grow. Most of the growth took place between 1977 and the mid-1990s when the total number of contract lobbyists hit its first plateau at about sixty-seven. Between 2003 and 2006 the number of contract lobbyists hit a new plateau of 75.

Table 22: Number of Registered Interests and Registered Lobbyists, by Type of Interest Group, 1986 and 2006

Special interest categories	# of registered interests 1986	# of registered interests 2006	# change	# of lobbyists registered 1986	# of lobbyists registered 2006	# change
Business/Industrial	84	134	50	108	236	128
Medical/Health Care	41	78	37	61	157	96
Professional	16	24	8	35	42	7
Insurance	29	41	12	49	81	32
Education	30	29	-1	70	59	-11
Energy, Oil & Gas	30	29	-1	43	51	8
Banks/Savings and Loan	13	27	14	28	58	30
Utilities	7	10	3	16	24	8
Agricultural/Rural	12	28	16	27	58	31
Cities	14	13	-1	17	26	9
Religious	6	4	-2	10	7	-3
Environment	6	5	-1	9	7	-2
Chamber of Commerce	12	13	1	19	25	6
Civil Rights/ Ethnic	1	11	10	3	17	14
Inter-govt. Relations	22	49	27	33	88	55
Labor/Unions	7	4	-3	12	6	-6
Real Estate	4	6	2	4	14	10

Railroads	4	6	2	8	6	-2
Construction/Land Devl.	11	16	5	20	30	10
Telephone and Comm.	14	21	7	30	58	28
"Sin" and Morality Groups	2	4	2	10	5	-5
Aged	5	9	4	11	21	10
Legal Profession	11	11	0	15	34	19
Liquor Interests	11	18	7	17	29	12
Highway/Safety	9	5	-4	23	8	-15
Social Problems	15	13	-2	26	20	-6
Women's Groups	4	5	1	5	6	1
Registered Individuals	15	2	-13	15	2	-13
Other/Unclassified	24	32	8	27	45	18
Totals	**459**	**647**	**188**	**751**	**1220**	**469**

Sources: Data for 1986 come from A. J. Cigler and D. C. Kiel, "The Changing Nature of Interest Group Politics in Kansas," in Marvin Harder, ed., *Politics and Government in Kansas* (Topeka KS: University of Kansas, 1989), table 1, p. 155; *Kansas Lobbyists Directory* (Topeka KS: Kansas Secretary of State, 2006).

The last column of table 21 shows that since 1997 contract lobbyists account for more than half of all lobbying registrations. By 2006 sixty-four
percent of all registrations were made by contract lobbyists. As noted by
McGill, even though each contract lobbyist in a firm is assigned a primary
responsibility for an account, all of the lobbyists in a firm will register for
every account handled by the firm, a practice that allows lobbying firm to
mobilize all of its lobbyists to address the emergency needs of each of its
clients.

The individualistic nature of lobbying and interest groups in Kansas is
highlighted in table 22, which breaks down the registrations by the type of
interests represented for the years 1986 and 2006. The story presented in
table 22 suggests that business and industrial, medicine, professional services, and financial interests, all of which were well represented in 1986,
have become even better represented in 2006. Over the course of twenty
years business and industrial interests increased their numbers from 84 to
134, medical interests from 41 to 78, and the other three areas by an average
of 14. Other business interests associated with construction, agriculture, and
communications also increased their numbers of registrations.

As one might expect during the hyper-pluralism era, there was an increase in registrations for groups promoting equality or moral order, but
these increases were minor by comparison to business interests. Representation for civil rights and ethnic interests increased from 1 to 11, for sin and
morality groups from 2 to 4, and for aged from 5 to 9.

Registrations for intergovernmental relations agencies increased from 22
to 49, while registrations for the legal profession rose by 7, from 11 to 18.
Finally, a few groups experienced minor decreases in registrations, the most
surprising of which is in the area of education.[17] Table 22 also analyzes the
number of registered lobbyists by type of interest represented. The finding
here largely reinforce the trends noted above; representation by probusiness
interests grew the most dramatically during this twenty-year time frame.

With the increase in business interest representation, a natural question is
the extent to which these business interests influence the policy direction of
Kansas. There is systematic evidence suggesting that business, industrial,
and professional groups exercise substantial influence in the legislature,
especially compared to the policies of other states. The Pacific Research
Institute (PRI) released a report in November 2004 that noted that Kansas is
the most economically free state in the union. PRI used 143 variables that
focused on tax rates, state spending, occupation licensing, environmental
regulations, income redistribution, right-to-work laws, minimum wage, and
tort law. According to PRI, Kansas' number one ranking is "largely due

to its respect for property rights: It engages in less income redistribution and attracts less tort litigation than most states." As noted by PRI, the index captures "states with the fewest regulatory and fiscal roadblocks, everything else considered."[18] Chapter 8 of this volume reinforces PRI's conclusion. It discusses the large number of business-friendly tax cuts passed by the legislature during the 1990s and 2000s.

As noted earlier, another byproduct of the hyper-pluralism era is the growth of association lobbyists, or in-house lobbyists, who work only for the specific organization by which they are employed. If one subtracts the number of contract lobbyists from the total number of lobbyists (table 21), one may infer that most registered lobbyists in the Kansas legislature are in-house lobbyists. This said, association lobbyists numbers have been on the decline over the past decade as the work load of contract lobbyists has increased.

Within their organization in-house lobbyists typically wear multiple hats, among them public relations, local government liaison, and community development, and are often stationed outside of Topeka. When the legislature is in session, the job of association lobbyists is to advocate and protect the interests of their business, association, advocacy group, or government agency. Unlike contract lobbyists who must balance their clients' time requirements and sometimes conflicting agendas, in-house lobbyists are one hundred percent loyal to the organization employing them.[19]

The interest group literature points out that there are several types of state-level association lobbyists. In this respect Kansas is typical. Examining the *Kansas Lobbyists Directory* for 2003 shows that occupational groups and professional associations such as for bankers, physicians, dentists, hospitals, builders, labor unions, trial lawyers, chambers of commerce, retailers, hair dressers, cattlemen, and wheat producers typically have in-house lobbyists. In Kansas a number of companies (regulated companies such as utilities and communications and companies with large government contracts such as cement and pavement companies) with perennial issues before the legislature traditionally supplement their professional association's lobbying with in-house lobbyists.

Many advocacy groups such as environmental, abortion, the ACLU, and tax rights also employ staff members who, among other things, are lobbyists. In some cases lobbying is one of the main duties of an advocacy group's executive director. Lobbyists for advocacy groups tend to be true-believers, who divide legislators by their support or opposition to a group's cause. Legislators who have been labeled as opposing the advocacy group are typically subjected to outside strategies, which are designed to generate negative publicity for enemy legislators.[20] In some cases these outside strategies have included recruiting and supporting challengers to the incumbent. The advocacy group Kansans for Life was notorious for using these strategies in the 1990s in order to unseat pro-choice Republican legislators in GOP primaries.[21]

By law state agencies cannot hire lobbyists. Nonetheless, many cabinet-level agencies and larger departments have personnel assigned to government relations. These individuals communicate with legislators, keep track of budgets, and promote or oppose legislation associated with their agency. They are association lobbyists in every sense of the word except name. In some cases subunits of larger state departments employ their own government relations personnel. For example, each of the universities of the Kansas Board of Regents employs a government relations official in Topeka during the legislative session. Even though each official's efforts should be coordinated through the Regents' office, each is primarily loyal to his or her university.

Most local units of government are members of a larger agency or voluntary association, which lobbies for all of its members. Thus the Kansas Department of Education has government relations staff members who represent the interests of all local school districts. The interests of counties are represented by the Kansas Association of Counties, while cities are represented by the League of Kansas Municipalities. However, in all three cases the largest of these local units of government has the resources to employ its own government relations officials.

A greater understanding of the backgrounds of contract lobbyists and the role that lobbyists play in the system can be seen by comparing the backgrounds of contract lobbyists with association lobbyists.[22] A random sampling of thirty association lobbyists and all sixty-seven contract lobbyists registered during the spring of 2003 was conducted. Twenty association lobbyists and thirty-two contract lobbyists returned completed surveys. Given the small number of completed surveys, a margin of error is difficult to define. Thus these findings have an impressionistic quality. However, because the survey findings coincide so closely with the existing literature on state-level association and contract lobbyists, these findings nonetheless provide a reasonable impression about these two types of lobbyists.[23]

Table 23 shows that there are several contrasting characteristics between contract and association lobbyists. Association lobbyists appear to be somewhat better educated than contract lobbyists. Ninety percent of association lobbyist respondents had at least a bachelor's degree, compared to only seventy-eight percent of contract lobbyists.

Table 23: Comparison of Backgrounds of Contract and Association Lobbyists

		Contract Lobbyists 1997	Contract Lobbyists 2003	Association Lobbyists 2003
Gender	Male	72.50%	71.60%	61.30%
	Female	27.50%	28.40%	38.60%
Education Level	6–11 years	–	–	–
	High School Graduate	–	–	–
	Some College	22.00%	21.90%	10.00%
	AA Degree	–	–	–
	Bachelor's Degree	14.60%	25.00%	40.00%
	Graduate Degree	63.40%	53.10%	50.00%
Primary Occupation	Lobbyist	73.20%	63.30%	16.70%
	Other	26.90%	34.30%	83.40%
Number of Years Registered	Less than 5	12.10%	25.80%	35.00%
	5 to 10	31.60%	22.60%	10.00%
	More than 10	56.00%	51.60%	55.00%
Lobbied in Other States	Yes	12.00%	12.50%	10.00%
Lobbied at the Federal Level	Yes	31.70%	35.50%	55.00%
Served in Public Office	Yes	39.00%	53.10%	10.00%
	. . . As a KS Legislator	75%	70.60%	50.00%

Sources: Data for 1997, Mandi Serrone, "Hired Guns: The Growth of Contract Lobbyists in Kansas" (unpublished honors thesis, University of Kansas, 1997), p. 23.

Table 24: Percentage of Women Lobbyists and Contract Lobbyists

Year	total women lobbyists	total lobbyists	percent women	total women contract lobbyists	total contract lobbyists	percent women
1967	9	266	3.38%	0	10	0.00%
1977	53	490	10.82%	0	22	0.00%
1987	125	662	18.88%	11	49	22.45%
1997	186	590	31.53%	18	65	27.69%
2003	226	571	39.58%	19	67	28.36%
2006	204	551	37.02%	17	75	22.67%

Sources: Data for 1967 to 1997, Mandi Serrone, "Hired Guns: The Growth of Contract Lobbyists in Kansas" (unpublished honors thesis, University of Kansas, 1997), p. 57; Data for 2003 and 2006, *Kansas Lobbyists Directory* (Topeka KS: Kansas Secretary of State, 2006).

There is an interesting contrast between contract and association lobbyists regarding their primary occupation. While about sixty-three percent of contract lobbyists view lobbying as their primary occupation, only seventeen percent of association lobbyists—forty-six percent fewer than contract lobbyists—responded the same. An association lobbyist is by definition an employee of the single client he or she represents. About fifty-six percent of association lobbyists indicated on the survey some form of association management work as their primary occupation. This result is also consistent with the literature. Finally, association lobbyists' duties require that they represent their association at the federal level much more frequently than do contract lobbyists. Over half (fifty-five percent) of the association lobbyists respondents have experience lobbying at the federal level, while approximately only thirty-five percent of contract lobbyists have done so.

Another difference between contract and association lobbyists is the percentage of each that have served in a public office. About fifty-three percent of contract lobbyists have served in public office. Of the twenty association lobbyists only two respondents—ten percent of the total—had served in public office. Only one of those two respondents had experience as a legislator. Very few association lobbyists have political backgrounds.

Finally, table 23 suggests that women are more likely to be association rather than contract lobbyists, but that lobbying as a whole tends to be a male-dominated profession. Only about twenty-eight percent of contract lobbyist as opposed to thirty-eight percent of association lobbyists are women. Table 24, based on an analysis of the *Kansas Lobbyist Directory*, reinforces these survey findings with public records, and, shows that women had been making steady progress in entering the lobbying field since the

1960s, growing from less than four percent in the late 1960s to almost forty in 2003. Up to 2003 women lobbyists continued to increase in numbers even as the total number of lobbyists in Kansas decreased between 1997 and 2003. However, between 2003 and 2006 the number of women lobbyists dropped from 226 to 204.

In comparison to other states, the percentage of women lobbyists appears to be greater in Kansas. In Anthony Nownes and Patricia Freeman's 1997 survey of three representative states (California, South Carolina, and Wisconsin), women lobbyists comprised twenty-seven percent of state house lobbyists. California had the highest percentage of women at twenty-nine percent.[24]

While women lobbyists as a whole have seen a large increase, this trend is less apparent among contract lobbyists. In a ten-year span, from 1987 to 1997, the number of women contract lobbyists increased by seven. But there was only one additional woman contract lobbyist registered in the six years between 1997 and 2003, and their numbers dropped from nineteen to seventeen between 2003 and 2006. This decline occurred despite the overall rise in contract lobbyists during this period.

Still, as a state Kansas again appears to be ahead of other states in the percentage of female contract lobbyists. Nownes and Freeman's study found that slightly less than twenty percent of contract lobbyists in their sample were women compared to from about twenty-two percent to twenty-eight percent in Kansas.[25] Nownes and Freeman concluded that the blame for this "occupational segregation" can partially be placed on a lack of experience. In their sample women averaged four fewer years of political experience than men. As noted in table 23, prior political experience is important to being a contract lobbyist. All of this data reinforces Nownes and Freeman's point that "the contract lobbyist 'gender gap' may actually be an 'experience gap.'"[26] Unfortunately, conditions that encourage the development of women contract lobbyists may not be improving in Kansas. The percentage of female legislators in Kansas declined from thirty-two percent in 1997 to twenty-nine in 2003.

In addition to divergent backgrounds, contract and association lobbyists also have some divergent opinions about each other. The survey asked both contract and association lobbyists to compare one another in different areas related to a lobbyist's ability to represent a client or clients. The results, shown in table 25, suggest that in almost every category contract lobbyists tend to hold themselves in higher professional regard as compared to association lobbyists. The major exception occurs with regard to each lobbyist's knowledge of substantive policy issues addressed in legislation relevant to

Table 25: Comparison of Attitudes and Opinions of Contract and Association Lobbyists

According to…	CONTRACT LOBBYISTS			ASSOCIATION LOBBYISTS		
	Better Informed	About the Same	Less Informed	Better Informed	About the Same	Less Informed
Knowledge of substantive policy issues addressed in legislation	28.1	34.4	37.5	5	30	65
Knowledge of the political and legislative process	71.9	25	3.1	35	60	5
	More Able	About the Same	Less Able	More Able	About the Same	Less Able
Utilizing grassroots support	32.3	41.9	25.8	5	15	80
Directing campaign donations	43.8	40.6	15.6	44.4	33.3	22.2
Committing one's efforts to a client's/association's cause	32.3	58.1	9.7	5	30	65

their clients-association. On this topic association lobbyists may have the advantage. Almost thirty-eight percent of contract lobbyists felt they were less informed than association lobbyists, with just over thirty-four percent claiming they have about the same knowledge. Exactly sixty-five percent of association lobbyists felt contract lobbyists were less informed, with thirty percent saying both groups of lobbyists were about the same.

Table 25 shows that contract lobbyists believe they have more knowledge of the political and legislative process than association lobbyists. According to contract lobbyists surveyed, over seventy percent felt they have more political knowledge than association lobbyists, and twenty-five percent felt their political knowledge was about the same. On the other hand, only thirty-five percent of association lobbyists agreed that contract lobbyists are better informed in this area, with sixty percent indicating that contract lobbyists and association lobbyists are equally informed. Said one lobbyist, "The association lobbyist is going to know his association's perspective very well. The problem is he's not going to know the legislative side of it." Indeed, the public office experience present among many contract lobbyists (but among only a few association lobbyists) is vital because it allows contract lobbyist to become experts in the processes and people involved in making law. As noted by one contract lobbyist,

> A good lobbyist, when talking to a legislator about an issue, needs to keep politics in mind. Part of it is that you're educating them about the issue, but also educating them about how this issue will fit into the political context—how this might play politically. A contract lobbyist should be obligated to provide the bigger political context. That's their expertise. That's what they're being paid for. Part of contract lobbying is being able to get the meeting with the person that you need to at the time you need it, and then you bring in your expert person to talk. You're a contact person. Once the client leaves, you remain behind and say: 'OK, this is what we want. You heard him explain it. Now, here is the bigger political context. These are the people who will likely be pissed off by it. These are likely supporters. Here's where we think the governor stands on it.'

Rosenthal states that "experience . . . leads to knowledge—of issues, process, and people. These are not separate commodities but warp and woof of the same fabric."[27] One contract lobbyist explained that he could not "regurgitate" as much information as the typical association lobbyist. However, his access to political officials and his understanding of how they operate allowed him to use the information he does have more effectively: "The information does you no good if you don't know how to apply it within the context of the political scene. It's easier to teach a contract lobbyist policy information than it is to teach an association lobbyist how to work with the legislature." This perception that contract lobbyists have greater knowledge of the legislative process may explain the increasing work load of contract lobbyists as opposed to association lobbyists in the state legislature.

Both groups of lobbyists were also asked which group was better able to utilize grassroots support. Kenneth Goldstein in *Interest Groups, Lobbying, and Participation in America* (1999) defines grassroots lobbying as "the identification, recruitment, and mobilization of constituent-based political strength capable of influencing political decisions."[28] The ability of a lobbyist to use grassroots efforts can be a significant factor for successfully representing an issue, especially given that "restrictive ethics laws . . . make it more difficult for lobbyists to establish relationships with legislators," making it necessary to mobilize public forces "outside the legislature for help."[29]

In 1997 ninety-two percent of Kansas legislators viewed a lobbyist gathering grassroots support as somewhat or very important.[30] Of the four activities listed that organized interests could be involved in, more legislators felt that grassroots support was at least somewhat more important than holding social events, providing campaign contributions, and advertising. As shown in table 25, association lobbyists overwhelmingly declared (eighty percent) that contract lobbyists were "less able" to utilize grassroots support than association lobbyists. Among contract lobbyists the answers were more spread out. About thirty-two percent felt they were "more able" to use grassroots support, and about twenty-six percent felt they were "less able" to use grassroots support, with about forty-two percent claiming both groups of lobbyists were equally capable. It seems that both types of lobbyists generally feel that association lobbyists have an edge when it comes to grassroots lobbying. This conclusion may explain why the largest and most powerful interest groups in Kansas use both professional and association lobbyists. In this manner they get the best of both worlds: association lobbyists with an innate knowledge of the issues facing the organized interest and better able to leverage grassroots support if needed, and contract lobbyists with their expertise in the legislative process.

The political career of Pete McGill shadows the evolution of interest group politics in Kansas from pluralism to hyper-pluralism. Like many other states, Kansas has a full range of interest groups pursuing a wide range of policy positions. But even in a state like Kansas, in which groups promoting moral order are active, the ranks of the interest groups lobbying the legislature are dominated by business groups, most of which are more in tune with the individualistic political culture. Representing these groups are a wide assortment of association and professional lobbyists of which approximately thirty percent are women lobbyists.

The findings suggest that Kansas is a typical state with regards to interest groups and lobbying. Like most states, Kansas has a healthy contract lobbying industry, with contract lobbyists representing a wide range of mostly business interests who can afford the lobbyists' services. Like other states, these contract lobbyists are more likely to know the legislative process because they are former legislators and government employees, and like other states, it is this in-depth knowledge of the legislative process that is their key advantage over association lobbyists. Association lobbyists, on the other hand, tend to wear numerous hats, including that of part-time lobbyist, and are becoming less numerous. When the legislature is in session and there is legislation important to their group, the association lobbyist is mobilized into action. Both contract and association lobbyists play important roles in the Kansas legislature by providing information, advocating their interests' positions, and when necessary attempting to hold legislators accountable for their votes.

CHAPTER SEVEN

State and Local Governments in a Federal Structure

Kansas governments operate within a federal structure in which contending cultural forces loom large. The U.S. Constitution and ever-broadening interpretations of national authority introduce a degree of hierarchy into the federal structure. Further, the authoritative acts of presidents, congresses, and federal courts, as well as national spending capacity, enforce a semblance of order and equality in this structure and occasionally diminish the sovereignty of Kansas governments. A preference for liberty, however, profoundly restrains direct national intervention and limits the tools of governance available for the exercise of national authority. Liberty diffuses political power and nurtures home rule, thus creating competition, conflict, and diversity across levels of government and among governments. In U.S. federalism raw coercion rarely succeeds. Conflicts are most often resolved and cooperation secured through negotiated agreements.

The age of individualism laid down fertile soil for local control in the body politic of Kansas, and Kansans have fashioned a multitude of governments in response to their perceived needs. Indeed, at the dawn of the twentieth century Kansans could proudly proclaim that roughly twelve thousand local bodies were engaged in delivering crucial public services throughout the state, one government on average for every 125 Kansans.[1] As Kansas entered the twenty-first century nearly four thousand local governments, more than found in all but four other states—California, Illinois, Pennsylvania, and Texas—were taxing and spending in behalf of their respective constituencies. Today, Kansans periodically elect over sixteen thousand of their neighbors to govern 105 counties, 1,299 townships, 627 cities, 1,533 special districts, and 324 school and community college districts.

A culturally restricted state government in Kansas became a more serious partner in federalism after the turn of the twentieth century. Progressive activists created new state agencies and expanded existing state authority, and state government began to exert a modest degree of order over relations between state and local governments. National spending through grants-in-aid further augmented state authority and in time prodded state government into becoming a cooperative partner in nation-state relations and into becoming more actively engaged in state-local relations. Today, state officials in dozens of state agencies administer hundreds of federal grants as well as a number of major state funds, which provide direct state service and community-based services throughout the state. Recent actions, including the diffusion of service delivery to a wide array of "third-party" governments, have moderated the nationalizing trends of grants-in-aid.

At present Kansas state officials often mediate this muddle of U.S. federalism by conducting state-nation and state-local diplomacy and by negotiating in an environment of contending cultural forces of liberty, order, and equality. Hierarchic forces constantly work at imposing more order upon and equality into this muddle, but Kansans instinctively value their liberty that nourishes home rule and local control. This chapter reviews the evolution and current state of Kansas governments in the federal structure.

NATION-STATE-LOCAL CONTEXT

Kansans took their first steps toward sovereignty under national supervision as provided in the Kansas-Nebraska Act of 1854. This congressional act provided for popular sovereignty in determining the slavery question and for administration of the territory through executive and judicial officers appointed with senate confirmation by the U.S. president. Legislative powers in the territory resided in a two-chamber legislative body of Kansans once elections were organized. Volatile territorial politics played out against the contentious and violent backdrop of what the nation would come to know as Bleeding Kansas. Ten territorial governors would come and go in less than seven years; five would be fired. Three early attempts at drafting a constitution would fail. On a fourth try Kansans took their first critical step toward statehood by drafting a state constitution at the Wyandotte convention of 1859.

The Wyandotte Constitution reflected cultural preferences for individual liberty and limited government that would fundamentally shape the framework of Kansas governments, both near term and well into the state's future. Frontier Kansas was in the forefront of national development: fifty million acres would be opened to settlement, railroads would be constructed, and new communities would be organized. But Kansas state government would be severely handicapped from direct engagement in that development. Two constitutional provisions—a cap on state debt of one million dollars and a prohibition on state participation in internal improvements—would shift action in the early years of statehood from state officials to local authorities who were free of constitutional constraints.

A prevailing political culture of individualism sought to encourage economic opportunity and entrepreneurship and at the same time limit government by diffusing political power. To accomplish these ends, state lawmakers liberally granted state residents powers of self-government in order to establish, organize, and operate counties, townships, cities, and schools throughout the state. Cities and counties were not only granted broad authority to tax, spend, and borrow for locally determined purposes but also both to subscribe for stock in and issue bonds to railroad companies and to aid private enterprise. Local self-government became the engine for state development and for the delivery of public services. Within the state's first three decades Kansans would organize 106 counties, 329 cities, 1,509 townships, and 9,284 schools.[2]

Federalism would be characterized in the state's formative years by an instrumental national presence and vigorous local self-government. Except for the Civil War national activism was restrained by cultural preferences that favored individual liberty, that abhorred national taxes, and that balked at the centralization of powers. The national government provided frontier security, wrested land from Indian control, dispersed public lands, aided railroad development, and ran the postal service. In this period federalism generally worked in line with the framers stated intentions of limiting the national government to certain powers "enumerated" in the U.S. Constitution. National lawmakers did enact the 1862 Morrill Land Grant Act, which prompted Kansas lawmakers to establish an agricultural college in Manhattan separate from the state university, but this action was the exception rather than the rule. In large measure the national government stayed within relatively narrow boundaries and rarely spent funds trying to tell state and local officials exactly what to do.

Local governments competed with financial incentives for county seats, state facilities, businesses, and railroads; carried out law enforcement, fire protection, public education, assistance to the poor, public health and sanitation, administration of justice, tax administration, and election administration; and financed roads, public works, and various community facilities. State lawmakers generally complied with national and local demands for development and followed through on their constitutional mandates to establish a state university, a penitentiary, and institutions for the "insane, blind, deaf and dumb," but not much more. At the start of the twentieth century state government in Kansas was skeletal, levying one dollar in taxes for all state purposes compared to seven dollars levied by local governments. Local debt exceeded state debt by a ratio of forty-seven to one.

The practice of laissez faire in state-local relations fostered competition, diversity, and local control in Kansas' local governments, most particularly among cities, but it also created chaos. Local debt mushroomed, and Kansas led the nation in municipal defaults in the late 1800s. Seventy-seven local governments defaulted between 1870 and 1905, one half of these being defaults for borrowing in behalf of railroads and private enterprise.[3] State lawmakers also assigned property tax assessment to local assessors, the result being gross disparities, both within jurisdictions and across the state, in violation of the state constitution's mandate for "uniform and equal" assessments. Constitutional prohibition of intoxicating liquors created further disorder in state-local relations. Ineffective enforcement by local officials led state lawmakers to initiate an extraordinary state takeover of local police operations in seven cities; such action quickly proved to be a political liability for Kansas governors, as well as inadequate as to effect, and was eventually abandoned.

Partially in response to the chaos Kansas state government became a more serious partner in federalism after the turn of the twentieth century. The progressive era crystallized Kansans' preference for political and moral order and ushered in an array of state reforms. State officials began to revise the imbalance between state and local government, and a marked shift in state-local relations began to take shape. In 1907, for example, state lawmakers initiated state regulation of waterworks and sewerage disposal; this regulation meant that the state had to take on oversight of city facilities and services. At the same time a state tax commission began reforms of local property tax assessments. In 1911 state regulation of public utilities eclipsed the role of cities in this field. In the same year state lawmakers called for a uniform system of accounts in counties, townships, and school districts. The state also established or substantially augmented various agencies. These agencies were responsible for public health, highways, public education, higher education, natural resources, mental health and retardation, and agriculture, among other duties, all of which would over time become the primary functions of state government. Even with these state actions a culturally based preference for local self-government and home rule would prevail well into the new century.

The progressive era also sparked national action that would in time reshape federalism profoundly in Kansas and across the country. A shift in political culture hastened by the progressive era broadened views of national power. In contrast with a strict interpretation of constitutional powers, national lawmakers and courts would increasingly draw upon implied powers in tandem with enumerated powers to gain preeminence in the federal structure. In this broadened view, for instance, the general welfare clause of the U.S. Constitution empowered Congress to provide for the "general welfare of the United States." The necessary and proper clause authorized Congress "to make all Laws which shall be necessary and proper for carrying into Execution" the enumerated powers. The supremacy clause stipulated that the Constitution and all laws adopted in accordance with it "shall be the supreme Law of the Land."

In 1913, in action critical to an expansive national role in federalism, progressive activists also secured adoption of the sixteenth amendment to the U.S. Constitution and bolstered the U.S. treasury with a potent revenue source, the income tax. Prior to that time the U.S. government finances had sputtered along, relying at various times upon excise taxes on alcohol, tobacco, and assorted luxuries; on import duties; and on miscellaneous fees. Between 1900 and 1915 U.S. revenues fell to one-third that of state and local governments, and the national government could afford little more than minimal national defense and postal service. With enactment of the income tax national revenues began to blossom, growing by 1920 to ten times the level of 1915 and double that of state and local governments. In the period 1919–21 tax rates on individuals in top-income brackets reached an early high of seventy-three percent and later shot to over ninety percent for the period of 1944 through 1963 before settling down to just under forty percent at the beginning of the twenty-first century.[4]

Federal Grants-in-Aid

An expansive view of national preeminence in the federal structure coupled with new financing ushered in an era of grants-in-aid that would come to characterize a key national role of federalism throughout most of the twentieth century. Grants-in-aid would not only elevate the nation's engagement with state and local governments, but it would also substantially augment state government's role vis-à-vis local government. A Kansas political culture that favored limited government and a diffusion of political power did not immediately embrace these shifts, as Kansans' response to the first grants-in-aid program, national assistance for roads, vividly illustrates.

ROAD BUILDING. From the beginning of statehood road building in Kansas had been local. Indeed, the Kansas Supreme Court ruled in 1871 that the constitutional prohibition on internal improvements banned state government from participation in the construction of "any roads, highways, bridges . . . streets, sidewalks, [or] pavements."[5] With counties, townships, and cities in charge of roads, the state ended up with a disparate, nonstandard, uncoordinated tangle of local roads, often bad roads that were funded with local property taxes. The emergence of the automobile would trigger a thirty-year political struggle across the cultural divide of local autonomy versus state authority over roads. Progressive activists called for change through a series of good-roads movements in the state but met fierce resistance. While most other states were organizing state highway departments, Kansans were literally stuck in the mud.

Congressional enactment of the Federal Aid Roads Act in 1916 became a catalyst for change in Kansas.[6] The act required states to raise state matching funds for roads and to establish state authority to administer road assistance, neither of which the Kansas state government was constitutionally authorized to do. Kansas officials moved to claim their share of federal money for Kansas roads, and thanks to their senior U.S. Senator Charles Curtis, they secured a waiver from the initial federal act that exempted Kansas from the requirement of state matching funds. State officials then moved haltingly through a series of convoluted steps to get around the state's constitutional prohibition.

Under federal pressure state lawmakers in 1919 crafted an ill-conceived but culturally logical constitutional amendment, a formula for distributing assistance to county roads. Curtis also succeeded in securing a second exemption for Kansas in 1921. By the mid-1920s, however, Kansas had become the only state in the union failing to provide state matching funds, and national officials tightened the noose. Finally, in 1925 the U.S. Bureau of Public Roads, frustrated by state government's lethargy in organizing and financing roads, suspended road aid to Kansas, based on a lack of "confidence in the organization as a whole."[7]

Cultural politics resisted change. Republican Governor Henry Allen (1919–23), a progressive era reformer, advocated stronger state authority; Democratic Governor Jonathan Davis (1923–25) pushed for local autonomy. Democratic State Representative P. L. Jackson of Ness City voiced Kansas' long-standing preference for political liberty on roads: "the idea of giving a highway commission, appointed by the governor, authority to drive into Ness County and order the construction of a road, probably pave a few miles and spend all our money without the sanction of county commissioners, is preposterous."[8]

State officials finally succumbed to federal pressure. In 1928 Governor

Ben Paulen called a special legislative session, and state lawmakers crafted a carefully worded constitutional amendment that authorized state government to "adopt, construct, reconstruct, and maintain a state system of highways" and to "levy special taxes, for road and highway purposes, on motor vehicles and motor fuels." Kansas voters adopted both amendments by more than a three-to-one margin. As a result federal aid resumed, and road building and state aid to local governments for roads would become primary obligations of state government. From 1916 to 1930 state financing for roads jumped from nothing to an annual twenty million dollars, which at the time represented sixty percent of total state revenues. Local officials were barred from taxing motor fuel and vehicles, but in return they secured a state promise, which has been kept to the present day, to share state road taxes with local governments. Politically the deep-rooted political culture underpinning local control gave ground to more centralized authority on roads through state and national governments.

State lawmakers have exercised their constitutional authority, particularly in the last third of the twentieth century, to make spending on transportation, primarily roads and highways, the third largest component of state expenditures, following education and human services. A mix of revenues from state highway taxes, sales taxes, and borrowing, supplemented by federal assistance, will bring transportation spending to $1.6 billion in 2009, one-quarter of which is expected to come from federal assistance.

Kansas adapted reluctantly and haltingly to the first grant-in-aid for roads. However, in the midst of a national depression and with the coming of the New Deal, Kansas state officials adopted a different tack in responding to the offer of federal assistance for those unemployed and destitute.

SPENDING FOR THOSE IN NEED. A specific concern for the vulnerable members of society found its way into the language of the Wyandotte Constitution of 1859. One provision called on the state to foster and support institutions for the "insane, blind, and deaf and dumb." The framers also wanted to assure that provision be made "for those inhabitants, who, by reason of age, infirmity, or other misfortune, may have claims upon the sympathy and aid of society." This genuine expression of care for those less fortunate stands in stark contrast with the prevailing culture of individualism that rejected the "paternal idea," in other words, that intervention through government would serve the best interests of society. However, the framers specifically assigned the task of providing for the poor to the county governments of Kansas—an assignment clearly in line with a cultural preference for restraint on state government. State lawmakers quickly passed laws providing for the appointment of local overseers in cities, townships, and counties to care for the poor and for county financing of asylums and aid for poor relief. However, the reliance on local property tax levies greatly restrained spending for those in need well into the twentieth century, and the diffusion of authority would create a patchwork of poor relief that varied from county to county and town to town.

The paternal idea gained strength during the progressive era and in its aftermath. According to Mary Rowland, new institutions were created along with a philosophy of social control "that [asserted] the state had an obliga-tion to regulate those forms of behavior that adversely affected the state's order."[9] The population of state institutions grew dramatically in a short pe-riod of time. State hospitals and homes added over twelve hundred patients, an increase of twenty-eight percent, between 1917 and 1929, peaking at over seven thousand by midcentury. State correctional facilities expanded by nearly eleven hundred inmates, an increase of fifty-two percent, in six years, 1924–30, and by 2008 had grown to over nine thousand.

The institutional bias in spending on behalf of vulnerable state residents continued well past midcentury. The institutional ethic of treatment and rehabilitation, though conducted by professional personnel, meant at the extreme a serious loss of liberty. Laws enacted in 1913 and 1917, for ex-ample, authorized the head of a state institution to initiate sterilization if he or she believed "that the mental or physical condition of any inmate would be improved thereby or that procreation by such inmate would be likely to result in defective or feeble-minded children with criminal tendencies, and that the condition of such inmate is not likely to improve so as to make pro-creation by such persons *desirable or beneficial to the state* [authors' em-phasis]."[10] Before the practice was halted in the 1950s and the law repealed in 1965, three thousand sterilizations were reportedly performed at state institutions in Kansas, making Kansas one of the top two or three states in using the procedure.[11]

The Great Depression of the 1930s would challenge political culture with respect to care for the poor in Kansas, much like the arrival of the automo-bile had set off a revision of federalism on roads.[12] Although elected to the presidency in 1932 on a promise of balancing the budget, Franklin Roosevelt would act aggressively to address the national depression and to embrace an expansive view of the U.S. Constitution in doing so. Roosevelt's New Deal sparked debate in Kansas political circles over the proper sphere of national authority, but state leadership in Kansas took a different approach than in earlier debates over roads. Also elected in 1932, Governor Alf Landon, with a political upbringing in progressive era politics, believed that state government should be a more active partner in the federal structure.[13] While reluctant to commit state funds, he moved swiftly to cooperate with the national administration, to procure all available emergency relief funds for Kansas, and to activate efficient state administration of those funds.

Upon his reelection in 1934 Landon called on state lawmakers to meet national requirements for relief and conservation programs and to maximize federal funds flowing into Kansas. Later, after the adoption of the Social Security Act in 1935, the U.S. Social Security Board advised state officials that the state's plan for administering assistance, relying as it did entirely on county administration, did not meet federal requirements nor assure an equitable distribution of assistance throughout the state.[14] In response Landon broke from his campaign for president in the summer of 1936 and called a special session of the legislature to propose constitutional amendments that would bring Kansas into compliance with the national law, that would allow for state financial participation, and that would make Kansans eligible for assistance. Kansas voters adopted these amendments by a margin of well over two-to-one in November 1936, and the following year, state lawmakers established state authority for administering federal assistance for social welfare in cooperation with county governments.

Lawmakers also enacted a state sales tax committing $2.6 million in revenues from the tax to social welfare spending at the county level. Through these commitments state government began spending state tax revenues in order to bolster the incomes of the state's poorest residents, even though state spending on social welfare would not be free of cultural resistance.[15] By 1960 state spending on social welfare administered through county governments had grown modestly to $13.2 million, a level slightly exceeding that of county spending on social welfare from property taxes.[16]

State government's commitment to equalizing conditions would be profoundly changed by participation in Medicaid, which was established through amendments to the Social Security Act in 1965. State officials readily agreed to participate in Medicaid, indeed determined from the start in 1967 to offer services and open eligibility beyond that required by the national act.[17] However, no state official at the time could have imagined how state spending would accelerate nor how the state's commitment to equalizing the quality of life of the state's most vulnerable citizens would be broadened and deepened.

Today, over three hundred thousand Kansans, nearly one in every eight residents, are assisted through Medicaid each year. Medicaid provides medical assistance to families with dependent children and to aged, blind, or disabled individuals with insufficient resources. It also provides rehabilitation and other services to help such families and individuals restore independence or self-care. In 2006 Medicaid paid sixteen million claims from over nineteen thousand vendors who offered assistance to eligible recipients. These providers included hospitals, physicians, dentists, pharmacists, local health departments, clinics, nursing homes, state institutions and community facilities serving the mentally ill and the developmentally disabled, among others. In 2006 expenditures through the program totaled $2.3 billion, sixty-six percent in federal assistance and thirty-four percent in state funds. Medicaid had become the behemoth of federal grants in aid to Kansas as well as to other state governments across the nation.

Accelerated state spending through Medicaid alarmed state lawmakers seeking to restrain spending. In 1969 legislators established the Special Committee on Medical Services and Fiscal Accountability of Welfare Programs to address the "financial crisis" associated with Medicaid spending.[18] Since that initial review over fifty reports from interim legislative committees and legislative post auditors have pointed with alarm to uncontrollable spending through Medicaid or its component parts. Recommendations to curtail state spending through reductions in the scope of services or in cutbacks in eligibility have been made on numerous occasions but have found no takers.[19] State government's principal mechanism for restraining costs has been to maintain low reimbursement rates for service providers. This practice has spawned lawsuits from the state's medical society, hospital association, and nursing home association as well as threats of lawsuits from others, and it has likely provoked some providers to refuse service for Medicaid clients. Such restraints, however, likely contributed to the state's ranking of second in the nation for low welfare spending by advocates of individual liberty and free markets.[20]

Even so, federal money has powered the state's commitment to egalitarian ideals through Medicaid. Money from the U.S. Treasury rather than from state coffers allows the state to serve the Kansas' most vulnerable citizens at thirty-four cents on the dollar, or $747 million from state taxpayers for $2.3 billion in services. This incentive helps explain why state lawmakers, with few exceptions, have consistently expanded rather than restricted services and eligibility. Federal inducements throughout the forty-year history of Medicaid have also prodded the state to augment coverage. Kansas took advantage of waivers from federal requirements beginning in the early 1990s, and now the state assists over 17,000 residents through home and community-based services. In 1998 Kansas took advantage of federal incentives and extended eligibility to 15,500 lower-income children, a number that by 2004 had grown to 32,000. In 2004 Governor Sebelius recommended that healthwave, an extension of Medicaid, be the vehicle for extending health insurance to additional uninsured Kansans, specifically 40,000 more children and 30,000 more working parents.[21]

In years past a prevailing political culture of individualism would have restrained the scope of state government and state spending, but the behemoth of Medicaid now has the politics of individualism working to advance rather than limit spending. At present a broad and diverse array of individuals and organizations have a direct and vital stake in Medicaid spending. The three hundred thousand eligible beneficiaries coupled with the nineteen thousand service providers and their employees easily total over five hundred thousand Kansans. When interested family members are added to the total, the livelihoods and quality of life of well over one million Kansans, two out of every five, depend directly or indirectly on Medicaid spending. No lawmaker can ignore the political potency of such an assemblage of beneficiaries.

The first grant-in-aid programs—for roads and social welfare—would establish a pattern for federalism in Kansas that would occur repeatedly throughout the balance of the twentieth century. Kansas officials would cooperate with national initiatives in medical assistance, transportation, education, housing and community development, food and nutrition, public health, environmental protection, wildlife conservation, unemployment, aging, criminal justice, juvenile justice, work-force development, and numerous other smaller endeavors. By 2005 federal grants-in-aid, primarily to state and local governments in Kansas, would reach $3.62 billion annually, over $1,300 for every Kansas resident. Grant categories surpassing $100 million annually in 2005 would include Medicaid and other human services ($1.87 billion), agriculture ($411 million), transportation ($402 million), education ($355 million), housing and community development ($195 million), and homeland security ($102 million).[22] State authority would in most cases be augmented by these grants, and national-state-local relationships reordered. Major departments of state government would in time be organized around related grant programs. In a few cases local authority would be diminished or completely eliminated.

Administering Grants-in-Aid

The onslaught of grants-in-aid in the 1960s and 1970s has introduced more complicated political dynamics into federal relationships. Federal grants often called for professional standards in grant administration, and as a result state and local agency officials and professional staff lodged within state and local bureaucracies gained power and political insulation from elected officials at both state and local levels.[23] With Medicaid, for example, over three hundred thousand Kansans currently receive medical and other assistance annually through twenty-five distinct services that are delivered through a network of thousands of independent vendors—state and local public agencies and for-profit and nonprofit organizations.

Only through dedicated work could an elected state official—a governor or state legislator—master and steer even parts of this behemoth. The complexity challenges gubernatorial and legislative staff and gubernatorial appointees. Professional and administrative staff within state agencies give order to the maze of intergovernmental relationships through ongoing communication and cooperation across levels of government on a daily, sometimes hourly, basis. Their expertise buttressed with federal money confers a substantial degree of immunity from political oversight and discretion in program management.

While most Kansas governors have followed Landon's cooperative precedent, making whatever state adjustments were required to secure federal aid, onerous grant requirements occasionally drew the ire of state officials. During the height of "galloping intergovernmentalism" in the late 1970s, for instance, Governor Bennett frequently chastised federal officials for their "arrogant disregard" of state advice in administering federal assistance.[24] In one instance Bennett flatly rejected federal money for juvenile justice stating that "the congressional approach of declaring another 'crisis,' creating another federal program to solve it, and building another federal bureaucracy to administer the program is ill-conceived and must be challenged. . . . This constitutes one more of the many federal programs designed to strip states of their sovereignty in return for federal dollars. I don't intend to stand idly by and see this state shackled for the political pleasure of fuzzy-minded bureaucrats of the east."[25] In response Bennett was accosted by interest groups in the state hoping to benefit from the funds and faced with threats that funds destined for Kansas would be reallocated to neighboring states. However, after federal officials adjusted the program to make it more palatable and upped the funding slightly, Bennett relented and recommended state participation, although not without incurring a few political liabilities on behalf of state sovereignty.

In recent years grants-in-aid have increasingly positioned state government between national and local governments, a placement that triggers never-ending dilemmas in state-local relations. In certain instances local officials have alleged that state officials are not allocating local governments their "fair" share of funds through state-administered grants. Local officials, either directly or indirectly through their associations, also frequently object to national policies that channel funds intended for local governments through state governments. On occasion local officials view state officials as simply agents of the national agencies who force unreasonable and unfunded mandates on local governments. On the other hand, state and local officials have in certain cases become allies in resisting burdensome federal requirements, and they appeal jointly to congressional representatives for relief.

Grants-in-aid profoundly shape the nature of national-state-local relations, but many Kansans feel the presence of their national government more directly in other ways. Every payday Kansans may take note of federal income and payroll taxes extracted from their paychecks, and on or before April 15 of each year, they dutifully record along with Kansas business owners the bulk of their annual contribution to the U.S. Treasury. The livelihood and care of many residents revolves around the nation's commitment to national defense through major defense facilities and veterans' hospitals in or near Leavenworth, Junction City, Topeka, and Wichita; veterans receiving pensions or other assistance; and defense procurement. Social Security payments and Medicare directly assist older and disabled Kansans. Agricultural subsidies aid farmers and ranchers and directly and indirectly assure the economic stability of residents and Main Street businesses in rural communities throughout the state.

How do Kansans fare in this complex equation of costs and benefits? The nonpartisan Tax Foundation estimates that in 2004 the national government spent $1.12 in Kansas for every $1 that Kansans sent to the U.S. Treasury, ranking Kansas twenty-third among the fifty states in benefits relative to costs.[26] This 2004 figure is up from $1.07 and a ranking of twenty-fourth in 1994. These estimates are supposed to include all taxes—income, Social Security, and excise taxes on individuals and businesses—and all forms of federal expenditures in Kansas. Based on Tax Foundation estimates, Kansans sent fifteen billion dollars to the U.S. Treasury in 2004 and received nearly nineteen billion in benefits. Those figures represent respectively 17.6 and 22.2 percent of the eighty-five-billion-dollar Kansas economy. In other words, over one in every six dollars in the Kansas economy flows through the U.S. Treasury. However, in 2004 national lawmakers spent more than they took in, and Kansans' share of this unfunded liability could be as high as two to three billion dollars.

National authority has also been accessible to those seeking equality.[27] Beginning in the 1950s and accelerating in the 1960s, the U.S. Supreme Court, presided over by Chief Justice Earl Warren, issued an array of decisions advancing equal rights and consequently diminishing state and local sovereignty. In 1954 the court overruled "separate but equal" education as inherently unequal and forced desegregation of local schools in the famous Kansas case of *Brown vs. Topeka Board of Education*. In 1961 the court ruled that citizens alleging grievances against state or local governments could apply directly to federal courts for remedies, and many have, one half of the forty thousand suits in 1986 being those incarcerated in state and local jails. In 1962 and in a series of follow-on cases, state and local officials were ordered by the court to implement "one-man, one vote," equally weighting votes for legislative bodies and forcing Kansas lawmakers to reapportion the Kansas House of Representatives, which had historically allocated at least one house seat to each Kansas county. In 1963 state and local governments were ordered to provide for the defense of indigents accused of a crime, and in 1966 they were ordered to protect the rights of crime suspects. In 1965 Congress acted further to assure voting rights for all citizens. The rights revolution elevated equality but eroded local control. More recent decisions of the U.S. Supreme Court, however, appear to have moderated nationalizing trends and drawn limits on congressional actions that diminish state and local sovereignty.[28]

Even with the rise in national intervention, the pursuit of liberty continues as a potent diffusing force in U.S. federalism and is undergoing a resurgence. Tax cuts at the national level over the past twenty-five years have restrained the galloping intergovernmentalism of the 1960s and 1970s. In the aftermath of the Reagan tax cuts of 1981 and of a temporary retreat in federal assistance, Kansas lawmakers undertook a series of state initiatives in the mid-1980s to address long-deferred issues so as to position the state for economic growth. Thorny issues of liquor and gambling that had festered for a century were resolved. Fundamental reforms of property assessment and taxation and of state income taxation were achieved. The economic development capacity of state government was transformed, and long-term investments in state infrastructure, particularly highways, were made. Similar initiatives have been taken in communities across the state

Throughout the 1980s and 1990s the delivery of public services has devolved from nation to state and from state to community. Long-standing national welfare entitlements that originated in the New Deal have been abandoned, elevating individual responsibility of recipients and shifting authority in administering aid from national officials to officials at the state and local levels. State institutions have been closed in favor of services based in the community. Waivers from rigid federal requirements give state and local officials more freedom in grant administration and allow individuals eligible for assistance a wider choice of services. Nonprofit organizations, for-profit businesses, and agencies of local government increasingly perform community services with state and federal funds but without close supervision.

As with most states, a preference for liberty in U.S. federalism has also spawned the delivery of public services in Kansas through third parties, "a hidden subcontinent of enormous size and complexity."[29] Third-party governments—a myriad of local governmental agencies, nonprofit organizations, and for-profit businesses—increasingly deliver critical services funded by state and national governments and exercise broad discretionary authority in doing so. One recent study identified over six hundred nonprofit organizations delivering human and health-related services in Sedgwick County.[30] According to Lester Salamon, Liberty rather than hierarchy characterizes this loose network: "what has emerged is less a smoothly operating, integrated system than a strange congeries of disparate parts that, while gigantic in aggregate scale, hardly fit together in any coherent sense."[31]

In the final two decades of the twentieth century Kansas governments have demonstrated new vitality in the federal structure. The rise in national preeminence evident throughout the prior six decades has given way to a political culture that warmly embraces liberty. As a result federalism favors more freedom, competition, and diversity and less order and equality.

STATE-LOCAL RELATIONS

Conflicting preferences for liberty, order, and equality undergird state-local relations in Kansas.[32] Constitutional framers preferred diffusion of political power and restraints on state government and therefore wrote provisions into the Wyandotte Constitution that were intended to "prevent the lumbering up of the statutes with local laws."[33] This cultural preference, however, was in direct conflict with a prevailing federal court ruling of 1868, which came to be known as Dillon's Rule, that local governments had no authority other than that expressly granted by state government. This legal dilemma of liberty versus order in state-local relations would plague state lawmakers, state courts, and local officials well past the midpoint of the twentieth century. As a result state statute books became littered with local laws, most of which were adopted in response to requests of local officials and many of which have over time become archaic.[34] Contradictory rulings by state court judges added to the confusion, and thus the legal foundation of state-local relations bordered on chaos for most of the state's first century.[35]

A watershed in the reconciliation of Kansans' cultural preference for local self-government and Dillon's Rule came in 1960 with the adoption of a constitutional amendment granting home rule to cities. The impetus for the home rule amendment came primarily from two sources. First, state lawmakers from urban areas began calling attention to the absurdities, inconsistencies, and confusion resulting from hundreds upon hundreds of local laws cluttering up state statutes. Second, the League of Kansas Municipalities initiated a discussion of constitutional home rule among city officials with proposals for an amendment. In the late 1950s a state legislative committee and a state commission on constitutional revision working independently of each other brought forth nearly identical recommendations for constitutional language that was drawn from the American Municipal Association's *Model Constitutional Provisions* and the constitution and statutes of Wisconsin. State lawmakers reworked and then submitted a proposed amendment to Kansas voters who adopted the amendment by a 55–45 margin in November 1960.

The city home rule amendment gives each and every one of Kansas' 627 cities autonomy through the power of initiative as well as providing a degree of immunity from state lawmakers. Thus the amendment gives cities a direct source of power for initiating legislation and also limits the power of state lawmakers with respect to cities. The amendment begins as follows: "cities are hereby empowered to determine their local affairs and government including the levying of taxes, excises, fees, charges and other extractions." In general, under home rule cities may enact legislation on: (1) any subject not addressed by state law; (2) subjects addressed by state laws that do not apply uniformly to all cities; and (3) subjects addressed by uniform state laws on which a city desires to enact provisions supplementary to state law. State lawmakers may exercise control over cities only through the enactment of state laws uniformly applicable to all cities. The language of the amendment ends with the following statement of intent: "powers and authority granted to cities pursuant to this section shall be liberally construed for the purpose of giving cities the largest measure of self-government."

In contrast to other local governments, Kansas cities have broad powers to expand their borders through annexation. Constitutional home rule specifically assigns the power for determining "the methods by which city boundaries may be altered" to the state legislature, but it requires that lawmakers enact "general law, applicable to all cities, for the incorporation of cities and the methods by which city boundaries may be altered." State lawmakers frequently hear protests from those pockets of state residents resisting annexation, but the requirement of uniform state law limits lawmakers from a patchwork response with special laws.[36]

County home rule came to Kansas in 1974 by statutory enactment rather than constitutional amendment. The statutory language begins with "the board of county commissioners may transact all county business and perform all powers of local legislation and administration it deems appropriate, subject only to the following limitations, restrictions or prohibitions."[37] County home rule applies to all 105 counties and is self-executing. While statutory home rule for counties was intended to work in ways procedurally similar to city home rule, state lawmakers may limit county home rule by simply writing exemptions into the county home rule statute as they have frequently done. Eight such limitations were written into the original home rule statute, and by 2003 that number had grown to thirty-five.

Local Governance

Cultural preferences have shaped local governance and administration in fundamental ways. For example, county government, much like state government, came of age in Kansas during a time in which a political culture favoring individual liberty prevailed. Consequently, political power was diffused, and governmental authority was restrained. State lawmakers parceled out the political powers of county government among a number of elected officeholders, among them a board of county commissioners, sheriff, clerk, treasurer, and register of deeds and proscribed the duties of these county officials in state statutes. As an extreme example the duties of county clerks today are specified in over nine hundred separate provisions of state statutes. This diffusion of authority in county government fosters a competition for power that frequently sparks courthouse disputes and disorder in county administration.

The progressive era reforms that restructured state government and many city governments in Kansas bypassed county government. With a few significant exceptions county governance structures of nineteenth-century origin have survived intact into the twenty-first century, and elected county officials, specifically sheriffs, clerks, treasurers, and registers of deeds, have organized frequently in recent years to block reform. For instance, a 1974 statute intended to grant county officials and electors some latitude in structural reform has never been effectively used for this purpose, in part due to procedural obstacles amended into the law. Further, in 1983 state lawmakers exempted these governance structures from change through county home rule. Without specific state legislative sanction, county officials and electors are consequently precluded from local self-governance with respect to county governmental structure. State paternalism reinforces the political liberties of elected county officials.

A few significant exceptions to state paternalism with respect to county governance have occurred over recent years. First, beginning in the 1970s, at the initiative of individual boards of county commissioners, the position of appointed county administrator has been established in twenty counties and brought a degree of administrative order to the diffusion of powers in those county governments. County administrators are generally charged with preparing county budgets, making recommendations on county policy, preparing the agenda for commission meetings, performing liaison with other local officials on behalf of the county, and coordinating the administration of county government. Belatedly in 1996 state lawmakers authorized county electors to petition and vote for the establishment of an appointed county administrator.[38]

Second, in 1976 state lawmakers authorized county boards or county electors by petition to expand the size of boards of county commissioners from three to five or seven members, subject to voter approval. This option has been exercised in nine counties, not including Wyandotte, Johnson, and Greeley counties that have expanded board size through special legislation.

Third, in five unique cases—Greeley, Johnson, Riley, Shawnee, and Wyandotte counties—state lawmakers authorized county electors to vote on structural change, and reforms were endorsed by voters in four of the counties:

In 1972 Riley County electors voted to eliminate the office of elected sheriff, consolidate city and county law enforcement, and establish an appointed county police chief.

In 1997 Wyandotte County voters consolidated county and city (Kansas City, Kansas) governments under one governing body, expanded the governing body to eleven members to be elected on a nonpartisan basis, established the position of appointed county administrator, and eliminated the elective offices of clerk, treasurer, public administrator, and surveyor.

In 1999 Johnson County voters adopted a charter for county government that eliminated the elective offices of clerk, treasurer, and register of deeds; established the office of board chair to be elected countywide for a four-year term; expanded the board of county commissioners to seven members to be elected on a nonpartisan basis; and established the position of appointed county manager.

In 2007 Greeley County voters adopted a plan for consolidating the governments of Greeley County and the city of Tribune without eliminating any elected county officials.

Shawnee County voters outside the City of Topeka, however, nixed a city-county consolidation plan, one requiring majority support from both city and noncity voters in that county. For the most part, though, county electors in Kansas, both urban and rural voters, appear ready to embrace reforms in county governance, but state paternalism in alliance with certain elected county officials has precluded this opportunity except in those instances outlined above.

In contrast to county governance, constitutional home rule has given city governing bodies and electors broad latitude in constructing city governance in accord with local desires, and they exercise this freedom without state interference. While state statutes outline basic governmental forms, cities may choose and have chosen variations in governance concerning partisan or nonpartisan elections, district or at-large elections or a mix of the two, establishment of primary elections, size of governing body, mayoral powers, terms of office, compensation of governing body members, powers and compensation of appointed officials, rules for the conduct of business, and nearly every other conceivable permutation in form of city government. As a result nearly half of the 627 Kansas cities operate under a form of government unique to that city in one way or another.

Freedom in city governance is tempered by order in city administration. Progressive era activists in Wichita conducted a vigorous grassroots campaign to end the disorder caused by political administration of city hall and demanded state authorization create a city manager selected on the basis of administrative ability.[39] In 1917 state lawmakers responded and authorized city electors to establish a city manager form, charging the manager with broad powers to prepare budgets, hire and fire personnel, and administer city operations. Since that time city voters in fifty-eight Kansas cities representing three-fourths of the state's total city population have embraced the manager form; another eighty-one cities have established a similar position of city administrator by ordinance. Today, over ninety percent of all city residents in Kansas live in cities administered by professional city managers or administrators. Order in city administration fortifies city home rule and freedom in city governance.

Over the course of Kansas history federalism has undergone fundamental change, even appearing on occasion to have been flipped topsy-turvy. National power rose in preeminence during much of the twentieth century; and state authority has been similarly augmented. Liberty has been tempered by the advance of cultural preferences for order and equality. Congress, the federal courts, presidents, and executive branch officials may act authoritatively in the federal structure and seek to enforce more order and to achieve more equality of conditions, but in U.S. federalism acts of preeminent authority are subject to challenge and often undergo change. Elections and political parties, interest groups, and citizen protests often contest authoritative action at any level. Conflicts are most often resolved through bargaining and compromise.

Against the rise of nationalizing influences, a preference for liberty infuses U.S. federalism and restrains the centralization of authority. State and local governments are empowered, as are third-party governments that deliver many public services. A preference for liberty and home rule characterizes state government's posture toward local governments in Kansas. Over sixteen thousand locally elected officials exercise wide latitude in determining the scope of local services and of spending priorities for those services. Cities may shape their governance in accord with local desires. The political liberties afforded elected county officials offer another form of local governance that occasionally borders on administrative chaos. Most important, Kansans have the freedom to choose where they live among these hundreds of jurisdictions based on their preferred mix of governance, services, and spending priorities. These choices reflect conflicting and shifting preferences for liberty, order, and equality and give U.S. federalism its dynamic, yet muddled character.

CHAPTER EIGHT

Taxing, Spending, and Borrowing

Alexander Hamilton and Andrew Jackson offered the nation competing visions of public finance. Hamilton championed a hierarchic view of the U.S. Constitution and envisioned national taxing and borrowing that would firmly elevate national power at the expense of state governments. Jackson vigorously challenged this view believing that freedom and equality could best be achieved and preserved through a diffusion of political powers by placing authority over finance close to the people at the lowest levels of government. Jackson prevailed in shaping mid-nineteenth-century thinking. The finance provisions of the Wyandotte Constitution of 1859 reflect Jacksonian ideals of limited government and equality. Taxing was to be "uniform and equal," spending was to be restrained and in certain cases prohibited, and borrowing was to be strictly limited.

State finance in Kansas has been dramatically transformed from those early days of state history in which government and its financing were largely local matters. State authority has been augmented often through enticements of federal grants-in-aid. Restraints on state taxing, spending, and borrowing have been substantially loosened, and the levers of finance have shifted from the local to the state level. The level of state taxing now exceeds that of local governments, today representing fifty-nine percent of combined state and local taxes, compared to fourteen percent at the beginning of the twentieth century.[1]

Cultural forces have energized this transformation. Issues of state finance reveal the motives of each of Kansas' dominant political cultures and spark intense conflict. The extraction of taxes underpins civil order yet may threaten individual liberty. Reforms in taxing and spending have been powered by cultural preferences for equality and order. At the same time the politics of individualism—the parochial interests of individuals, groups, and geographic areas—permeates state decisions to tax and spend as well, most often in resistance to preferences for equality and order. A dominant culture of individualism asks what's in it for me and then assesses how each financial transaction of state government affects my livelihood. State action on finance often represents direct economic transactions with individual Kansans, their families, or their businesses, and residents may know, or can determine with reasonable certainty, how a decision on taxes affects their personal pocketbook or how a decision on spending affects their quality of life. Egalitarian reformers seek taxes levied in accord with ability to pay and oppose taxing those who are politically weak. In response competitive individualists protest, organize, and throw the bums out to protect their liberties and avoid paying taxes. The story of this transformation of state finance— the critical shifts in taxing, spending, and borrowing over state history— may be examined through the cultural lens of liberty, equality, and order.

TAXING

In 2008 Kansas taxpayers paid $12.2 billion in state and local taxes, $7.2 billion in state taxes and $5.0 billion in local taxes. This tax burden equates to $4,401 per capita and 12.1 percent of personal income; Kansas ranks in the midrange among the fifty states in measures of state and local taxes but higher than surrounding states. In 2007 Kansas ranked twenty-third in state taxes per capita and twenty-sixth in state taxes as a percent of personal income; in 2006 the state ranked thirty-second in state and local taxes per capita and twenty-ninth in state and local taxes as a percent of personal income. On most measures of state and local tax burden, Kansas ranks lower than Nebraska but higher than Missouri and Oklahoma. In the recent rankings Colorado ranks lower than Kansas on state and local taxes in terms of personal income but higher on a per capita basis.

Taxes on property, income, and sales represented 87.1 percent of total state and local taxes in 2008, with property taxes at 33.6 percent, income taxes at 27.9 percent, and sales taxes at 25.6 percent. Taxes on motor fuels and vehicle registration comprised another 5.1 percent of the total, and unemployment compensation represented 2.3 percent. Taxes on insurance premiums and on the production of oil, gas, and coal through severance taxes generate slightly more than one percent of total state and local taxes.

State policy makers have unofficially adopted a tax policy of seeking a balance among the three primary tax sources, property, income, and sales. This policy was articulated by the Governor's Tax Equity Task Force of 1995 as follows: "The state and local tax system should be balanced and diversified. A diversified tax system offers a blend of economic tradeoffs. Because all revenue sources have their weaknesses, a balanced tax system will reduce the magnitude of problems caused by over reliance on a single tax source. It will also result in lower rates on each tax and reduce the pressure of competition from other states that have lower rates for a particular tax."[2] This policy has over the past seventy-five years steadily shifted the state and local tax burden from property taxes toward income and sales taxes.

Taxing Property

In crafting a finance article in 1859, the framers of the Wyandotte Constitution reflected Jacksonian ideals of equality and limited government and called for the legislature to provide for "a uniform and equal rate of assessment and taxation."[3] Uniform and equal promised fairness and limited future lawmakers in that they "could not hide taxes or impose taxes disproportionately on the politically weak."[4] In line with constitutional prescription, state lawmakers defined property in the broadest possible terms. Taxation of all property, or ad valorem taxation, was taxation according to value and at the time was viewed as the most equitable form of taxation. As articulated by Governor Thomas Carney in 1862, "let all protected by the State share equally its burdens in proportion to their property."[5]

Jackson also believed that administration of government should be "plain and simple," and ease of administration was considered to be a strength of property taxation. Property was assessed in accord with value, and a direct tax on property restrained spending. Tax collection would be assured, if necessary, by forcing the sale of a delinquent taxpayer's properties. With purely Jacksonian instincts state lawmakers in Kansas diffused powers of taxation to the lowest possible level and placed the authority to assess, levy, and collect property taxes in the hands of a few thousand locally elected county, township, and city officials. Administration of the tax would be up close and personal, literally neighbor to neighbor.

The egalitarian ideals on which the property tax was founded quickly met the full political force of a prevailing culture of individualism. Competitive individualists instinctively pursue their self-interest in avoiding taxes, and for the first half of state history that meant avoiding property taxes. Farmers complained early that the assessment of personal property was particularly unjust.[6] Homesteaders could avoid taxes by delaying the patent of land titles and frequently did. A few Kansas railroads took this practice to the extreme. According to Paul Gates, "as late as 1882, twelve years after construction was completed and twenty years after the lands were granted, the Kansas

Pacific had taken title to little more that one-sixth of its lands."[7] That would mean tax avoidance on well over three million acres, or nearly seven percent of all land in Kansas.

Governments could compete in tax avoidance as well. A friendly hometown assessor could help all taxpayers in his jurisdiction by lowering assessments, thereby shifting state or countywide property taxes to other jurisdictions. County officials desiring to settle delinquent accounts negotiated lower taxes. Lawmakers required oaths by both assessors and taxpayers "to prevent all forms of lying and collusion," but gaping disparities in assessment resulted within and across jurisdictions.[8] Shortly before his departure from office in 1889, Governor John Martin would observe that administration of property taxation "encourages partiality and injustice. . . . It is absurd to expect that these officials, holding their positions by the votes of those whose property they assess, will not each endeavor to secure for his neighbors and constituents all possible exemption from the burden of taxation."[9]

Students of Kansas finance would document Martin's observation on numerous occasions throughout the twentieth century. James Boyle concluded in 1908 that the constitutional prescription of equality was "imaginary" and called for the "gradual displacement of the general property tax." A study in the early 1920s documented for various classes of property that larger property owners were consistently under assessed compared to smaller property owners. In the mid-1950s Lawrence Leonard observed that "no assessment of the last 100 years has attained even approximate equality of assessment between state or locally assessed properties, individual properties, classes of property, or geographic locations. The nearly universal rule has been inequality and regressivity. The properties with the highest sales values . . . tended to be relatively under assessed." Leonard concluded that "imperfect property tax administration may be the price of local democracy." In the mid-1980s Glenn Fisher observed that comparing property sales to assessments gave evidence that "the quality of assessment was incredibly bad."[10]

A contest of political cultures would shape state policy and local administration of the property tax throughout the twentieth century. Shortly after the close of the nineteenth century progressive reformers would seek to save the property tax by bringing order into its chaotic administration and restoring its equity. In stops and starts these reformers made repeated attempts throughout most of the new century to increase state supervision of local assessment and could occasionally claim success. For example, in the first major reform (1907–9) property valuation increased five times over, and tax rates were correspondingly slashed from near five percent of property value to less than one percent. Reform, however, was short-lived. Order and equity would give way to the political forces of an individualistic political culture. State authority in tax administration would be restrained, and local autonomy preserved. After each reform property taxation would revert and reflect the competing interests and political potency of individuals and groups.

The impact of self-interest politics would be seen in lowered assessments, broadened exemptions, and constitutional exemptions from uniform and equal. Assessments were most often skewed to the benefit of homeowners, farmers, and owners of large properties. Two early attempts (1914 and 1920) to strip "uniform and equal" from the constitution were rejected by voters, but voters would look favorably on future departures from uniform and equal taxation: voters exempted mineral products in response to the distressed coal industry (1924), intangible properties in response to bank failures (1924), household personal property in response to homeowners (1963), motor vehicles in response to vehicle owners (1974), and agricultural land in response to landowners (1976). In addition, state lawmakers repeatedly responded to pressures to broaden exemptions for "benevolent and charitable purposes." The 1976 amendment authorizing the taxation of agricultural land under "use value" rather than "uniform and equal" marked the beginning of the end of uniform and equal.[11]

Over the twenty-year period, 1976–96, in a boiling cauldron of self-interest politics, voters would abandon uniform and equal and lock into place winning and losing property taxpayers. A state court judge would further order state officials to take charge of property tax assessment. Voter adoption in 1986 of a "classification" amendment—classifying property for purposes of taxation—represented the watershed event of the period. In place of uniform and equal, classes of property would be assessed and taxed at varying rates of appraised value, generally as follows: property of homeowners (twelve percent), commercial and industrial equipment (twenty percent), commercial and industrial real estate (twenty-five percent), use value of agricultural land and mineral leaseholds (thirty percent), and public utility properties (thirty percent).[12] Inventories of merchants and manufacturers, farm machinery and equipment, and livestock were completely exempted from property taxation. The deal making mirrored the political calculus of individualism in Kansas. Homeowners, farmers, and ranchers were the big winners as were merchants and manufacturers, and public utilities and commercial and industrial property owners were losers.

Along with classification progressive reformers—state lawmakers and state court judges—would rebalance the century-long Jacksonian preference for local autonomy in property tax administration. In 1985, with a nudge from state courts, state lawmakers ordered statewide reappraisal of all properties, expanded state funding and staffing to oversee and direct property appraisal, required computer-assisted mass appraisal, authorized the state director of property valuation to certify local appraisers, and if an appraiser was determined to be incompetent, to remove him or her from office.

These state actions to bolster state authority in property tax administration were further assured by state Judge Terry Bullock, who ordered steps toward equity in school finance. In 1992 Bullock ordered the state director of property valuation to exercise supervision over property tax administration, specifically "over all county, city, and township officials involved in the process." As a result state tax officials entered into a consent decree with the court in 1993 that spelled out a deadline for every county to meet specific standards for appraisal.[13] The court order and consent decree put backbone into state authority and fortified the actions of state officials with respect to administration of the property tax. A substantial degree of hierarchy was instituted in tax administration, and the property tax was indeed saved as progressive reformers had hoped, if not in the form constitutional framers had envisioned.

Those state officials who led the reforms and cut the deals in the mid-1980s made property tax administration in Kansas among the best in the nation, but they also suffered retaliation from taxpayers who lost out. A chief proponent of reform, former Governor John Carlin, was defeated in his bid to return to the governorship in 1990 as well as in his race for Congress in 1992. Governor Mike Hayden, who as speaker of the house supported and as governor implemented classification and reappraisal, was also targeted. Commercial real estate interests organized a million-dollar campaign for one of their own to unseat Hayden in the Republican primary of 1990. They failed but undermined Hayden to the point that he was defeated in the general election. At the local level affected taxpayers pressured county commissioners to fire their appointed appraisers. Local officials in mineral-rich southwest Kansas threatened to secede from the state. Political revenge, however, produced little change in tax policy or administration.

By the end of the twentieth century the politics of individualism had left the historic ideal of uniform and equal in shambles. Mineral interests, bankers and financiers, homeowners, farmers and ranchers, merchants and manufacturers, and many others with powerful voices in the state capitol had secured constitutional and statutory protections from the property tax, dramatically reducing the property tax base to an astounding seven percent of the full market value of property in the state.[14] Exemptions of personal property of business and agriculture had made the property tax increasingly a tax on residential and commercial real estate. Still, even with a greatly diminished base modernized appraisal was boosting the value of assessed property, which jumped by 24.3 percent in 1989 and has grown on average over four percent a year since then. Property tax revenues have increased even more rapidly at an annual rate of 5.7 percent. After state lawmakers reduced the state-mandated property tax for schools in 1996 and again in 1997, public attention to the property tax burden had calmed to such a degree that in 1999 lawmakers suspended all statutory levy limitations on property taxation by local governments except on schools.

Even with abandonment of uniform and equal assessment the property tax continues as the largest single revenue source for state and local governments as well as serving as the backbone of local finance in Kansas. Schools, counties, and cities claim 91.8 percent of the $4.10 billion in annual revenues from the tax, compared to 1.2 percent committed to state purposes. In 2008 $1.81 billion went to schools, $1.16 billion to counties, and $794 million to cities. The remaining $290 million went to the other twenty-nine hundred local jurisdictions that levy property taxes.

Taxing Income

As the egalitarian foundation of the property tax eroded, Kansans began to consider other sources of revenue and eventually began to look with favor on taxing incomes through a graduated income tax. Egalitarians viewed an income tax based on one's ability to pay, with tax rates graduated for those with higher incomes, as the ideal in taxation. What better way to enforce equality of conditions, a core egalitarian principle. Additionally, some individualists viewed the income tax as a way to shift the tax burden from their property wealth to other forms of wealth. A mix of motives and political cultures was in play with the adoption of a state income tax in Kansas.

Proposals for income taxes and graduated income taxes are traceable in Kansas to an egalitarian movement, the populist uprising of the late 1880s and the early 1890s.[15] At that time farmers expressed a growing discontent with the inequities of taxes, both state and national. State and local property taxes fell heavily upon farmland and the personal property of farmers, not to mention the added burden caused by what farmers believed to be the careless issuance of county bonds for railroad construction and other private endeavors. At the same time dealers in stocks and bonds as well as the railroads were escaping taxation. Farmers also came to see protectionist tariffs at the national level as favoring manufacturers while adding to the cost of products essential to farming.

Distressed farmers eventually organized into a Populist Party that consistently endorsed a graduated income tax as a solution to inequitable taxation. Leading Kansas populist William Peffer, elected to the U.S. Senate in 1891 by a populist majority in the state legislature, championed a graduated income tax at the national level, but surprisingly, populist legislative majorities in the Kansas legislature through the mid-1890s, as well as two populist governors, failed to raise the issue of a state income tax.[16] Kansas populists obviously saw the income tax as a national rather than as a state solution.

Kansas progressives did vote in the 1911 legislative session to ratify an amendment to the U.S. Constitution authorizing taxation of incomes but showed little interest in a state income tax before 1919.[17] The 1913 legislative session in which Democrats held majorities in both houses for the only time in state history did support an open-ended constitutional amendment eliminating "uniform and equal," allowing classification, and authorizing graduated income taxes as well as other taxes, but voters rejected the amendment in 1914. In his legislative message of 1919 Progressive Republican Governor Henry Allen became the first Kansas governor to suggest income taxation as a partial answer to "inequality in the distribution of the tax burden."[18] In response state lawmakers proposed a constitutional amendment that would give themselves complete freedom from constitutional constraints on taxes, but voters spurned the proposition in 1920. Governor Jonathon Davis, the third Democrat elected to the governorship, also proposed a state income tax in 1923 but found little support in a Republican-dominated legislature.[19]

Real progress on a state income tax would begin in the mid-1920s with political groundwork by organized agricultural groups, led by the Kansas Farm Bureau with the aid of an extension service economist at Kansas State Agricultural College in Manhattan.[20] Motivated by a desire to relieve the property tax burden on farm properties, which carried nearly one-half of the load, the Kansas Farm Bureau endorsed a state income tax in 1924 and began to lobby for its enactment.[21] In the gubernatorial campaign of 1928 progressive Republican Clyde Reed pledged "modernization of the state tax system in order to reduce the land-tax load" and once elected lent his support to task force recommendations calling for state taxation of incomes. A factional Republican legislature agreed to submit a constitutional amendment for a graduated, progressive income tax to voters, but the measure again fell to defeat at the hands of voters in 1930, although only by a few thousand votes.[22]

The farm lobby led again by the Kansas Farm Bureau immediately pushed for resubmission of the amendment for a graduated income tax in the 1931 legislative session. The farm lobby was aided by the Kansas Chamber of Commerce but opposed by the American Taxpayers' League, a somewhat shady lobby of wealthy business interests active nationally at the time in promoting state sales taxes and opposing state taxes on incomes and corporations.[23] The farm lobby gained support as well from newly elected governor Democrat Harry Woodring, who had prevailed in the bizarre 1930 gubernatorial election in which goat-gland doctor John Brinkley garnered thirty percent of the vote as a write-in candidate. Woodring issued a special legislative message on taxation calling for resubmission "to lift a part of the load now borne by real and tangible personal property, and so far as possible to distribute it to other forms of wealth which hitherto either in whole or in part have escaped the tax burden."[24] Resubmission gained the necessary two-thirds vote of a Republican-controlled legislature in which, according to Francis Schruben, 89 of 165 state legislators "had a direct interest in agriculture."[25]

The state income tax became an issue in the gubernatorial campaign of 1932. In seeking reelection Woodring endorsed the income tax, as did his Republican challenger Alf Landon. In announcing for governor Landon called for tax relief that "required economy in public expenditures and an equitable distribution of the tax burden [;] taxes must be shifted to accumulated wealth by imposing taxes on income and investments."[26] In November 1932 voters elected Landon and adopted the amendment with a fifty-eight to forty-two percent margin, thus granting state lawmakers "the power to levy and collect taxes on incomes from whatever source derived, which taxes may be graduated and progressive."

As governor Landon called for an income tax on the second day of the 1933 legislative session, not as "just another tax" but so "the tax on property be proportionately reduced." A unified farm lobby—the Kansas Farm Bureau, the Kansas Farmers Union, the state Grange, and the Cooperative Grain Dealers Association—moved into action. The measure was approved in the house by a good margin but ran into difficulty in the senate. Lobbyists for corporations and utilities pushed for a sales tax in place of the income tax and tried to scuttle the bill. Opponents criticized the bill for not mandating a direct offset on property taxes. On the last legislative day, after three conference committees and an agreement on reduced rates, a state income tax was enacted into law, with graduated rates of one to four percent on individuals and two percent on corporations.

Kansas agricultural interests had pushed the income tax on the state legislative agenda and provided the primary political force in assuring its enactment. Farm interests were also well represented, indeed overrepresented, in the state legislature throughout this period, particularly in the malapportioned state house. Economic distress also played a part, for as the economy fell beginning in 1929, property taxes rose precipitously to an astounding 12.6 percent of personal income, the highest in state history.[27] The new state tax was justified as an egalitarian measure to achieve more equitable distribution of the tax burden, but the interests of farmers would be well served by a steady shift of that burden over the coming decades from wealth in property to wealth based on individual and business incomes.

State lawmakers made no adjustments in income tax rates for over twenty years after 1933, and then in the twenty-year period beginning in 1957, rates were adjusted upward on five occasions—three times under Democratic governors (1957, 1958, and 1970) and twice under Republican governors (1965 and 1977). Fundamental reform of the state income tax occurred in 1988 and 1989 at the initiative of Governor Hayden in response to national tax reform. Top rates were reduced from 9.0 to 5.3 percent, income brackets were cut from eight to two, the tax base was broadened, and tax liabilities for low income taxpayers were reduced or completely eliminated. In 1992, in connection with reform of school finance, three tax brackets were adopted with rate increases on the top two brackets.

Income tax politics has created liabilities for Republican governors and likely contributed to the shortening of political careers. Most prominent was the reelection defeat of Governor Bill Avery who in 1965 aggressively promoted the enactment of unpopular tax measures, as the instituting of income tax withholding for the first time and the raising of tax rates across all brackets of individual and corporate incomes as well as increasing state sales tax and cigarette tax rates. On the last day of the 1977 legislative session Governor Robert Bennett was trapped by a coalition of legislators—Democrats and defecting Republicans—with the passage of a bill raising income tax rates on upper bracket taxpayers to the all-time high of nine percent. Although he had vetoed a similar bill earlier in the session, Bennett wanted to shed any image of protecting high-income taxpayers from his Johnson County base and allowed the bill to become law without his signature. His inaction failed to prevent his becoming a one-term governor. National income tax reform in October 1986 occurred a few days before Hayden's election as governor and produced an immediate bump in state income tax collection. State taxpayers demanded a "return of the windfall," and the issue dogged Hayden through most of his governorship and became a liability in his unsuccessful bid for reelection.[28]

More generally, the state income tax has fallen victim to the politics of individualism—the politicking of self-interested individuals and groups for special deals to avoid paying income taxes. The simple egalitarian principle of taxation according to ability to pay frequently gives way to deal making that favors a particular class of income tax payers and adds to an accretion of special exemptions, deductions, credits, adjustments, abatements, and checkoffs. Today, the state income law comprises nearly one hundred pages of single-spaced small type in state statutes, at least ten times the space required for the original act of 1933. Even with expert assistance few state lawmakers can master this complexity and often succumb to those pushing a special deal.

Individual and corporate income taxes today represent the backbone of state government finance. Nearly all income tax revenues are allocated to the state general fund, which finances the primary obligations of state government; in 2008 these revenues comprised 56.9 percent of the state general fund. This heavy reliance on the income tax, however, makes state government susceptible to economic volatility. In the aftermath of 9/11 income tax revenues fell by $315 million from 2001 to 2003, a drop of 14.3 percent, and state lawmakers were forced to take desperate measures to address the crisis. After that time the economy recovered, and income tax revenues bounced back, averaging annual growth of 12.3 percent in the period 2003–8. In 2008 individual and corporate income taxes totaled $3.3 billion but were again projected to decline by $100 million in 2009 as a consequence of the global economic meltdown.

Taxing Sales

As noted in chapter 7, enactment of the Social Security Act in 1935 triggered a series of events that eventually led to adoption of a state sales tax in Kansas.[29] The state's culturally diffused, locally administered welfare structure fell well short of compliance with the national act, and on recommendation of Governor Landon in 1936 state lawmakers proposed constitutional amendments to bring Kansas into compliance. Kansas voters adopted the amendments, and shortly thereafter the 1937 legislative session faced the immediate issue of how to implement and finance state participation in the national act.

A state sales tax had been given consideration by state officials prior to 1937, but few had stepped forward to justify the tax. A state tax code commission had embraced a state income tax in 1929 but also concluded that no form of sales taxation offered a satisfactory solution in Kansas.[30] The Kansas farm lobby had opposed taxation of sales in 1931 and 1933 and was joined in their opposition by organized labor in 1935. A few business interests had promoted a state sales tax in the early 1930s but more from a desire to scuttle enactment of the state income tax than from principles of taxation. While neither candidate in the 1936 campaign for governor raised the issue of a sales tax, Democrat Walter Huxman called for state relief for needy and elderly citizens and state assistance to schools through some form of "direct taxation." Against a less-than-positive backdrop a two percent tax on retail sales sailed through both houses of a Republican-controlled legislature by wide margins in April 1937.[31]

Once elected governor, Huxman acknowledged, as did most state legislators, that the sales tax was a regressive tax that fell more heavily on the poor. Huxman gave lukewarm support to a one percent sales tax as a source of needed revenue and did sign the final bill. In final legislative action on the sales tax bill, a number of opposing lawmakers decried the inequities of the tax for adding to the financial burden of those least able to pay for the necessities of life. However, a few lawmakers saw the tax as "equal and just." In justifying his support for the sales tax, Representative G. W. Crouch, a Republican farmer from Maple Hill, stated that "the time has come when all good citizens should realize they are a part of our government, and should be willing to bear some share of its burdens as well as share in its benefits."[32] Crouch may have voiced the logic that most lawmakers preferred to leave unspoken. Revenues from a sales tax would benefit lower income citizens, and they should therefore "share" in its burden. A legislative staff report affirmed this logic later in 1937: "one of the avowed purposes of the sales tax was to 'broaden the tax base,' by compelling those classes to pay taxes who can be reached through neither the general property nor the income tax."[33]

The practical politics of self-interest may have played a more critical role than logic in the adoption of a state sales tax. In the final bill lawmakers had fashioned a deal that spread the benefits of the tax among a number of interested parties: $2.6 million allocated for state financial participation in implementing provisions of the Social Security Act; $2.5 million apportioned for school aid; $200,000 set aside for the crippled children's commission; and most of the remaining balance, estimated at $3.9 million, distributed to local governments for an immediate reduction in property taxes. In other words, spending from sales tax revenues would be earmarked for a variety of purposes mostly carried out through local governments. Those with an interest in social welfare, public education, or property tax relief would benefit. Legislative staff reported that the enactment of the sales tax introduced a new policy of "state-collected, locally-shared taxes."[34]

State lawmakers would increase the sales tax rate only twice from 1937 through 1985 but would bump up the rate four times in the twenty years after 1985 to its current level of 5.3 percent. Sitting governors approved the six rate increases (2.5 percent in 1958, 3 percent in 1965, 4 percent in 1986, 4.25 percent in 1989, 4.9 percent in 1992, and 5.3 percent in 2002); three were Republicans and three were Democrats. Additionally, in 1970 lawmakers authorized cities and counties to enact local sales taxes collected by the state and subject to a referendum of local voters. As of 2006 two hundred and ten cities and eighty-five counties had imposed a local sales tax with rates ranging from .25 to 2.0 percent. In 2008 state and local sales taxes generated $3.1 billion in revenues, $2.26 billion for state purposes and $861 million for local governments.

As with property and income taxes the sales tax has also endured a constant barrage from the politics of individualism. Special interests—both worthy and greedy—have tried to avoid paying the tax by chipping away at those sales subject to taxation. Lawmakers have on rare occasion extended the tax base, but more often, any change has added to the accumulation of those sales exempted from taxation. The original four exemptions have ballooned to sixty. Rarely does a legislative session now pass without the addition of exemptions, large and small, that erode the base. By one estimate over seventy-six percent of all sales are now exempted from taxation.[35]

SPENDING

The Wyandotte Constitution of 1859 was drawn in a prevailing culture of individualism that sought to restrain the scope of state government and spending by state government. The necessity to levy a property tax each legislative session was one way to constrain state spending. Another was an outright constitutional prohibition on spending for "internal improvements," which meant, according to state courts, no state spending on any kind of roads or waterworks or for economic development. These bans would hamstring spending by state lawmakers well into the twentieth century.[36]

As outlined in chapter 7, federal initiatives through grants-in-aid on road building and social welfare broke through the restraints of an individualist culture and eventually led to a posture of accepting federal assistance across the entire scope of state government. The availability of federal assistance in combination with a variety of emerging demands, crises, and missed opportunities persuaded Kansans to broaden the scope of state government through constitutional amendments freeing state lawmakers from the spending restrictions of the internal improvements prohibition.[37]

A desire for good roads plus the threat of losing federal funds led in 1928 to the authorization for spending on state highways. Floods followed by droughts in the early 1950s convinced Kansans in 1958 to authorize state financial participation in federal initiatives addressing flood control and conservation and development of water resources. The availability of federal funds prompted approval in 1980 of state spending on improvements in which the national government participated. Serious downturns in the Kansas economy in the early 1980s finally loosened the long-standing prohibition almost completely. A 1986 amendment authorized state spending designed to stimulate economic development, and it further extinguished the spending prohibition by allowing the state to undertake "any work of internal improvement" once authorized by an extraordinary vote of state lawmakers.

In addition to the constitutional amendments loosening the prohibition on internal improvements, voter adoption of other amendments has augmented state authority and broadened the scope of state spending. Kansans' approval of taxes on motor vehicles and fuels in 1928 put state government in charge of highway finance. Voter authorization of graduated and progressive taxation of incomes in 1931 gave state lawmakers a potent new revenue source. State government's entry into the field of social welfare followed voter approval of state financial participation in the Social Security Act of 1935. An overhaul of the education article of the Kansas Constitution in 1966 marked a critical shift from local to state financing of public schools. Centralized administration and financing of the state judiciary came with voter endorsement of court unification in 1972. Approval of classification for purposes of property taxation in 1986 prompted substantial centralization in property tax assessment. Voter approval of a state lottery also in 1986 significantly augmented state spending for purposes of economic development.

State spending has also historically followed the availability of new revenues. When property taxes provided the dominant source of revenues, state spending was restrained, indeed severely restrained. New taxes on motor vehicles and fuels coupled with federal funds dramatically boosted state spending on roads and highways. Enactment of a state sales tax in 1937 brought about new state spending on social welfare and schools as well as bringing state aid in reducing local property taxes. The availability of federal funds and cooperation with federal agencies beginning in the late teens and peaking in the 1960s and 1970s prompted additional state spending in a wide range of new fields such as law enforcement, environmental protection, public health, medical care, and special education. Tax increases in 1965 and 1992 accompanied huge spending hikes in state aid for public schools.

The scope of state spending has often been enlarged by state lawmakers in order to shift the financing of public services from property taxes to income and sales taxes. In 1975 state lawmakers' takeover of the administration of social welfare from county government was motivated to a significant degree by a desire to reduce reliance on property taxes. The overhaul of school finance in 1965, 1973, 1992, and 2006 substantially shifted the tax burden from local property taxes to state income and sales taxes, as did reductions in state-mandated property tax levies for schools in 1997 and 1998.

With the expanding scope of state government and the upward adjustments in income and sales tax rates, state spending from the state general fund as a percent of state personal income edged upward throughout most of the twentieth century, but since 1990 it has generally stabilized around 5.5 percent of personal income. Spending on education (all levels) and human resources (which includes income maintenance, social services, medical assistance, state hospitals, and public health) comprise the primary obligations of state government. Since 1990 these two functions of state government have increased their claim on the state general fund, jumping from seventy-nine percent of state general fund spending in 1990 to eighty-eight percent in 2006.[38] The stimulus of Medicaid, as outlined in chapter 7, helps explain the accelerating growth of human resources spending, and education spending now claims two out of every three dollars in state general fund spending. A closer look at aid to public schools, the single largest component of education spending and indeed of the entire state budget, sheds light on an aspect of state spending that is largely powered by state initiative.

School Finance

On the issue of school finance the Kansas Constitution says simply that "the legislature shall make suitable provision for finance of the educational interests of the state." This language, as well as the entire education article, was adopted by voters in 1966 as the first and only amendment to this article. This language became particularly relevant after 1973 when the U.S. Supreme Court weighed in on behalf of state jurisdiction in educational finance and declined to apply the equal protection clause to evident inequities in a Texas school case, *Rodriquez v. San Antonio School District*. This ruling coupled with the vagueness of the state constitution left school finance in the hands of state lawmakers; it has also spawned numerous legal challenges over the past forty years as to the constitutionality of decisions on school finance made by lawmakers. Lawmakers and state courts have been embroiled in determining exactly what represents "suitable" provision for school finance.

For most of state history spending and taxing for public schools was carried out locally by locally elected school boards levying property taxes. Local control was encouraged by a prevailing cultural preference that restrained state government and diffused political power to the lowest level. Kansans embraced local control with a vengeance establishing by the start of the twentieth century over nine thousand school districts, including many one-room schools. The deep-seated preference for local control immunized Kansas schools and school funding in the state from other cultural forces well into midcentury. By 1950 Kansas would still have forty-five hundred school districts and would rank high among the handful of states dependent on local property taxes for school finance.

State lawmakers' first serious step toward state aid of local schools came with the enactment of a state sales tax in 1937.[39] This aid was allocated, as required by the original education article in the Wyandotte Constitution, in proportion to the number of students in a school district. Over the next twenty-five years state lawmakers would enact additional measures of school aid, characterized in the mid-1960s as "a hodgepodge of at least a dozen funds from county and state sources."[40] Even so, the level of state aid in 1960 still represented a modest twenty-seven million dollars, roughly one dollar in state taxes for every six in property taxes levied at the local level for schools.[41] School spending varied widely across the state, most often in direct correlation with the property wealth in school districts.

Belatedly, after midcentury demands for order and equity in school finance would challenge the state's long-standing dedication to local control. These demands gathered steam with time, and after revision of the education article, they forced state lawmakers and state courts to address four basic issues in school spending: What is a "suitable" level of funding for schools as required by the state constitution? What is equality of education for students and is it required? What is equitable for state and local taxpayers in the financing of schools? What degree of order and rationality is required in determining suitable funding, equal education, and equitable financing? State lawmakers would initially address these demands in the School Foundation Finance Act of 1965 and under instructions from state court judges enact fundamental revisions through the School District Equalization Act of 1973 and finally through the School District Finance and Quality Performance Act of 1992. After 1965 school finance increasingly became a consuming occupation of state legislators, and lawmakers would make annual adjustments in response to educational interests.

Deep-seated cultural conflicts energized the ongoing debates over school spending. Calls for equality and order were made most forcefully by state court judges. In 1991, for example, District Court Judge Terry Bullock of Shawnee County asserted that the constitutional language for "suitable" financing meant strict equality of education and total state control of financing: "The mandate is to furnish each child an educational opportunity equal to that made available to every other child. . . . [Any variation from equality requires] a *rational educational explanation* for the differential. . . . Does this mean 100% 'state financing' is required for public schools? The clear and simple answer is 'yes.'"[42] Bullock dismissed any value in the one-hundred-and-thirty-year state history of local engagement in educational finance and ordered state lawmakers to fix school finance in compliance with his demands for educational equality, state control, and rational prescription before the end of the 1992 legislative session.

In each of the three overhauls of school finance, state lawmakers addressed the four primary issues: suitable provision, educational equality for students, equity for taxpayers, and order and rationality in these determinations. First, the level of funding for schools was substantially increased, presumably accomplishing more suitable provision of school finance. Second, measures were taken to equalize spending per pupil by limiting high-spending districts, by encouraging low-spending districts, and by basing aid on estimates of educational costs unique to each district.[43] Third, financing of schools was shifted fundamentally from locally levied property taxes to state-levied taxes, primarily income and sales taxes, thus shifting school finance from a less equitably distributed property tax base to presumably more equitably distributed income and sales tax bases. Finally, each overhaul sought to advance the state toward a more ordered and rational basis for school finance.

Even with these direct moves toward enhanced suitability, educational equality, tax equity, and rationality in school finance, state lawmakers could not accept the court's hierarchic view and enfeeblement of local engagement in school finance. Each overhaul granted local school boards and local electors an escape from state controls that gave them the ability to embellish school spending. For instance, the 1992 overhaul that mandated the most rigid limits on local spending allowed school boards either on their own or with the consent of local electors to adopt a "local option budget" to increase spending by twenty-five percent above their base budget. As of 2006 298 of the 300 districts had adopted local option budgets ranging from 2 to 27 million dollars, generating statewide additional school spending of $663 million, roughly sixteen percent of total state and local spending on schools.

A new round of litigation began in 1999 with two local school districts claiming that state financing of schools fell short of constitutional requirements, and again the Kansas courts assumed the role of superintending the financing of public schools. In January 2005 the Kansas Supreme Court unanimously ordered lawmakers to ignore politics as well as past spending patterns and fund schools based on cost analyses in accordance with standards of equity and rationality, and the court eventually forced the governor to call lawmakers back into a special session in June 2005.[44] The court then took an unprecedented action by mandating that "the legislature shall implement a minimum increase of $285 million" over the prior year and by promising to monitor lawmakers' actions on school funding into the future. The court's interpretation of "suitable" financing of schools eclipsed the legislature's power of appropriating funds and placed the court in charge of the financing of schools.

The seven years of litigation came to an end in 2006. After the Kansas legislature had substantially increased state funding of schools in 2005 and 2006 and committed the state to increases in future funding through 2009, the supreme court finally relented and dismissed the case declaring the Kansas legislature in "substantial compliance with our prior orders." The split decision of the court suggested that the justices had tired in their assumed roles as superintendents of school finance. The court appeared to back off on earlier declarations on equality, saying that "equity does not require the Legislature to provide equal funding to each student or school district." Further, the court ignored legislative action allowing local districts wider latitude in spending that will obviously result in growing disparities among districts. On the other hand, court action did force the legislature to add just over seven hundred and fifty million dollars to the funding of schools within a four-year period, the 2005–6 through the 2008–9 schools years.

Legislative and judicial actions on state spending for schools over the past fifteen years leave school finance in an ongoing conundrum. The state's share of state-local funding for schools has jumped dramatically in this period, from slightly over forty percent in 1992 to nearly seventy-five percent today. However, with diminished powers for financial stewardship, local school boards will continue to be motivated to maximize the state share of school funding. Any enterprising school district will face minimal political risk in appealing to state court with claims of inequality of funding, real or imagined, and pleading for the court to order more exacting standards of equity and rationality in school finance. The question is not if but when another round of litigation will begin. Without more precision in the constitutional language on school finance, school funding will remain a political question to be resolved between state lawmakers and state courts.

Kansas is not alone in facing court challenges over funding of schools. As of 2005 twenty-three states were actively embroiled in litigation similar to Kansas; another twenty-two had earlier confronted similar suits.[45]

Thomas Jefferson and Andrew Jackson could point with pride to their indelible imprints on state borrowing in Kansas. In a political culture of individualism that feared borrowing and sought to restrain government, framers of the Wyandotte Constitution placed strict limits on borrowing by state government. The state constitution set a cap of one million dollars on state debt and required the consent of state voters for any issuance of debt to exceed the cap. The constitutional language of 1859 remains untouched today. State lawmakers proposed exceeding the debt cap on only one occasion—to borrow twenty-five million dollars to pay benefits to veterans of World War I. That proposition was approved by voters in 1922 and paid off in 1948, and the constitutional vehicle for authorizing debt has not been used since.[46]

Within the first ten years of statehood state lawmakers used debt sparingly to pay current expenses and to aid in constructing state facilities, but state borrowing quickly reached the debt cap and came to a standstill in 1869.[47] Republican Governor John St. John (1879–83) extended the freeze on debt for another forty years by forcefully proclaiming in 1881 that "we are creating no new debts, but pay as we go." Kansas state government did indeed reach debt free status by 1916. The pay-as-we-go policy, however, did not apply to local governments that were free of constitutional constraints. State lawmakers liberally granted borrowing authority to cities and counties, and by the beginning of the twentieth century local debt exceeded state debt by a ratio of forty-seven to one. Kansas municipalities also led the nation in defaults.

Kansas would break free from constitutional restrictions on state debt through a series of friendly state court rulings beginning in the 1930s. In 1934 the Kansas Supreme Court ruled that the state debt cap applied only to "debts to be paid by a general property tax," and as a result state lawmakers began to authorize debt that would be repaid from revenues other than the property tax. Debt backed by anticipated non-tax revenues would be used frequently beginning in the 1950s to finance various capital projects such as dormitories, a state office building, student unions, parking facilities, a fish hatchery, and a turnpike. Debt backed by anticipated tax revenues would be used more conservatively, as for example, beginning in 1972 to build state freeways with borrowing repaid by fuel taxes and vehicle registration fees. Lawmakers slowly replaced pay as we go with a philosophy of pay as we use.

Even with constitutional restrictions loosened, Kansas lawmakers authorized debt sparingly, and well into the last quarter of twentieth century the state still ranked near the bottom of the fifty states in the use of debt for state purposes. The historic reluctance to use debt began to change with Governor Hayden who advocated more aggressive use of debt financing to reverse declining investments in state infrastructure.[48] At Hayden's initiative state lawmakers established the Kansas Development Finance Authority in 1987 to coordinate the issuance of state debt and in 1989 authorized $890 million in borrowing as part of an eight-year, $3.7 billion comprehensive highway program. Hayden proposed that the borrowing be repaid solely with increased highway user fees, but in response to heavy lobbying from truckers, he agreed to a compromise with state legislators that increased the state sales tax for highway financing along with increased user fees.[49]

The success of the 1988 highway program prompted Governor Graves to initiate a second wave of aggressive borrowing that focused on transportation. Graves, whose family had long standing ties to the trucking industry, named the state's top trucking lobbyist to head his transportation task force. The governor proposed even heavier borrowing without any tax increase to finance his plan, but in 1999 legislators instead increased highway user fees and boosted transfers of sales tax revenues to finance an additional debt of $995 million. As a result primarily of the 1989 and 1999 highway plans, tax-supported debt in Kansas ballooned from $424 million in 1992 to $2.4 billion in 2002, ranking the state near the top of all states in the rate of growth in debt and highway spending.

In the late 1990s financial missteps compounded by fallout from 9/11 accelerated state borrowing even more. During the good times of the late 1990s when revenues were flowing into state coffers at rapid rates, state lawmakers became accustomed to cutting taxes while increasing spending. In 1997 and again in 1998 lawmakers cut property taxes for schools statewide and substantially shifted school finance to state revenue sources, that is, state income and sales taxes. A phase down of property taxes on motor vehicles from 1996 through 2000 added more obligations onto state revenues. Further, individual income tax rates were reduced for single filers in 1997 and 1998, as were insurance company taxes in 1997. Special interests were granted dozens of new exemptions, deductions, and assorted adjustments from property, income, and sales taxes, all of which eroded those tax bases. During this period annual growth in state spending surged at two to three times that of the cost of living.

Lawmakers first turned to highway debt to cover their tax cuts and spending spree. They immediately reneged on prior commitments of sales tax transfers for highway purposes, and with the economic downturn of 2001 the heavy reliance on sales tax revenues for highways hit a wall. State general fund revenues dipped by $300 million between 2001 and 2003, an absolute drop of eight percent. Lawmakers completely stopped sales tax transfers in 2003 and 2004 and instead authorized another $487 million in highway debt, increasing the original $995 million authorization by nearly fifty percent. Further, in 2003 state highway officials refinanced $389 million in prior debt to "create near term cash flow savings and mitigate the risk of funding shortfalls."[50] As a result, borrowing for highways was dramatically increased and extended well into the future.

Lawmakers next turned to pension debt. Even with surging revenues in the 1990s state lawmakers chose to cut taxes rather than pay state government's actuarially based share of public employee retirement obligations. Consequently, unfunded pension liabilities quadrupled from 1993 to 2003.[51] To rectify this financial lapse, lawmakers authorized an unprecedented $550 million in pension bonds in 2003 to shore up the unfunded liabilities that had accumulated during the good times and to pay off some current obligations. Additionally, state officials structured the borrowing to help cover over their current predicament, dedicating some bond proceeds for meeting current obligations, postponing any payment on the bonds for five years, and extending the term of the debt for thirty years.[52]

Tax-supported debt in Kansas mushroomed to $4.5 billion in 2006, more than ten times the level of 1992, and pushed Kansas into the upper ranks of state borrowers. According to Moody's, Kansas ranked fourteenth in tax-supported debt per capita in 2005, up from forty-third in 1989, and fifteenth in tax-supported debt per capita as a percent of personal income in 2005, up from forty-third in 1989.[53] Kansas tax-supported debt per capita as a percent of personal income has jumped from 0.5 percent in 1992 to 4.0 percent in 2005, compared to the surrounding states that ranged from 0.1 percent in Nebraska to 1.5 percent in Missouri.

The financial actions of state lawmakers over the past ten year reflect a dramatic departure from the state's historic reluctance to use debt in meeting state obligations. Pay as you go was initially replaced by pay as you use. In other words, the burden of paying for major improvements was placed on those who benefited from the improvement rather than upon current taxpayers. More recently, however, lawmakers have increasingly turned to borrowing in order to lighten the financial burden on current taxpayers at the expense of future taxpayers. Borrowing has been increased and extended in the aftermath of an economic downturn, which has been exacerbated by prior tax cuts and spending increases. These financial practices have allowed state lawmakers to meet prior spending commitments, as for example on highways, but have also brought state government in Kansas and a few other states under the scrutiny of national bond-rating agencies in the period 2002–5. The state's aggressive use of debt may result in higher borrowing costs, may limit the state's debt capacity, and may restrain financial flexibility in future years.

Cultural forces have powered the transformation of state finance in Kansas. Calls for more equitable taxation justified the adoption of income taxes and later sales taxes. Demands for equality and order have turned school finance topsy-turvy from local to state control. State courts and federal agencies have ordered state lawmakers to confront the inequitable distribution of resources and to establish a more rational basis for state finance by equalizing conditions through spending on social welfare and education.

Individual interests have occasionally aided in reform. Farm groups championed income taxes to gain relief from property taxes. Advocates of sales taxes wanted all residents including those with little property or income to share in the tax burden. Expanding services and eligibility through Medicaid finds support from those benefiting from an improved quality of life that Medicaid spending provides.

More often, however, individualism gives advantage to strong, well-organized interests against the weak. Tax policy becomes riddled with the deal making of parochial interests and of groups that push and pull to have taxes paid by someone else. More borrowing shifts state obligations from current to future taxpayers.

An unusual cultural combination has moved historically debt-resistant Kansas into the front ranks of aggressive state borrowers in recent years. Preferences for equality and order bolster state spending, while preferences for liberty and limited government press for outright tax cuts as well as other restraints on taxes. These cultural forces have combined to secure more spending and less taxing and to make up any differences through more state borrowing; these practices move state finances toward a condition of structural imbalance. More spending, less taxing, and more borrowing are not likely to be sustainable in the long-term and represent a formidable challenge to state lawmakers.[54] As this volume goes to press, the economic collapse of 2008 is making the future of state finances more grim, with state officials projecting a general fund deficit of eight hundred and eighty million dollars in 2010, an amount roughly equivalent to fifteen percent of general fund revenues, and with more red ink being predicted in future years.[55]

The clash of cultural forces can make the politics of taxing, spending, and borrowing most wicked, as is the case with school finance. First, the tax bases of rural, sparsely populated jurisdictions become eroded and constrained as a result of tax exemptions promoted by individual interests. State lawmakers adjust school funding to account for skewed tax bases, but school officials challenge funding as irrational and inequitable. State courts then order lawmakers to finance schools on a more rational and equitable basis. Such orders not only threaten local liberty in controlling schools but also force wealthier urban and suburban residents to underwrite the high costs of education in small tax-poor jurisdictions that resist losing local control through consolidation with neighboring schools. State lawmakers comply, at the same time enacting more tax exemptions, and as a result another set of school officials go to court alleging irrationality and inequity in school funding.

CHAPTER NINE

Kansas Politics in State and Nation

The clash of political cultures has placed Kansas in the national spotlight at various times throughout state history and has made Kansas politics an intriguing topic for both casual observers and serious scholars. Abolitionists, prohibitionists, populists, progressives, and more recently polar alliance Republicans have shaped the state's political landscape and also left their imprint on national politics to an extent clearly out of proportion to the state's population. The prism of political cultures helps understand the historic moments of high drama and their connection to the current conflicts and contradictions in everyday political affairs. This concluding chapter summarizes the major findings of this book, places them within the context of national politics, and assesses the future directions of Kansas politics.

THE CLASH OF POLITICAL CULTURES

Kansas political history shows that each clash of political cultures is different than the one before. In the state's early history those who supported abolition challenged supporters of slavery, and the conflict became a precursor to the Civil War. The abolitionists, with their feet firmly planted in the strong evangelical Protestant religions of the nineteenth century, won this battle but not without bloodshed, making the birth of Kansas somewhat unique in the annals of U.S. history. These early immigrants to Kansas came imbued with religious fervor and left an indelible imprint on the politics of the state.

As the wounds of Bleeding Kansas healed, the passion to establish a higher moral order were transferred in part to a new movement, the prohibition of intoxicating liquors. In the 1870s Kansas started its own version of the Hundred Years War by prescribing individual behavior with respect to booze through the force of law. Kansas became the first state to adopt a constitutional amendment banning the sale of intoxicating liquors. Even though prohibition was antithetical to the individualistic credo of the Gilded Age, Kansas politics was able to make its peace with prohibition, perhaps setting a crucial precedent for the polar alliance politics that would characterize state politics in the last decade of the twentieth century. Fifteen years after the nation abandoned its attempts at prohibition and nearly eighty years after Kansas constitutionally prohibited the sale of booze, Kansas in 1948 finally allowed for the legal sale of beer, wine, and spirits on a limited basis. Not until 1986 did Kansans choose to allow what the dry forces labeled open saloons.

From the 1880s through the 1920s Kansas would be an early adopter of two other movements that would sweep through the nation. At the end of the nineteenth century the populists and their penchant for egalitarian policy prescriptions would collide headlong with the cultural forces of laissez faire individualism. William Allen White's editorial "What's the Matter with Kansas?" assailed the populists as rubes and bellicose complainers who blamed their personal misfortunes on anyone but themselves. As the economy surged out of its depression in the late 1890s, the cries of the populists were replaced by the businesslike good government reformers of the progressive era. The conflict between the progressives and party oligarchs would rage for three decades in Kansas before finally subsiding, and by the end of this battle the face of state and local governments in Kansas would be changed.

Signaling a temporary lull in the cutting-edge politics of Kansas, Governor Alf Landon, a defender of the free market ideology, was soundly defeated by FDR's New Deal coalition in the 1936 presidential campaign. The Kansas politics of small government was firmly rejected by the nation as well as by Kansas, and in so doing, Kansas politics receded from the headlines to be replaced by national leaders, who though Kansas reared to be sure, represented the mainstream of U.S. politics. Gone were the rants of Kansas radicals, abolitionist John Brown, populist William Peffer, and prohibitionist Carrie Nation, replaced by the more reasonable discourse of President Dwight D. Eisenhower; U.S. Senators Frank Carlson, James Pearson, Bob Dole, and Nancy Landon Kassebaum; and Governors John Anderson, Robert Docking, and Robert Bennett. These Kansans who served past the midpoint of the twentieth century produced a more sedate brand of politics that steered down the middle of the political road. They worked largely within the state's political structures instead of outside them.

Even as mainstream politics settled into Kansas, a new clash of cultures was lurking beneath the political surface, returning Kansas to its place on the cutting edge of politics. One movement would emerge in opposition to the size and scope of government and with a desire to constrain government and to cut taxes. Another movement would reemerge to oppose abortion in the late 1980s, to challenge the teaching of evolution in public schools in the late 1990s, and to attack stem cell research and gay marriage in the 2000s. These issues, which grip the nation as well, have spawned a unique political alignment within the GOP, named here as polar alliance Republicans, who seek on the one hand to apply the force of government on social issues such as abortion and marriage and on the other to limit the powers of government on economic issues such as taxing, spending, and regulation. These polar alliance Republicans and their associated constituencies have established litmus tests, as for example on abortion and no-tax pledges, to enforce compliance on their issues and to pressure moderate Republicans to either join up or defect. Whether this political alliance of countervailing cultural forces will last is open to question.

These cultural movements throughout Kansas' political history have influenced state governmental structures as well. Perhaps in no place is this influence more evident than in the state's constitution, which has undergone a series of reforms, many of which were designed by progressives in the early 1900s and their moderate successors in the 1970s and most of which were designed to modernize the constitution. These reformers set the stage for political change by strengthening gubernatorial powers, loosening restraints on the legislature, unifying the court system, classifying property for tax purposes, removing restrictions on amending the constitution, deleting statutory prescriptions, and cleaning up archaic language. In 2005 polar alliance Republicans also left their mark on the state's constitution with an amendment that banned gay marriages and civil unions and that passed with seventy percent of the statewide vote.

The common wisdom is that Kansas elections and party politics are somewhat insulated from national political tides or, if anything, may lead them. An extensive analysis of county voting patterns for president, U.S. senators, and governor in Kansas shows that this common wisdom is not supported. Even though Republicans have dominated state party politics since 1861, there have been a number of party realignments in Kansas, each roughly coinciding with a major national alignment: the post–Civil War / Progressive alignment (1900 to 1928), the New Deal alignment (1930 to 1978), and the New Right alignment (1980 to the present). Of the three the timing of the New Right alignment appears to be at odds with other journalistic accounts that emphasize the Summer of Mercy in Wichita (1991) as being a key event in spurring the rise of polar alliance Republicans and three-party politics. Our analysis suggests that the rise of polar alliance Republicans is a manifestation of the Reagan revolution and the politics unleashed by Reagan. In

Kansas the emergence of polar alliance Republicans is nationally significant because it may be a harbinger for other states in which Republicans dominate and split into moderate and polar factions.

Like the state constitution, the Kansas legislature reflects the influence of a historically dominant political culture of individualism. Its status as a part-time citizen legislature fits nicely with the individualistic norm that the best legislature is one that meets infrequently for short periods of time and that the best legislators are those who are not career politicians. Indeed, when the legislature goes home in May, editorial pages across the state breath a collective sigh of relief that the opportunity for mischief has diminished.

To maintain its part-time status, the legislature has institutionally adjusted to increase legislative capacity with measures such as a legislative research department to conduct nonpartisan research for committees and legislators, a legislative post audit operation to oversee executive implementation, a unified appropriations process in which the governor is charged with the responsibility of preparing a balanced budget based on existing tax revenues, and an interim committee process to hear testimony and to draft legislation between legislative sessions. In addition, power in both chambers tends to be centralized in the leadership, represented by the speaker of the house and the president of the senate. Even though the president's power is filtered through a leadership committee, both leaders exercise considerable control over the flow of legislation within their respective chambers. This centralization of power helps to provide order to a legislative process that could be far more chaotic and time consuming.

Finally, Kansas Republicans have split into factions beginning with the 1995 legislative session. This split has led to occasions when moderate Republicans join Democrats in a centrist coalition. Although traditional two-party politics remains the norm, factional disputes have prompted primary challenges to sitting incumbents, divided control of the senate and house leadership between moderates and polar alliance Republicans, and fostered the formation of moderate coalitions to support or oppose legislation on critical votes such as on educational finance.

The Kansas governorship has emerged over state history to become a preeminent position in state politics and government. When something goes wrong, Kansans most often look to the governor for answers. The evolution of gubernatorial powers follows national patterns to a large degree with a dramatic transformation beginning in the 1970s. The modern governorship is the one office in state government with the potential to give order and direction to state politics through agenda setting, maintenance of fiscal stewardship, management of executive operations, and representation of Kansans as chief of state.

Gubernatorial politics has departed from what might be expected in a strong Republican state. This departure might be explained in part by the impact of political cultures. Republican governors have grappled with the cultural dilemma presented by their party's alliance of liberty and order, and eleven of twenty-nine have left office in defeat. Without a firmly established cultural coalition in Kansas, Democrats have been more entrepreneurial in campaigning for and performing as governor and have succeeded in winning the office in eleven of the last eighteen elections. In stark contrast, Kansans have not elected a Democrat to the U.S. Senate since 1932.

The interest group politics of Kansas has in large measure also followed national trends. Just like national government and many other states, Kansas has experienced a proliferation of interest groups in the post-WWII era as well as a change in the way that interests are represented in the halls of government. Since the 1960s and 1970s Kansas' interests are increasingly represented by either professional contract lobbyists like Pete McGill, the state's first professional contract lobbyist, or association lobbyists, who are employed by their organization in a variety of capacities, one of which is lobbying the legislature and other governmental bodies.

Patterns of taxing and borrowing parallel the trends in state-local relations in Kansas. At the beginning of the twentieth century the ratio of local-to-state taxes was seven to one while today it is to four to six. A political culture that historically has restrained state taxing and spending has given way to reordered and equalized state finances in response to national initiatives, public demands, and state court actions, among other influences. Consequently, the state takes a progressive approach that calls for a balance among property, income, and sales taxes in order to support state spending that is focused primarily on education and assistance to those in need.

The financial future of the state, however, is not rosy because a variety of national and state initiatives coupled with missteps in state finance have placed the state on an unsustainable course. Aggressive borrowing for state highways beginning in the 1990s that was compounded by additional borrowing needed to shore up state pensions has boosted Kansas into the upper tiers of state borrowers, far ahead of surrounding states. In educational finance those with a preference for equality won an important battle in state courts that forced the state to fund education on a "rational" basis. The practical effect of this court intervention is that such areas as suburban Johnson County in the Kansas City metropolitan area with high incomes, sales, and assessed valuations underwrite the high costs of education in sparsely populated rural areas with constricted tax bases and in communities with large numbers of high-risk children. National initiatives such as Medicaid only exacerbate the state's budgetary dilemma and lead the state to expend an ever-increasing percent of the state's general fund revenues on medical assistance for the poor.

As conflicting cultural forces push for higher state spending to achieve order and equality on the one hand and for tax cuts to preserve liberty and limited government on the other, the present direction of state finance may not be sustainable. Further, the fiscal disparities between urban and rural Kansas present an ongoing financial quandary because of the higher costs of delivering services like education, welfare, and healthcare to sparsely populated rural areas.

THE FUTURE DIRECTIONS OF KANSAS POLITICS

Will the clash of political cultures wither away in the politics in the twenty-first century? This volume has examined the state's politics through the prism of political cultures, but as noted in the introduction, an urban-rural divide lurks beneath the surface of Kansas as a fault line that may give way if enough political force is applied. Most often, however, established mechanisms for political expression—political parties, interest groups, and elections, along with cultural forces—relieve the tension on this fault line. In the process of finishing this book in 2007 and 2008, Governor Kathleen Sebelius and her administration was embroiled in a major controversy over their refusal to grant an air permit for two seven-hundred-megawatt coal-fired electrical plants in southwest Kansas. In October 2007 the issue had all the makings of a urban-rural, east-west dispute. The *Wichita Eagle* opined against the plants. The Lawrence City Commission also issued a statement against building the coal plants. Officials from Sunflower Electric fired back on this eastern urban intrusion; Sunflower spokesman Steve Miller told the *Salina Journal* (November 3, 2006) that he would "make it my crusade to make sure all our western Kansas dollars are diverted as far away from Lawrence as they can be, because they have unfairly stuck their nose in western Kansas' business."

Despite this puffery, once the issue materialized in the 2008 legislative session, urban-rural conflicts were replaced by party loyalty. Most Democrats, except for a handful from western Kansas, supported the governor's veto of the bills permitting the plants, while the lion's share of Republicans, except a few in Johnson County, voted to override the veto. The Sebelius veto was sustained on three different occasions in the house.

Even though the urban-rural split has not been a persistently dominant force in past or current politics, this divide may emerge more prominently in the future of Kansas politics. Why? First, cultural and political forces may be aligning on the urban-rural divide. Seventy to eighty percent of voters in rural counties supported a constitutional ban on gay marriage in 2005, compared to fifty-five to sixty-five percent in most urban counties.

Second, rural counties more commonly elect polar alliance Republicans, whereas most urban counties elect a diversity of representatives, including Democrats, moderate Republicans, and polar alliance Republicans. Urban Sedgwick County with the state's largest city elects more than its fair share of polar alliance Republicans and provides a stark exception to an alignment of culture and demography. If urban counties, especially Sedgwick, move to elect a greater proportion of Democrats and moderates in the future, polar alliance Republicans may become more confined to rural Kansas.

Third, the politics of consolidation will likely make a return visit to Kansas in the coming years. State budgetary shortfalls, whether as a result of recession, debt repayment, school finance, or some combination thereof, will likely spark consideration of consolidation alternatives. With over three hundred unified school districts covering the state, nearly half of which enroll fewer than five hundred total students, school consolidation will be a high-priority target for many urban legislators. Other targets of opportunity might include overturning Kansas' one judge per county mandate or merging the state's administration of welfare, health, and aging services in a manner similar to the consolidation of welfare services carried out by the Kansas Department of Social and Rehabilitative Services in 2006.

Rural populations may frame the next bout of consolidation as a reflection of the cost of providing quality services to rural communities. Conversely, egalitarian populist sentiments may resurface after a century-long hiatus to dominate the rural landscape. Unfortunately, in contrast to the populists of the late nineteenth century, rural voters today have become a minority, one that is diminishing with time. Unless they find sympathetic coalition partners in urban or suburban counties, rural communities will endure these changes without the ability to hold state policy makers accountable to any large degree.

For rural communities consolidation will only fuel their depopulation. On the plus side, the twenty or so rural trade centers that dot the state may boom as Kansas' rural population clusters in those communities where government and retail services are still available. These factors may facilitate the emergence of the urban-rural divide as a consistent force in state politics, but Kansas' dominant political cultures will persist. For the past and the future Kansas politics is best understood as a clash of political cultures.

Appendixes

I. THE KANSAS COURT SYSTEM

Prior to 1900 the Kansas Supreme Court consisted of a chief justice and two associate judges popularly elected to overlapping terms.[1] In 1900 a constitutional amendment was ratified expanding the court to seven justices. In 1965 the legislature enacted the Judicial Department Reform Act, which grouped existing district courts into six judicial districts, with each one supervised by an associate justice of the supreme court. The Office of Judicial Administrator was also established to assist with this work and to help manage case loads in each judicial district.

As noted in chapter 2, the Missouri Plan for choosing supreme court justices was ratified in 1957, and a revised judicial article, ratified in 1972, created a unified Kansas court system with a supreme court, state district courts, and municipal and small claims courts. Finally, in 1975 the state legislature created the Kansas Court of Appeals, which handles appeals between the state district courts and the supreme court. The creation of the appeals court relieved the workload on the supreme court, which prior to 1975 heard all appeals from state district courts. In 2000 the Kansas court system terminated over four hundred and sixty thousand cases. About thirty-eight percent of these were civil cases, nine percent criminal cases, and forty-two percent traffic cases; the remainder ranged from juvenile cases to miscellaneous probate actions.[2] In a typical year the Kansas Court of Appeals will hear about twenty-two hundred appeals. Even though the entire ten-judge Court of Appeals may choose to hear a case, for most cases, three judges are impaneled. By contrast, the Kansas Supreme Court terminates about three hundred cases a year. In about two-thirds of these cases a written opinion is issued.[3]

Reflecting Kansas' rural character, the state legislature has decreed that every county must have a district or magistrate judge assigned to it. In return, every county must provide courtroom facilities and a clerk of the court. Rural district court judges, who have smaller local case loads, are often assigned cases in other district courts in order to help alleviate case backlogs.

2. SUMMARY OF LEGISLATION
GOVERNING LOBBYING IN KANSAS

KSA 46-222

"Lobbyist means: 1. Any person employed in considerable degree for lobbying; 2. Any person formally appointed as the primary representative of an organization or other person to lobby in person on state-owned or leased property; or 3. any person who make expenditures in an aggregate amount of $100 or more, exclusive of personal travel and subsistence expenses, in any calendar year for lobbying." 1974–91.

KSA 46-225

Lobbying is defined as: 1. "Promoting or opposing in any manner action or nonaction by the legislature on any legislative matter or the adoption or nonadoption of any rule and regulation by any state agency or 2. entertaining any state officer or employee or giving any gift, honorarium or payment to a state officer or employee in an aggregate value of $40 or more within any calendar year if at any time during such year the person supplying the entertainment, gifts, honoraria or payments has a financial interest in any contract with, or action, proceeding or other matter before the state agency in which such state officer or employee serves, or if such a person is the representative of a person having such a financial interest." 1974–91.

KSA 46-232

State officers or employees cannot lobby their own agency for compensation. 1974.

KSA 46-236

No state employee or candidate for office can elicit gifts, money, and so on from a special interest for which the employee knows that the purpose of the major donor is to influence the performance or official duties of an officer. 1974–2000.

Exceptions:

Contributions in compliance with campaign finance act

Commercial Loans

Beneficial charitable organization

KSA 46-237

No state officer or employee shall accept any economic incentive of forty dollars or more in any given calendar year. No person with a special interest shall offer forty dollars or more in a given calendar year. No person of a state agency shall given forty dollars or more to another agency or employee. No food or drink shall be given to influence a state officer. No state officer or employee shall accept payment for speaking engagements, except that legislators, part-time officers or employees, and employees of the executive branch of government shall be allowed to receive reimbursement for reasonable expenses to be determined by the Gov. Ethics Commission. Gifts from foreign nations having value of one hundred dollars and more shall be accepted on behalf of the state of Kansas. No legislator shall solicit any contribution to be made to any organization for the purpose of paying for travel, subsistence, and other expenses in attending and participating in meetings. The legislator can accept reimbursements for the purpose of education and for informing and strengthening the legislature in all states. 1974–2000.

KSA 46-255

Any individual may file with the commission a verified complaint in writing of alleged violations of any provision. 1974.

KSA 46-26

Every lobbyist must register with the sos. On or after October 1 any person may register as a lobbyist for the proceeding year. If a lobbyist anticipates spending less than one thousand dollars in a given year, he or she must pay a fee of thirty-five dollars for registration. If a lobbyists anticipates on spending more than one thousand dollars in a given year, he or she must pay three hundred dollars for registration. If a lobbyist belongs to a lobbying firm, he or she must pay three hundred and sixty dollars for registration for the year. All of these funds go the Gov. Ethics Commission fee fund. 1974–2000.

KSA 46-267

No person shall pay or promise compensation for a desired result to be obtained; payment shall not be contingent upon outcome. No person shall pay or promise contingent compensation for the referral of a person to a lobbyist for lobbyist services. No lobbying contract shall be valid or enforceable in a court of law unless it is in writing, signed by all parties, and was executed prior to the lobbyists commencement of lobbying for the represented person under such contract. 1974–97.

KSA 46-268

Every lobbyist must file an employment report and expenditure forms on the tenth day of February, March, April, May, September, and January. 1974–95.

KSA 46-269

Provided a lobbyist spends more than one hundred dollars, he or she must file a report must be filed; six categories are to be itemized. 1974–2000.

1. Food and Beverages
2. Entertainment, gifts, and so on
3. Mass media communications
4. Recreation and hospitality provided
5. Communications for the purpose of influencing the legislature
6. Other

KSA 46-271

No lobbyist shall offer to pay for anything that is ten dollars or more in any calendar year to any state employee or candidate for state office with a major purpose of influencing such officer or employee in the performance of official duties. 1974–91.

KSA 46-272

No lobbyist shall pay any state officer or employee or candidate for office or associate a fee-compensation for the sale or lease of any property or furnishing services that is substantially in excess of that which another person in the same occupation would charge. 1974.

KSA 46-273

No lobbyist shall offer employment to any state officer or employee or associated person thereof for representation with the intent of obtaining improper influence over a state agency. No lobbyist shall use threat or the promise of official action in an attempt to influence a state agency in any representation case. 1974.

KSA 46-275

Giving false lobbying information is a class b misdemeanor, for which the punishment is not however listed however. A class b misdemeanor is not universal. 1974–75.

KSA 46-277

Intent is required for an act to constitute a punishable violation. 1974.

KSA 45-280

There is a civil penalty for not filing reports. 1978–2001.

KSA 46-287

No person can advertise a position on a legislative statue or legislative action without the word "advertisement" and without the name of the person of the organization sponsoring the ad. No person shall broadcast paid advertisements promoting or opposing an action by the legislature unless followed by a statement with a disclaimer about the person who purchased said ad. 1988–90.

KSA 46-288

Violations of acts 46-215 through 46-286 will incur the following pen-
alties:

First offense carries a fine of up to five thousand dollars

Second offense carries a fine up to ten thousand dollars

Third offense carries a fine of up to fifteen thousand dollars,

1988–2001.

Notes

INTRODUCTION

1. The sometimes tense relations between religion and public schools are traceable to the beginning of statehood; see James C. Carper, "A Common Faith for the Common School? Religion and Education in Kansas," *Mid-America: An Historical Review* 60, no. 3 (October 1978). An antievolution movement also materialized in the late 1920s in Kansas but fell short of gaining political power; see Barbara Jean Beale, "Gerald Burton Winrod: Defender of Christianity and Democracy in the United States" (master's thesis, Wichita State University, 1994), 12–25.

2. Carl Manning, "Evolution Debate Tops State's Stories," *Topeka Capital-Journal*, December 27, 1999.

3. The Kansas State Board of Education's ten seats are staggered. Only half of the positions are up for election on even years.

4. Jim McLean, "Conservatives Lose Control of Education Board," *Topeka Capital-Journal*, August 2, 2000.

5. Connie Morris defeated Sonny Rundell, and conservative Iris Van Meter defeated Val DeFever.

6. John Hanna, "Board Member: Evolution a 'Fairy Tale,'" *Topeka Capital-Journal*, June 14, 2005; Barbara Hollingsworth, "Science Standards Supporter Wraps Up Case Today," *Topeka Capital-Journal*, May 12, 2005.

7. See James R. Shortridge, *Peopling the Plains: Who Settled Where in Frontier Kansas* (Lawrence: University Press of Kansas, 1995).

8. *Emporia Gazette*, April 25, 1922, in *The Editor and His People: Editorials by William Allen White*, selected by Helen Ogden Mahin (New York: Macmillan, 1924), 174.

9. Craig Miner, *Kansas: The History of the Sunflower State, 1854–2000* (Lawrence: University Press of Kansas, 2002), 290.

10. Neal R. Peirce and Jerry Hagstrom, *The Book of America* (New York: Norton, 1983), 585–601.

11. Peirce and Hagstrom, *Book of America*, 585.

12. Thomas Frank, *What's the Matter with Kansas? How Conservatives Won the Heart of America* (New York: Metropolitan, 2004).

13. At least three factors contribute heavily to this pattern of population change. First, agricultural practices have become industrialized, a process that leads to a reliance on large machinery, hybrid grains, and the use of fertilizers, pesticides, and other high energy agricultural practices. All of these trends have enabled farmers and ranchers to increase the size of their operations while at the same time to decrease the number of people employed in agriculture. Federal crop subsidies, which have for the most part encouraged greater production than markets can bear, have generally exacerbated this process. Second, the boom and bust economic cycles associated with the agricultural economy have accelerated depopulation, hastening the movement of rural populations into urban centers during bust cycles. Third, an ever-increasing proportion of jobs are located in urban centers. This shift started during the industrial revolution and has continued as the state's economy has become increasingly dependent on information age and service sector employment.

14. Mark Drabenstott and K. H. Sheaff, "The New Power of Regions: A Policy Focus for Rural America," in *The Main Street Economist* (Kansas City MO: Federal Reserve Bank of Kansas City, 2004), 1–5.

15. For this analysis we used a statistical technique called cluster analysis on variables representing each county's population, population change, household income, and occupational employment patterns. The categories of counties parallel those discussed in Timothy S. Parker and Linda Ghelfi, "Using the 2003 Urban Influence Codes to Understand Rural America," *Amber Waves* 2 (2004): 12–13.

16. Donald D. Stull and M. J. Broadway, *Slaughterhouse Blues: The Meat and Poultry Industry in North America* (Belmont CA: Wadsworth, 2004).

17. The lives of countless rural communities trudged on in the aftermath of the consolidation of rural schools and the reapportionment of the state legislature. Interesting enough, the pain and suffering caused by these events have gone largely unrecorded by current history. In fact, two recent treatments of Kansas history fail to reference any of these events in their indexes. See Miner, *Kansas*, 509–34, and Shortridge, *Peopling the Plains*, 471–80.

18. David E. Kromm and Stephen E. White, eds. *Groundwater Exploitation in the High Plains* (Lawrence: University Press of Kansas, 1992); Preston Gilson and Joseph A. Aistrup, "The Value of Ogallala Aquifer Water in Southwestern Kansas," in *Symposium 2001: State of Water Issues of the Great Plains* (Dodge City KS: Great Plains Foundation, 2002).

CHAPTER ONE: POLITICAL CULTURES

1. This chapter and particularly the conceptual framework that directly follows draws upon theoretical work of Aaron Wildavsky and his associates, primarily from Michael Thompson, Richard Ellis, and Aaron Wildavsky, *Cultural Theory* (Boulder: Westview Press, 1990), 25–38. The conceptual work of these cultural theorists has much in common but also departs significantly from the widely cited work of Daniel J. Elazar, *American Federalism: A View from the States* (New York: Crowell, 1966). For a comparison of these two approaches see H. Edward Flentje, "State Administration in Cultural Context," in *Handbook of State Government Administration*, ed. John J. Gargan (New York: Dekker, 2000), 75–77.

2. See Flentje, "State Administration," 70–74. A political culture of fatalism is likely present in Kansas politics, but this volume focuses on the three more visible and active political cultures.

3. Thompson, Ellis, and Wildavsky, *Cultural Theory*, 34.

4. Thompson, Ellis, and Wildavsky, *Cultural Theory*, 35.

5. This section on liberty and the following section on equality draw heavily upon excellent analyses of Kansas populism and its antecedents, specifically: John D. Hicks, *The Populist Revolt: A History of the Farmers' Alliance and the People's Party* (1931, repr. Lincoln: University of Nebraska Press, 1961); O. Gene Clanton, *Kansas Populism: Ideas and Men* (Lawrence: University Press of Kansas, 1969); Peter H. Argersinger, *Populism and Politics: William Alfred Peffer and the People's Party* (Lexington: University Press of Kentucky, 1974); Norman Pollack, *The Just Polity: Populism, Law, and Human Welfare* (Urbana: University of Illinois Press, 1987); Scott G. McNall, *The Road to Rebellion: Class Formation and Kansas Populism, 1865–1900* (Chicago: University of Chicago Press, 1988); Gary Lee Malecha, "A Cultural Analysis of Populism in Late-Nineteenth-Century America," in *Politics, Policy and Culture*, ed. Dennis J. Coyle and Richard J. Ellis (Boulder: Westview Press, 1994).

6. John J. Ingalls to Percy Daniels, August 7, 1888, in Percy Daniels, *Swollen Fortunes and the Problem of the Unemployed* (1908), 36–38, and in People's Party pamphlets, Kansas State Historical Society, VI, quoted in Clanton, *Kansas Populism*, 43.

7. *The Smoky Hill and Republican Union*, May 29, 1862, quoted in Homer E. Socolofsky, "How We Took the Lands," in *Kansas: The First Century*, ed. John D. Bright, vol. 1 (New York: Lewis Historical Publishing, 1956), 295.

8. Miner, *Kansas*, 103.

9. Clanton, *Kansas Populism*, 28.

10. Hicks, *Populist Revolt*, 26.

11. McNall, *Road to Rebellion*, 119, 121.

12. *The Advocate* (Topeka), December 30, 1891, quoted in Clanton, *Kansas Populism*, 67; *Peoples Herald* (Lyndon), September 29, 1890, quoted in Clanton, *Kansas Populism*, 81. *The Advocate* served as a leading mouthpiece for the people's party.

13. Quoted in Richard J. Ellis, *American Political Cultures* (New York: Oxford University Press, 1993, 54.

14. Lorenzo Lewelling, Inaugural address, January 9, 1893, Gubernatorial papers of Governor Lorenzo Lewelling, Kansas History Center, Kansas State Historical Society, Topeka.

15. In a political movement as fluid as populism, specifics in the populist program became identified with a sometimes diverse multitude of leaders, spokesmen, and gatherings associated with the movement at various times. At its core, particularly in the beginning, the populist agenda focused on money, transportation, and land reform. See Argersinger, *Populism and Politics*, 5.

16. McNall, *Road to Rebellion*, 186, 197, 204–8, 230–34.

17. James C. Malin, *A Concern about Humanity: Notes on Reform, 1872–1912 at the National and Kansas Levels of Thought* (Lawrence: Malin, 1964), 191–93.

18. Francis W. Schruben, *Kansas in Turmoil, 1930–1936* (Columbia: University of Missouri Press, 1969), 45–46.

19. Schruben, *Kansas in Turmoil*, 44.

20. The review of Kansas history with respect to prohibition draws on the excellent work of Robert Smith Bader, *Prohibition in Kansas* (Lawrence: University Press of Kansas, 1986).

21. Bader, *Prohibition in Kansas*, 15–16.

22. Bader, *Prohibition in Kansas*, 37.

23. Kansas Supreme Court Justice David Brewer wrote the unanimous opinion on the constitutionality of the amendment; see *Prohibitory Amendment Cases*, 24 Kans 499, 706.

24. *Kansas Session Laws of 1885*, chaps. 149 and 169.

25. *Kansas Session Laws of 1887*, chap. 100.

26. *Kansas House Journal*, 1889, 62.

27. Bader, *Prohibition in Kansas*, 133–55.

28. W. G. Clugston, *Rascals in Democracy* (New York: Smith, 1941), 39; Bader, *Prohibition in Kansas*, 160.

29. *Kansas Session Laws, 1903*, chaps. 214 and 223; *Kansas Session Laws, 1909*, chap. 257; *Kansas Session Laws, 1913*, chaps. 179 and 181.

30. *Kansas Session Laws, 1913*, chap. 294; *Kansas Session Laws, 1915*, chap. 268.

31. *Kansas Session Laws, 1909*, chap. 164; *Kansas Session Laws, 1911*, chaps. 165 and 237.

32. *Kansas Session Laws, 1909*, chap. 215.

33. *Kansas Session Laws, 1915*, chap. 394.

34. Kansans voted against repeal of prohibition in 1934; fifty-six percent opposed repeal, with voters in 89 of 105 counties electing to retain prohibition; see Bader, *Prohibition in Kansas*, 123–25.

35. Even though the center of gravity in Republican Party politics shifted away from economic liberty toward economic order during the progressive era, voices advocating individualism were not suppressed. One Kansas banker wrote Progressive Republican Governor Hoch in 1906 denouncing the state guarantee program as "impractical, unjust . . . populistic, socialistic and paternalistic and repugnant to the spirit of our institutions and to those qualities of individualism and individual responsibility which our forefathers sought to preserve, encourage and establish through the Constitution"; J. B. Adams to Governor Hoch, December 21, 1906, Edward W. Hoch Gubernatorial Papers, Kansas State Historical Society, quoted in Robert Sherman La Forte, *Leaders of Reform: Progressive Republicans in Kansas, 1900–1916* (Lawrence: University Press of Kansas, 1974), 124.

36. *Kansas Session Laws, 1915*, chap. 389; *Kansas Session Laws, 1917*, chaps. 297, 86, and 312.

37. Ying Huang, Robert E. McCormick, and Lawrence J. McQuillan, *U.S. Economic Freedom Index: 2004 Report* (San Francisco: Pacific Research Institute, 2004). See also the websites of Kansas organizations promoting individualism: http://www.flinthills.org; http://www.kansastaxpayers.com; http://www.americansforprosperity.org/kansas.

38. Richard Ellis and Aaron Wildavsky, *Dilemmas of Presidential Leadership from Washington through Lincoln* (New Brunswick NJ: Transaction, 1989), 5, 111–83, 193, 197.

39. The interconnections of the thirteen Republican governors with their progressive-era predecessors have not been thoroughly researched and deserve further study. Partial documentation of these interconnections can be found in various sources. For example, the connection of Reed and Landon with their progressive predecessors is well documented in the Landon biography by Donald R. McCoy, *Landon of Kansas* (Lincoln: University of Nebraska Press, 1966). Other connections may be found in the excellent biographical sketches of Kansas governors by Homer E. Socolofsky, *Kansas Governors* (Lawrence: University Press of Kansas, 1990). See, for example, Ratner's ties to Landon (183), Schoeppel's ties to Ratner (187), Carlson's ties to Landon (190–91), and Arn's ties to Ratner and Schoeppel (197). The connections of more recent Republican governors, Avery, Bennett, Hayden, and Graves, in politics and policy are better known.

40. The word "polar" accurately characterizes this new party dynamic. *Webster's New Riverside University Dictionary* defines polar as "occupying or marked by opposite extremes."
41. *Wichita Eagle*, January 20, 1995.
42. *Wichita Eagle*, January 29, 1995.
43. See chapter 1 and Joel Paddock, "Democratic Politics in a Republican State: The Gubernatorial Campaigns of Robert Docking, 1966–1972," *Kansas History* 17, no. 2 (Summer 1994).

CHAPTER TWO: THE CONSTITUTION

1. James W. Drury, *The Government of Kansas*, with Marvin G. Stottlemire, 6th ed. (Topeka: Public Management Center, University of Kansas, 2001), 1–5.
2. Much of this history is based on the work of Francis Heller, *The Kansas State Constitution: A Reference Guide* (Westport CT: Greenwood Press, 1992), 1–4. This book is one of the best references on the Kansas Constitution.
3. Heller, *Kansas State Constitution*, 4–9.
4. Kristi Lowenthal, *The Equal Rights Amendment and Conservative Thought in Kansas* (PhD diss., Kansas State University, 2008), 52–53.
5. Marilyn Schultz Blackwell, "Meddling in Politics: Clarina Howard Nichols and Antebellum Political Culture," *Journal of the Early Republic* 24, no. 1 (Spring 2004): 31.
6. Lowenthal, *Equal Rights Amendment*, 52–53.
7. Lowenthal, *Equal Rights Amendment*, 53.
8. Constitutional amendments required a two-thirds vote of both chambers of the legislature and a majority of voters ratifying it in a general election. The Wyandotte Constitution also limited revisions to one subject per amendment. Finally, it prescribed that no more than three amendments could appear on the general election ballot at any one time. A constitutional convention to revise the entire document or a subset of articles as decreed by the legislature could be called by a two-thirds vote of both chambers. This call had to be ratified by a majority of voters, and any subsequent outcome of the convention also had to be ratified by a majority of voters. See Heller, *Kansas State Constitution*, 133–35.
9. Even though there have been numerous calls for constitutional conventions, only two have been held, in 1879 and 1891. In both instances the revised constitutions failed to be ratified by a majority of voters. See Drury, *Government of Kansas*, 25.
10. Marvin A. Harder, "Electoral Politics in Kansas: A Historical Perspective," in *Politics and Government in Kansas: Selected Essays*, ed. Marvin A. Harder (Topeka: Capitol Complex Center, University of Kansas, 1989), 41–46.

11. Miner, *Kansas*, 383.

12. Miner, *Kansas*, 382–85.

13. Heller, *Kansas State Constitution*, 20–21.

14. The legislature pledged to use the gaming proceeds to fund economic development programs.

15. Harder, "Electoral Politics in Kansas," 41–46.

16. Kansas Secretary of State, *Kansas Constitution*, 29–34.

17. Kansas Secretary of State, *Kansas Constitution*, 29–34.

18. In 1923 voters ratified an amendment providing property tax relief for the coal industry and for property with evidences of debt. The implementation of this property-tax classification system in the late 1980s led to an increase in the property taxes of many businesses and remains a topic of much controversy. See Heller, *Kansas State Constitution*, 22–23.

19. One of the amendments ratified by voters in 1970 was struck down by the Kansas Supreme Court because it tried to revise two articles in one amendment.

20. Heller, *Kansas State Constitution*, 26–29.

21. Heller's work provides a complete history of this period; see Heller, *Kansas State Constitution*, 32–34.

22. This amendment officially ended the tradition of redistricting the state legislative boundaries once every thirty or so years and then only under extreme duress from urban constituencies.

23. Heller, *Kansas State Constitution*, 34–35.

24. *Serrano v. Priest*, 487 P.2d 1241 (Cal. 1971); David C. Thompson, David Honeyman, and R. Craig Wood, *Educational Fiscal Equality in Kansas under the School District Equalization Act* (Manhattan KS: UCEA Center for Education Finance, Kansas State University), 2–4.

25. Drury, *Government of Kansas*, 298.

26. This act withstood two court challenges in the mid-1990s, one by Unified School District Number 229 (local control and equal protection rights) and the other by a coalition of twenty mid-sized school districts (weighting formula for high and low enrollment leads to unequal funding).

27. Actual costs were determined by a study commissioned by the state legislature called the Augenblick and Meyer study. In the special session the state legislature ordered the office of the auditor to conduct its own assessment of the actual costs to educate K–12 students.

28. Fred Mann, "School Plan Passes: $148 Million More," *Wichita Eagle*, July 2, 2005; Chris Moon, "Relief, Concern Follow Dismissal of School Finance Case," *Topeka Capital-Journal CJOnline*, July 29, 2006, http://cjonline.com/stories/072906/leg_eduruling.shtml.

29 *Montoy v. State*, 275 Kan. 145, 62 P.3d 228 (2003).

30. Moon, "Relief."

31. Heller, *Kansas State Constitution*, 47–61.

32. For a classic example of a model state constitution, see Committee on State Government, *Model State Constitution*, 5th ed. (New York: National Municipal League, 1948).

33. See the comments of Bruce Cain at a workshop sponsored by Rutgers University, School of Law; "Workshop One: What Should a State Constitution Do?" May 17, 2005, http://www-camlaw.rutgers.edu/statecon/wrkshpla.htm.

34. Derek Schmidt, "Testimony in Support of Senate Concurrent Resolution 1606 Proposing Senate Confirmation of Supreme Court Justices," Kansas State Senate, Senate Judiciary Committee, February 21, 2005.

35. See the comments of Allan Tarr at the Rutgers's workshop; "Workshop One: What Should a State Constitution Do?" May 17, 2005, http://www-camlaw.rutgers.edu/statecon/wrkshpla.htm.

36. Drury, *Government of Kansas*, 125.

37. John Harrigan and David C. Nice, *Politics and Policy in States and Communities*, 8th ed. (New York: Pearson Education, 2004), 18.

38. Article 15, section 15, states that "victims of crime, as defined by law, shall be entitled to certain basic rights, including the right to be informed of and to be present at public hearings, as defined by law, of the criminal justice process, and to be heard at sentencing or at any other time deemed appropriate by the court, to the extent that these rights do not interfere with the constitutional or statutory rights of the accused."

39. Jack Treadway, "Adoption of Term Limits for State Legislators: An Update," *Comparative State Politics* 16, no. 3 (June 1995): 1–3.

40. For those interested in a complete description of the Kansas court system and its operation, see Drury, *Government of Kansas*, chap. 11.

CHAPTER THREE: ELECTIONS AND POLITICAL PARTIES

1. Thomas Frank characterizes Kansas as a state that is "deep in the heart of redness"; see Frank, *What's the Matter with Kansas?* chap. 2.

2. See Allan Cigler and Burdett Loomis, "Kansas: Two-Party Competition in a One-Party State," in *Party Realignment and State Politics*, ed. Maureen Moakley (Columbus: Ohio State University Press, 1992).

3. GOP factionalism is in part responsible for the election of Democratic governors in 1882, 1896, 1912, 1930, 1956, 1966, and 1990.

4. Harder, "Electoral Politics in Kansas."

5. A close reading of Harder suggests that historically the outcomes emerging from Republican factionalism, particularly at the gubernatorial level, fall into

two general categories. The losing GOP faction temporarily abandons the party, resulting in higher likelihood of Democratic victory. Or alternatively, it splinters the party so as to temporarily form a third party, thus resulting in a higher likelihood that Democratic candidates win. In other words, GOP factionalism creates an electoral environment that often reflects the outcomes of a two-party competitive system.

6. See also Frank, *What's the Matter with Kansas?* chap. 5.

7. Indeed, many moderate Republicans sported yard signs that read "Another Republican Supporting Sebelius." These Republicans may have voted against their party's nominee for governor (or U.S. representative in the case of Johnson County Mods) when that nominee represented a faction other than their own, but they remained true to the GOP for most other offices.

8. Cigler and Loomis, "Kansas"; Richard P. Heil's work, focusing on party competition, echoes their conclusions; see Heil, "Indices of Party Strength: The Case of Kansas" (PhD diss., University of Kansas, 1983).

9. This definition represents an amalgamation of several perspectives about realignments and party alignments. See Walter Dean Burnham, *The Current Crisis in American Politics* (Oxford, UK: Oxford University Press, 1982); Edward G. Carmines and James A. Stimson, *Issue Evolution: Race and the Transformation of American Politics* (Princeton NJ: Princeton University Press, 1989); J. R. Petrocik, *Party Coalitions* (Chicago: University of Chicago Press, 1981); and James L. Sundquist, *Dynamics of the Party System*, rev. ed. (Washington DC: Brookings Institution, 1983).

10. Harder's historical framework is informative, but he does not specifically use a party alignment approach. Cigler and Loomis in "Kansas" do take a party alignment approach, but the bulk of their analysis concentrates on the 1970s and 1980s when party registration data and polling data became available for analysis. Given the age of this research and its more narrow analytical focus, we conducted our own independent analysis of Kansas party alignments.

11. The details of this analysis, data, methods, and findings are available upon request from the authors.

12. James R. Shortridge, *Cities on the Plains: The Evolution of Urban Kansas* (Lawrence: University Press of Kansas, 2004), chap. 3.

13. The counties are weighted by population so that Sedgwick County (location of the City of Wichita) with its large population is given a greater weight than Wichita County with its smaller rural population.

14. Cumulatively these variables did a poor job of explaining GOP support ($R2 = .089$). We suspect that if nationality and religious denomination variables were included in this analysis, the variance explained would improve. These variables, however, were not available in the 1910 census.

15. Burnham, *Current Crisis*, 1982; Carmines and Stimson, *Issue Evolution*, 1989; Petrocik, *Party Coalitions*, 1981; Sundquist, *Dynamics of the Party System*, 1983.

16. Cigler and Loomis, "Kansas," 168.

17. Taken as a whole, these demographic variables explained 66.6 percent of the variance in the structure of GOP voting.

18. T. B. Edsall and M. D. Edsall, *Chain Reaction* (New York: Norton, 1992), 132.

19. David Mayhew, *Placing Parties in American Politics* (Princeton NJ: Princeton University Press, 1986), 70; see also Cigler and Loomis, "Kansas," 172. Other studies reinforcing this finding include Marvin A. Harder, "Party Factionalism in Kansas" (PhD diss., Columbia University, 1959), and Ronald A. Averyt, "The Minority Party in a Non-competitive State: The Case of Kansas" (PhD diss., University of Kansas, 1970); both cited in Cigler and Loomis, "Kansas," 172.

20. Much of the following scholarship first appeared in Joseph A. Aistrup and Mark Bannister, "Kansas," in *State Party Profiles*, ed. Andrew M. Appleton and Daniel S. Ward (Washington DC: Congressional Quarterly, 1997). The authors would like to thank Mark Bannister for his contributions to this section.

21. Norbert Dreiling, chairman of Kansas Democratic Party, 1966 to 1974, interview conducted by Joseph A. Aistrup and Mark Bannister on June 15, 1995; Robert Bennett, Republican governor of Kansas, 1975 to 1979, and chairman of Kansas Republican Party, 1982 to 1983, interview conducted by Joseph A. Aistrup and Mark Bannister on July 14, 1995.

22. Bennett, interview; Lyle D. Pishny, vice-chairman of Kansas Republican Party, 1989 to 1990, interview conducted by Joseph A. Aistrup and Mark Bannister on July 14, 1995.

23. Pishny, interview.

24. Cornelius Cotter, James L. Gibson, John F. Bibby, and Robert J. Huckshorn, *Party Organizations in American Politics*, (New York: Praeger, 1984), chap. 2.

25. Bennett, interview.

26. Kansas Democratic Party, Uncataloged party correspondence, Kansas Historical Society, 1981.

27. Dreiling, interview.

28. Dreiling, interview; see also Joel Paddock, "The Gubernatorial Campaigns of Robert Docking, 1966–1972," *Kansas History* 17 (Summer 1994).

29. Kansas Democratic Party, correspondence.

30. John Bird, executive secretary, 1970 to 1974, and chair, 1991 to 1993, of the Kansas Democratic Party, interview conducted by Joseph A. Aistrup on July 11, 1995.

31. John Hanna, "Graves Takes Aim at GOP Platform," *Topeka Capital-Journal*, June 17, 1995.

32. Hanna, "Graves Takes Aim."

33. Laura Rozen, "Trouble in 'Holy City'," Salon.com, September 3, 1999, http://www.salon.com/news/feature/1999/09/03/kansas/index.html.

34. Chris Moon, "Conservatives Shrug It Off," *Topeka Capital-Journal*, December 9, 2005.

35. Michael Smith, "Kansas: The Three Party State," *Campaigns and Elections* 24, no. 10 (October–November, 2003): 36–37.

CHAPTER FOUR: THE STATE LEGISLATURE

1. On even years the constitution limits legislative terms to a maximum of ninety days. On odd years there is no constitutional limitation, but by custom the legislature's leadership keeps the session length between ninety and one hundred days.

2. Several works describe the basic characteristics of the Kansas legislature. Please see Marvin A. Harder, "Introducing the Kansas Legislature," in *Politics and Government in Kansas: Selected Essays*, ed. Marvin A. Harder (Topeka: Capitol Complex Center, University of Kansas, 1989), chap. 9; Drury, *Government of Kansas*, chaps. 3 and 4; and Heller, *Kansas State Constitution*.

3. For a discussion of legislative professionalism, see Peverill Squire, "Legislative Professionalism and Membership Diversity," *Legislative Studies Quarterly* 17 (1992), and Peverill Squire, "Professionalization and Public Opinion of State Legislatures," *Journal of Politics* 55 (1993). These data are obtained through *National Conference of State Legislatures*, "NCSL Backgrounder," October 2005, http://www.ncsl.org/programs/press/2004/backgrounder_ful landpart.htm.

4. In a news analysis John Hanna notes that conservative lawmakers are beginning to argue that the state legislature needs to meet for longer periods. The conservatives believe that they need more time to dive into, analyze, and reduce the state's growing budget, which in 2007 was over twelve billion dollars. See John Hanna, "Analysis: Some Legislators Want Longer Time to Study Budget," *Topeka Capital-Journal*, April 30, 2007. An alternative to lengthening the sessions is for the two budget committees to begin their sessions earlier than all of the other committees.

5. Heller, *Kansas State Constitution*, 16.

6. See James L. Sunquist, *The Dynamics of the Party System*, rev. ed. (Washington DC: Brookings Institution, 1983), chaps. 6 and 7.

7. Heller, *Kansas State Constitution*, 16.

8. Heller, *Kansas State Constitution*, 16.

9. Miner, *Kansas*, 200–205; Heller, *Kansas State Constitution*, 16.

10. Miner, *Kansas*, 204.

11. Heller, *Kansas State Constitution*, 16; Miner, *Kansas*, 204.

12. Drury, *Government of Kansas*, 39–40.

13. Michael A. Smith and Brenda Erickson, *Kansas: A Retro Approach to Law-making* (National Conference of State Legislators–Council of State Governments Joint Project on Term Limits, 2005), table 1.

14. Drury, *Government of Kansas*, 31.

15. In 1871 the house voted to seat 133 members, including eight members who were in unnumbered districts. This number exceeded the constitutional limitation of 100 seats. In 1873 voters ratified a constitutional amendment increasing the limit to 125 house seats and 40 senate seats. The house nonetheless ignored the amendment, seating 137 members in 1881. In the 1880s the population of Kansas would grow from slightly over one million to over one and a half million, with Wichita and Topeka leading the way. As the population soared, so did the acrimony over apportionment, leading in 1886 to a special session of the legislature, which also failed to resolve the one house member per county issue. See Drury, *Government of Kansas*, 31.

16. Prior to the federally mandated reapportionment of the 1960s, both chambers were required by the Kansas Constitution to reapportion seats every five years. But, alas, reapportionment was a rare event. After apportioning its forty seats in the 1870s, the senate reapportioned only in 1933, 1947, and 1962. About fifty years passed in the house before it once again reapportioned its twenty urban districts in 1959. See Drury, *Government of Kansas*, 31–33.

17. Drury, *Government of Kansas*, 38.

18. Marvin A. Harder, "The Participants," in *Politics and Government in Kansas: Selected Essays* , ed. Marvin A. Harder (Topeka: Capitol Complex Center, University of Kansas, 1989), 136.

19. Heller, *Kansas State Constitution*, 71, 112–15.

20. This action led to a mini-constitutional crisis because the 1974 amendment prescribed the legislature to reapportion seats in 1989. In 1988 the legislature passed and the voters ratified a constitutional amendment allowing the state legislature to redraw the districts in 1989 using the most "recent" census data (1980s updates) and then to redraw the district boundaries again in 1992 and every ten years thereafter using U.S. Census data. See Drury, *Government of Kansas*, 33–34.

21. The late Republican state Senator Stan Clark, who represented the "big" 40th district in the northwest part of the state from 1994 until his death in 2004, believed that the decline of rural communities in Kansas and the rest of the United States could be directly tied to one person–one vote. Clark observed that "when rural counties lost their house seats, the flow of money headed to the urban centers to address their problems, taking tax dollars out of rural

areas, thus making it difficult for them to deal with their issues of population decline." Senator Clark made these comments to a state and local politics class at Fort Hays State University on April 6, 2001, in response to a student's question about why rural Kansas has continued to lose population and wealth.

22. *Montoy v. State*, 275 Kan. 145, 62 P.3d 228 (2003).

23. Drury, *Government of Kansas*, 35.

24. Senator Schmidt met with a Kansas politics class from Kansas State University on February 13, 2006, on the floor of the senate chambers. His comments were made in response to a question about school finance and the urban-rural divide in Kansas.

25. Drury, *Government of Kansas*, 55, 57.

26. Drury, *Government of Kansas*, 55–61; Heller, *Kansas State Constitution*, 16.

27. Drury, *Government of Kansas*, 58

28. Smith and Erickson, *Kansas*, 13–14.

29. Smith and Erickson, *Kansas*, 13–14, 18.

30. Burdett A. Loomis, *Time, Politics, and Policy: A Legislative Year* (Lawrence: University Press of Kansas, 1994); Smith and Erickson, *Kansas*, 11–12.

31. Marvin A. Harder, "The Cabinet System," in *Politics and Government in Kansas: Selected Essays*, ed. Marvin A. Harder (Topeka: Capitol Complex Center, University of Kansas, 1989), 217.

32. Drury, *Government of Kansas*, 120.

33. Gubernatorial appointees must be approved by the senate.

34. Harder, "Cabinet System," 221.

35. Drury, *Government of Kansas*, 61.

36. John Hanna, "Sebelius Budget Plan Protects Education, Hits KDOT," *Topeka Capital-Journal*, January 15, 2003.

37. Hanna, "Analysis"; Alan Cobb, "Bloated Budget Signal That Many Lawmakers Lack Will for Fiscal Restraint, Says Americans for Prosperity," Americans for Prosperity, press release, May 2, 2007.

38. Harder, "Cabinet System," 116.

39. Lawrence C. Dodd and Bruce I. Oppenheimer, "The House in Transition: Partisanship and Opposition," in *Congress Reconsidered*, ed. Lawrence C. Dodd and Bruce I. Oppenheimer, 3rd ed. (Washington DC: CQ Press, 1985).

40. Two outstanding works in the field of comparing state legislatures include Malcolm E. Jewell and Marci L. Whicker, *Legislative Leadership in the American States* (Ann Arbor: University of Michigan Press, 1994), and Malcolm E. Jewell, *Representation in State Legislatures* (Lexington: University Press of Kentucky, 1982).

41. See Loomis, *Time, Politics, and Policy*, chap. 2, for an outstanding summery of how these types of institutional parameters can shape the actions of Kansas state legislators and the Kansas legislature.

42. Gerald C. Wright and Brian F. Schaffner, "The Influence of Party: Evidence from the State Legislatures," *American Political Science Review* 96 (2002).

43. Malcolm E. Jewell, *The State Legislature: Politics and Practice* (New York: Random House, 1962), and Ronald D. Hedlund and Keith E. Hamm, "Political Parties as Vehicles for Organizing U.S. State Legislative Committees," *Legislative Studies Quarterly* 21 (1996), explore the possibility that the this type of strong party model is not always conducive to responsible or even responsive representation. This question is important, but it is beyond the scope of this chapter.

44. Smith and Erickson, *Kansas*, 6–7; Drury, *Government of Kansas*, 40–41

45. Marvin Harder and Carolyn Rampey, *The Kansas Legislature: Procedures, Personalities, and Problems* (Lawrence: University Press of Kansas, 1972).

46. Smith and Erickson, *Kansas*, 7.

47. Loomis, *Time, Politics, and Policy*, 55.

48. Speaker Mays met with a Kansas politics class from Kansas State University on February 13, 2006, in the gallery of the house chambers. His comments were made in response to a question about how he maintained party discipline.

49. Drury, *Government of Kansas*, 41.

50. Joseph Cooper, *The Origins of Standing Committees and the Development of the Modern House* (Houston: William Marsh, Rice University, 1971).

51. Smith and Erickson, *Kansas*, 7.

52. Smith and Erickson, *Kansas*, 9–10. Wayne L. Francis and James W. Riddlesperger, "U.S. State Legislative Committees: Structure, Procedural Efficiency, and Party Control," *Legislative Studies Quarterly* 7 (1982), note that the trend toward committee's taking a heavier load in state legislatures has been taking place for many years.

53. Twenty-eight million dollars of which represented increased state general fund spending, and $23.5 million of which represented increased local authority to raise property taxes in communities with expensive housing costs. See John Milburn, "House Advances $155 Million Education Plan," *Topeka Capitol-Journal*, March 25, 2004.

54. In August 2004 Kassebaum lost in the GOP primary to Shari Weber, who was former majority leader of the house and whom he had beat in 2002.

55. The phrase "unholy alliance" was used by Derek Schmidt (R-Independence); see John Hanna, "Senate: Bipartisan Bill's Success Leads President to Urge 'Attack of Conscience,'" *Topeka Capital-Journal*, February 14, 2002.

56. Joshua Akers, "District Map Fight Continues," *Topeka Capital-Journal*, April 15, 2002.

57. Hanna, "Senate."

58. Lacking an initiative process to amend the state constitution, other prominent

national reform movements that limit the powers of legislatures to tax and spend (ranging from Proposition-13 types of amendments to the taxpayers bill of rights or TABOR) have not gained traction in Kansas.

59. Frank, *What's the Matter with Kansas?* chap. 5.

60. Within the contexts of American politics this type of dynamic is not uncommon. The most common referent comes from the congressional literature. Given the liberal bent of the New Deal Democratic coalition, especially in the wake of the civil rights and voting rights movements of the early 1960s, conservative southern Democratic members of Congress would often break ranks with their more liberal northern Democratic colleagues to vote with Republicans. The "Conservative Coalition" was the product of a regionally based ideological split within the Democratic party. It remained active until the Democrats surrendered control of the Congress after the 1994 elections. In the comparative state legislative politics literature, R. Harmel and K. Hamm, "Development of a Party Role in a No-Party Legislature," *Western Political Science Quarterly* 39 (1986), observed the formation of a conservative coalition in the Texas legislature (suburban Republicans and rural Democrats) when the GOP was starting to grow in Texas. However, as the GOP became more competitive over time, this coalition began to fray, eventually losing most of it coherence as a coalition. The Kansas case of the moderate coalition has some similarities and differences when compared to the Conservative Coalition in Congress and Texas. Like the Conservative Coalition, ideology plays a significant role in defining the split in the large majority Republican party. The moderate coalition, however, diverges from the Conservative Coalition model in at least one important way. Conservative and liberal Democrats in Congress were insulated from primary challenges from each other. Thus liberal northern Democrats did not go to southern districts to challenge conservative Democrats in the primaries. The regional divide between the North and South reinforced the Democratic Party's ideological cleavage. This geographical divide meant that their conflicts were confined to policy and leadership choices within the institution of Congress. This is not case in Kansas. Moderates and polar alliance Republicans can, if they choose, regularly challenge each other in primaries.

61. It is important to note that when V. O. Key examined intraparty Democratic strife in the South in the first half of the twentieth century, he studied all primary challenges, including those for open seats. Competition for open seats within the Kansas Republican Party has always been strong. Because it is such a constant over the entire period of this study, we do not conduct a separate analysis of intraparty competition for open seat nominations.

62. Carl Manning, "Majority Leader Fails in Write-in Campaign," *Topeka Capital-Journal*, November 5, 2002.

63. John Milburn, "In House Republican Rematch, Weber Defeats Kassebaum," *Topeka Capital-Journal*, August 4, 2004. Interestingly, Cindy Neighbor, another moderate Republican from Shawnee, who also favored greater funding for K–12 education went down to defeat in 2004 at the hands of Mary Pilcher-Cook. Like the race between Weber and Kassebaum, that between Pilcher-Cook and Neighbor was a repeat of the 2002 primary, which was won by Neighbor.

64. Chris Moon, "GOP Sides Split," *Topeka Capital-Journal*, August 5, 2004.

65. It is important to note that the number of primary challenges to GOP house incumbents appears to increase in the two elections after each reapportionment (1992 and 2002), although the peak was much higher in the wake of the 2002 reapportionment.

66. "Republicans Part Company on Issues," *Wichita Eagle*, July 13, 1994.

67. Smith and Erickson, *Kansas*, 8.

68. Although we recognize that newspapers and their reporters have a political bias, this bias is not an important concern for this content analysis. Our content analysis was not focused on which side won or lost or the arguments for or against a particular piece of legislation. Rather, the content analysis focused on whether the issue covered in the news story was a partisan issue, in which the parties or party factions divided on the issue, and if so, what types of partisan coalitions formed either in favor or in opposition to the issue. Focusing on these points allowed us to avoid any fallacies that might occur due to biased reporting.

69. We also considered analyzing roll-call votes as a way to research this topic. Even though the Kansas House records all votes, the Kansas Senate does not. By rule the senate only records the roll-call votes for the first five votes of each day's session. After the first five only the final vote tallies are recorded. As one senator noted, who wishes to remain anonymous, this practice is "very convenient." Often this process means that the first five votes of every session are procedural rather than substantive. Given our focus on the interrelationship between the house and senate, we concluded that news reports would be a more fruitful venue in uncovering patterns of moderate coalition politics.

70. A graduate student and an author independently content analyzed each story. The inter-coder reliability coefficient was .876. We note that when there were differences in coding, these differences tended to be regarding ordinal scale judgments of magnitude.

71. This result corresponds with the multistate analysis of state legislatures done by Melissa P. Collie, "Voting Behavior in Legislatures," *Legislative Studies Quarterly* 9 (1984). Collie found that most roll-call votes in most state legislatures are not structured by partisan conflict.

72. The threat of a moderate coalition is the most frequent when polar alliance Republicans control the house and moderate Republicans control the senate.

CHAPTER FIVE: THE GOVERNOR

1. This chapter focuses upon the forty-one Kansans who have been elected to the office of governor and draws upon an invaluable volume on Kansas governors compiled by Socolofsky, *Kansas Governors*. Four volumes of gubernatorial papers compiled at Wichita State University have been useful as well, specifically H. Edward Flentje, ed., *Selected Papers of Governor Robert F. Bennett: A Study in Good Government* and *"Civics Book" Politics* (Wichita: Center for Urban Studies, Wichita State University, 1979); Joe P. Pisciotte, ed., *Selected Papers of Governor John Carlin: An Index of Social and Political Change* (Wichita: Hugo Wall School of Urban and Public Affairs, Wichita State University, 1993); Warren B. Armstrong and Dee A. Harris, eds., *Populism Revived: The Selected Records of Governor Joan Finney, 1991–1995* (Wichita: Hugo Wall School of Urban and Public Affairs, Wichita State University, 1998); H. Edward Flentje, ed., *Selected Papers of Governor Mike Hayden: Advancing a Progressive Agenda* (Wichita: Hugo Wall School of Urban and Public Affairs, Wichita State University, 2002). Two biographies of governors and two histories on Kansas politics in the early part of the twentieth century have been useful in placing the Kansas governorship in historical context: McCoy, *Landon of Kansas*; Homer E. Socolofsky, *Arthur Capper: Publisher, Politician, and Philanthropist* (Lawrence: University of Kansas Press, 1962); La Forte, *Leaders of Reform*; Schruben, *Kansas in Turmoil*.
2. For details on this period, see Socolofsky, *Kansas Governors*, 1–30.
3. Socolofsky, *Kansas Governors*, 8.
4. Three governors without prior elective experience were Lewelling who served as a local official in the People's Party, Woodring who served as an officer in the American Legion, and Landon who had been active as a Republican Party official and manager of the gubernatorial campaign of Clyde Reed in 1928.
5. The governor's salary is set by statute and is adjusted upward also by statute, usually on an annual basis along with the salaries of other elected state executives in line with adjustments for all other state employees in the classified service; see *Kansas Statutes Annotated* 75-3101 and 3111a. Further reference to *Kansas Statutes Annotated* is as KSA.
6. Kansas Division of the Budget.
7. There was an earlier executive residence purchased by the state in 1901 with Stanley as the first occupant; see Socolofsky, *Kansas Governors*, 131.
8. For details on Kansas politics in this time frame, see La Forte, *Leaders of*

Reform, and Marvin A. Harder, *Electoral Politics in Kansas: A Historical Perspective* (Topeka: Capitol Complex Center, University of Kansas, 1981).

9. The nineteen governors defeated in reelection bids included eleven Republicans (Robinson in 1862 party convention, Carney in 1864 party convention, Anthony in 1878 party convention, St. John in 1882 general election, Morrill in 1896 general election, Bailey in 1904 party convention, Reed in 1930 primary election, Hall in 1956 primary election, Avery in 1966 general election, Bennett in 1978 general election, and Hayden in 1990 general election), six Democrats (Glick in 1884 general election, Hodges in 1914 general election, Davis in 1924 general election, Woodring in 1932 general election, Huxman in 1938 general election, and George Docking in 1960 general election), and two populists (Lewelling in 1894 general election and Leedy in 1898 general election).

10. Socolofsky, *Kansas Governors,* 166; McCoy, *Landon of Kansas,* 104, 108, 110. For more on the Brinkley campaign, see Schruben, *Kansas in Turmoil.*

11. Rhoten A. Smith and Clarence J. Hein, *Republican Primary Fight: A Study in Factionalism,* Case Studies in Practical Politics (New York: Holt, 1958), 1.

12. Socolofsky, *Kansas Governors,* 21; Smith and Hein, *Republican Primary Fight,* 1–2; Paddock, "Democratic Politics in a Republican State," 111–13; 2002 election summaries on campaign finance compiled by the Kansas Governmental Ethics Commission.

13. For 1970 estimate, see Larry Sabato, *Goodbye to Good-Time Charlie: The American Governor Transformed, 1950–1975* (Lexington MA: Lexington Books, 1978), 157; for 1980 data, see Thad L. Beyle, ed., *Re-Electing the Governor* (New York: University Press of America, 1986), 23; and for 2002 data, see the Kansas Governmental Ethics Commission.

14. See Joseph A. Schlesinger, "The Politics of the Executive," in *Politics in the American States: A Comparative Analysis,* ed. Herbert Jacob and Kenneth N. Vines (Boston: Little, Brown, 1965); Thad Beyle, "The Governors," in *Politics in the American States: A Comparative Analysis,* ed. Virginia Gray and Russell L. Hanson, 8th ed. (Washington DC: CQ Press, 2004); and H. Edward Flentje, "The Political Nature of the Governor as Manager," in *Being Governor,* ed. Thad L. Beyle and Lynn R. Muchmore (Durham NC: Duke Press Policy Studies, 1983), 85–92.

15. An elected insurance commissioner was created by statute in 1900. The superintendent of public instruction was removed by constitutional amendment in 1966.

16. Jack F. McKay and Howard Hallman, *State Governmental Organization in Kansas, 1965–1950* (Lawrence: Bureau of Governmental Research, University of Kansas, 1950), 8–13.

17. Kansas Commission on Executive Reorganization, *Reorganizing Kansas State Government for Maximum Effectiveness, Efficiency and Economy* (Topeka, January 1971), v, 6–7, 9.

18. Chapter 260 of *Kansas Session Laws, 1925* (Topeka: Kansas State Printer, 1925). The legislative history of the budget office may be tracked through KSA 75-3714a and following.

19. In 1965 Schlesinger ranked the Kansas governorship thirty-second in a tie with five other states; see Schlesinger, "Politics of the Executive," 229. In 2004 Thad Beyle ranked Kansas twenty-first in terms of the governor's institutional powers, excluding party control; see Beyle, "The Governors," 212–13.

20. See Bader, *Prohibition in Kansas*, 36–62, and H. Edward Flentje, "Capital Finance and Public Infrastructure," in *Kansas Policy Choices*, ed. H. Edward Flentje (Lawrence: University Press of Kansas, 1986), 115–16.

21. See chapter 1 for a more detailed summary of enactments in the progressive era.

22. See chapter 8 for a more detailed summary of gubernatorial involvement in tax policy.

23. Democrats held a razor-thin 63–62 majority in the Kansas House during the first half (1991 and 1992) of Finney's term.

24. See Loomis, *Time, Politics, and Policies*.

25. See KSA 74-8001 and following; KSA 74-8101 and following; and KSA 74-99b01 and following.

26. See KSA 74-2622; KSA 47-2302; and KSA 47-2002.

27. Flentje, *Selected Papers of Governor Robert F. Bennett*, 215–29.

28. Flentje, *Selected Papers of Governor Robert F. Bennett*, 264.

29. *Topeka Capital-Journal*, September 13 and 15, 1984.

30. Richard Ellis and Aaron Wildavsky suggest that chief executives may be viewed in cultural context as follows: "Presidents and citizens exist within political cultures that guide and restrain how they behave. Presidents . . . face constraints of two kinds: conflicts within the culture (or cultures) to which they adhere, and conflicts between opposing cultures. Such conflicts—being torn between opposing forces—create the dilemmas with which presidents grapple." See Ellis and Wildavsky, *Dilemmas of Presidential Leadership*, viii.

31. Ellis and Wildavsky, *Dilemmas of Presidential Leadership*, 6.

32. Ellis and Wildavsky, *Dilemmas of Presidential Leadership*, 2.

33. Lewelling, Inaugural address, January 9, 1893.

34. Socolofsky, *Kansas Governors*, 120–21.

35. Malin, *Concern about Humanity*, 191–93.

36. See Harder, *Electoral Politics in Kansas*.

37. Ellis and Wildavsky, *Dilemmas of Presidential Leadership*, 2.

38. La Forte, *Leaders of Reform*, 111–12, 115–17.

39. Socolofsky, *Arthur Capper*, 87.

40. Quoted in Socolofsky, *Arthur Capper*, 223.

41. Socolofsky, *Arthur Capper*, 88, 95–96.

42. Socolofsky, *Arthur Capper*, 76–77, 86. See also *Addresses and Messages by Arthur Capper, Twenty-Second Governor of Kansas* (Topeka: Capper Printing Company, n.d. [likely 1919 or shortly thereafter]). In only four of forty-one Republican gubernatorial primaries was there no contest.

43. McCoy, *Landon of Kansas*, 46.

44. McCoy, *Landon of Kansas*, 165, 118, 151, 166, 168, 173–74, 146, 170. For gubernatorial addresses, see Kansas State Library, http://www.kslib.info/ref/message/index.html.

45. McCoy, *Landon of Kansas*, 196, 174, 278, 293–94. Landon also discouraged any talk of a return to public office but kept a hand in state politics, eventually becoming the elder statesman of Kansas. He was mentioned as a candidate for a U.S. Senate seat in 1938 or for another try for the presidency in 1940 or for cabinet appointment. He periodically engaged in national political discussion but eschewed public office for the balance of his life.

46. See chapter 8 for details

47. Paddock, "Democratic Politics in a Republican State," 109–11, 117–18, 123.

48. Paddock, "Democratic Politics in a Republican State," 109–11, 117–18, 123.

49. Harder and Rampey, *Kansas Legislature*, 44–59.

50. Paddock, "Democratic Politics in a Republican State," 122–23.

51. Harder, *Electoral Politics in Kansas*, 7.

52. See Pisciotte, *Selected Papers of Governor John Carlin*.

53. Armstrong and Harris, *Populism Revived*, 6.

CHAPTER SIX: INTEREST GROUPS AND LOBBYING

1. Allan J. Cigler and Dwight C. Kiel, "The Changing Nature of Interest Group Politics in Kansas," in *Politics and Government in Kansas: Selected Essays*, ed. Marvin A. Harder (Topeka: Capitol Complex Center, University of Kansas, 1989); Mandi Serrone, "Hired Guns: The Growth of Contract Lobbyists in KS" (senior honors thesis, University of Kansas, 1997); Jeremy Stohs, "Hired Guns II: Pete McGill, the Growth of Contract Lobbying, and Client Relations in Kansas" (senior honors thesis, Kansas State University, 2003).

2. William Allen White, *The Autobiography of William Allen White* (New York: Macmillan, 1946).

3. Cigler and Kiel, "Changing Nature of Interest Group Politics," 151; Burdett A. Loomis and Allan J. Cigler, "Introduction: The Changing Nature of Interest Group Politics," in *Interest Group Politics*, ed. Allan J. Cigler and Burdett Loomis, 6th ed. (Washington DC: CQ Press, 2002).

4. White, *Autobiography*, 181–96.

5. White, *Autobiography*, 424–36, 472–96, 516–28.

6. Cigler and Kiel, "Changing Nature of Interest Group Politics," 151; Loomis and Cigler, "Introduction."

7. Another difference between the party politics era and interest group pluralism era is that corruption was not as rampant, and while the interest groups and parties were interdependent, they remained independent entities in the interest group pluralism era.

8. Cigler and Kiel, "Changing Nature of Interest Group Politics," 151; Loomis and Cigler, "Introduction."

9. Allan Rosenthal, *The Third House*, 2nd ed. (Washington DC: CQ Press, 2001), 30–40.

10. John Hanna, "Lobbying Industry Shaped by Pete McGill," *Topeka Capitol-Journal*, May 28, 1996.

11. The interviews with Pete McGill were conducted by Jeremy Stohs on March 25, 2003, in Topeka KS and on March 30, 2003, at McGill's home in Overland Park KS. Given that most of the changes in lobbying in Kansas follow national trends and fit into the lobbying patterns of other states, it would be incorrect to conclude that McGill caused these changes. Rather, McGill was the first to ride the waves of transformation and as such to establish a strong foundation for the development of professional contract lobbying in Kansas.

12. McGill's statement corresponds with existing political science literature that suggests there is a negative relationship between the ability of interest groups to control the legislative process and the extent of professional staffing of legislators' offices; see Thomas R. Dye, *Politics in States and Communities*, 10th ed. (Upper Saddle River NJ: Prentice Hall, 2000) 117. Further, McGill's statement regarding the dominance of a few interest groups in the 1960s corresponds with previous research regarding interest groups in Kansas; see Neal R. Pierce, *The Great Plains States of America* (New York: Norton, 1973), 238, and Cigler and Kiel, "Changing Nature of Interest Group Politics," 152.

13. Rosenthal, *Third House*, 30–40.

14. KSA 46-215 and following.

15. Kansas is not unusual in this respect. Washington DC is full of K-Street lobbying firms employing a multitude of former U.S. representatives and U.S. senators; see Jeffrey M. Berry, *The Interest Group Society*, 3rd ed. (New York: Longman, 1997).

16. Serrone, "Hired Guns."

17. The largest decreases occurred in registered individuals and highway-safety. The latter decline reflects the intense effort to push safety and stricter drunk-driving standards during the 1980s.

18. Pacific Research Institute, "Kansas as No. 1," press release, November 24, 2004, http://liberty.pacificresearch.org; Pacific Research Institute, "Economic Freedom: Bush States Have It and Kerry State Don't," press release, November 23, 2004, http://liberty.pacificresearch.org.

19. Rosenthal, *Third House*, 30–40.

20. Rosenthal, *Third House*, 40.

21. Frank, *What's the Matter with Kansas?*

22. In 2003 Stohs conducted parallel surveys of contract and association lobbyists using standard self-administered mail survey practices (cover letter, anonymous prepaid return, and two follow-ups). Many of the survey items came from Serrone's 1997 and Cigler and Kiel's 1986 studies; see Serrone, "Hired Guns," and Cigler and Kiel, "Changing Nature of Interest Group Politics." As in Serrone's study a contract lobbyist is defined as "a person who represents two or more clients of which two clients are of completely different nature"; see Serrone, "Hired Guns," 5–6. Identification, as well as names and addresses, of lobbyists may be obtained from the *Kansas Lobbyist Directory*, 2003.

The surveys were mailed or hand delivered in early February 2003 to all contract lobbyists in the state of Kansas (sixty-seven total) and to a sampling of thirty randomly selected association lobbyists. After three weeks twenty association lobbyists had returned surveys, however, only twenty-two contract lobbyist surveys had been returned. At the beginning of March 2003 a second mailing of contract-lobbying surveys was sent out. After this mailing the response rate for contract lobbyists increased to forty-eight percent. Data for the association lobbyists are impressionistic; however, the findings presented here do coincide with the extant literature.

23. The margin of error for any survey is determined primarily by two factors, the size of the sample and the heterogeneity of the population being surveyed. In most cases social scientists assume that the population is heterogeneous: see Herbert M. Blalock Jr., *Social Statistics*, rev. 2nd ed. (New York: McGraw-Hill, 1979), chaps. 8–12. However, among association and contract lobbyists this assumption may be less applicable. Given the consistency of these findings with works in other states (Rosenthal, *Third House*) and similar surveys in Kansas (Cigler and Kiel, "Changing Nature of Interest Group Politics"; Serrone, "Hired Guns"), a strong case can be made that while the interests represented by lobbyists are diverse, the type of people who become lobbyists and their opinions about the profession, among other things, may be more homogeneous. Therefore a survey of fewer lobbyists may be a valid representation of the opinions and characteristics of all lobbyists.

24. Anthony J. Nownes and Patricia Freeman. "Female Lobbyists: Women in the World of 'Good Ol' Boys,'" *Journal of Politics* 60 (1998): 1185.

25. Nownes and Freeman, "Female Lobbyists," 1185.

26. Nownes and Freeman, "Female Lobbyists," 1187.

27. Rosenthal, *Third House*, 34

28. Cited in Rosenthal, *Third House*, 153.

29. Rosenthal, *Third House*, 153.

30. Serrone, "Hired Guns," 57.

CHAPTER SEVEN: STATE AND LOCAL
GOVERNMENTS IN A FEDERAL STRUCTURE

1. The number is both misleading and telling—misleading in that nearly ten thousand of the local authorities were school districts set up by county school superintendents but telling in that the principle of local control found fertile ground in the body politic of Kansas.

2. County seat wars in Garfield County eventually resulted in a court challenge (*State ex rel. Ives v. Commissioners of Garfield County*, 1893) and a ruling that the county did not meet the state constitutional requirement of at least 432 square miles. Garfield consequently became a township in neighboring Finney County reducing the number of counties to the current number of 105.

3. Kenneth E. Beasley, *State Supervision of Municipal Debt in Kansas: A Case Study* (Lawrence: Governmental Research Center, University of Kansas, 1961), 8.

4. David Hoffman, ed., *Facts and Figures on Government Finance*, 37th ed. (Washington DC: Tax Foundation, 2003), 51–54; 114–31.

5. *Leavenworth County v. Miller*, 7 Kans. (1871), 493.

6. This discussion draws from Mary Rowland, "Kansas and the Highways, 1917–1930," *Kansas History* 5, no. 1 (Spring 1982), and Sherry Lamb Schirmer and Theodore A. Wilson, *Milestones: A History of the Kansas Highway Commission and the Department of Transportation* (Topeka: Kansas Department of Transportation, 1986), chap. 2.

7. Jane Perry Clark, *The Rise of Federalism: Federal-State Cooperation in the United States* (New York: Columbia University Press, 1938), 203; 240. See also A. Bower Sageser, "Political Patterns of the 1920s," in *Kansas: The First Century*, ed. John D. Bright, vol. 2 (New York: Lewis Historical Publishing, 1956), 84–85.

8. Quoted in Craig Miner, "Interpreting Kansas History: A County Perspective" (paper, annual conference of the Kansas County Commissioners Association, Wichita, May 9, 2003), 7.

9. Mary Scott Rowland, "Social Services in Kansas, 1916–1930," *Kansas History* 7, no. 3 (Autumn 1984): 213.

10. *Kansas Session Laws, 1917* (Topeka: Kansas State Printer, 1917), 443. See also *Kansas Session Laws, 1913* (Topeka: Kansas State Printer, 1913), 525–26.

11. Moya Woodside, *Sterilization in North Carolina* (Chapel Hill: University of North Carolina Press, 1950), 194. See also Dwayne L. Oglesby, "What Has Happened to Kansas' Sterilization Laws?" *Kansas Law Review* 2, no. 2 (December 1953).

12. This discussion draws from Nancy McCarthy Snyder, "Organization of Human Services," in *Kansas Policy Choices, 1990*, ed. H. Edward Flentje (Wichita: Hugo Wall Center for Urban Studies, Wichita State University, 1990), 108–12.

13. This discussion of Landon's role draws from McCoy, *Landon of Kansas*, particularly 140–44, 172–76, 181–98, 268.

14. Clark, *Rise of Federalism*, 209.

15. Robert W. Richmond, "Kansas in the Late 1940s," in *Kansas: The First Century*, ed. John D. Bright. vol. 2 (New York: Lewis Historical Publishing, 1956), 470–71.

16. *Kansas Governor's Budget Report for the Fiscal Year 1960* (Topeka: State Printer, 1959), 214–15.

17. The description of the evolution of Medicaid spending in Kansas was assisted by telephone interviews with Robert C. Harder, conducted in April and May of 2005. Harder served in the Kansas legislature from 1961 to 1967 and later on the staff of Governor Robert Docking, 1967–69. He was appointed head of social welfare in 1969, first as director of the Department of Social Welfare and in 1973 as secretary of the newly created Department of Social and Rehabilitation Services. He continued as secretary through 1987, serving under four governors.

18. This committee functioned through 1972 and laid the groundwork for establishing the Department of Social and Rehabilitation Services through an executive reorganization order issued by Governor Robert Docking in 1973 and for state assumption of authority for social welfare in 1975. See "Report and Recommendations of the Special Committee on Medical Services and Fiscal Accountability of Welfare Programs, Proposal No. 50," in *Report on Kansas Legislative Interim Studies to the 1973 Legislature*, pt. 5 (Topeka: Legislative Coordinating Council, Kansas Legislature, 1972).

19. State legislators have also come to expect supplemental appropriations each year for Medicaid spending as routine. This practice essentially renders the appropriation bill enacted each legislative session for the upcoming fiscal year meaningless as a control on spending. Executive branch and departmental officials operate under an unwritten understanding with legislative leaders that the existing scope of services and eligibility for services will determine the level of state spending and that this level of spending will be covered if necessary through supplemental appropriations in the following legislative session. This practice entrusts departmental officials with broad discretion in Medicaid spending.

20. Huang, McCormick, and McQuillan, *U.S. Economic Freedom Index: 2004 Report*, 45.

21. Office of the Governor, news release, November 9, 2004.

22. *Book of the States*, vol. 40 (Lexington KY: Council of State Governments, 2008), 42–45. A Rand Corporation study reports that Kansas colleges and universities received $119 million in fiscal year 2002 for the conduct of research and development, although the overlap of this figure, if any, with the U.S. census figures cited by the *Book of the States* is uncertain; see Donna Fossum et al., *Vital Assets: Federal Investment in Research and Development at the Nation's Universities and Colleges* (Santa Monica CA: Rand Corporation, 2004), 13.

23. See Elazar, *American Federalism*, 147–54, and Deil S. Wright, *Understanding Intergovernmental Relations*, 3rd ed. (Pacific Grove CA: Brooks/Cole, 1988), 83–86.

24. Flentje, *Selected Papers of Governor Robert F. Bennett*, 299–318.

25. Flentje, *Selected Papers of Governor Robert F. Bennett*, 302.

26. See *Federal Tax Burdens and Expenditures by State*, Special Report no. 139 (Washington DC: Tax Foundation, 2006).

27. This paragraph draws from Martha Derthick, *Keeping the Compound Republic: Essays on Federalism* (Washington DC: Brookings Institution Press, 2001), 138–52.

28. See Derthick, *Keeping the Compound Republic*, 153–61.

29. Lester M. Salamon, *Partners in Public Service* (Baltimore: Johns Hopkins University Press, 1995), 3.

30. Melissa A. Walker, Tricia Thomas, Jason Osterhaus, Matthew Stiles, and Yusi Zheng, *A Preview of Nonprofit Organizations in Wichita and Sedgwick County, Kansas* (Wichita: Hugo Wall School of Urban and Public Affairs, Wichita State University, 2007), 10–11.

31. Salamon, *Partners in Public Service*, 12.

32. This section draws from H. Edward Flentje, "Kansas," in *Home Rule in America: A Fifty-State Handbook*, ed. Dale Krane, Platon N. Rigos, and Melvin B. Hill Jr. (Washington DC: CQ Press, 2001), 156–65.

33. James W. Drury, *Home Rule in Kansas* (Lawrence: Governmental Research Center, University of Kansas, 1965), 15. Original constitutional language called for "general laws" in the organization and financing of cities and in the conferring of corporate powers, and special legislation was specifically prohibited in Article 2, Section 17, as follows: "All laws of a general nature shall have a uniform operation throughout the state; and in all cases where a general law can be made applicable, no special law shall be enacted." These provisions were designed to limit the state legislature's powers with respect to interfering in the governance of a particular local government but in practice were to little avail.

34. For a careful examination of state actions designed to control cities prior to home rule, see Barkley Clark, "State Control of Local Government in Kansas: Special Legislation and Home Rule," *Kansas Law Review* 20 (1972).

35. This mishmash of state statutes appears on the surface to be onerous state mandates on local governments, but their bark is with few exceptions greater than their bite. City and county governing bodies may exempt themselves from a significant number of these statutes through the exercise of home rule powers. Many have accumulated in state statute books since the beginning of statehood and are archaic, obsolete, and irrelevant. Many others lack enforcement: larger, more sophisticated jurisdictions maneuver around them, and smaller jurisdictions ignore them. For more details on this subject, see H. Edward Flentje, "State Mandates on Cities and Counties in Kansas: An Overview," in *An Inventory of State Mandates on Cities and Counties in Kansas*, comp. H. Edward Flentje, Darron Leiker, and Mark Detter (Wichita: Hugo Wall School of Urban and Public Affairs, Wichita State University, 1994).

36. In 1987 state lawmakers enacted the most recent uniform state law authorizing three options for annexation by cities. First, within certain statutory limitations cities may unilaterally annex city-owned land, platted land adjoining the city, land lying mainly within the perimeter of a city, land that will make city boundaries straight and harmonious, and tracts of land in which two-thirds of the boundary of a tract adjoins the city. Unilateral annexation requires the city to prepare a plan for extending services to the area proposed for annexation, give notice to property owners, and hold a public hearing on or near the property proposed for annexation. Cities are prohibited from annexing agricultural lands of twenty-one acres or more without the consent of the owner. Second, cities may annex adjoining lands with the consent of landowners. Finally, cities may annex land by order of the board of county commissioners, who act as a quasi-judicial boundary commission, after the board follows statutory procedures and considers a number of statutory factors in making an order. Aggrieved parties in annexation proceedings, including cities, may appeal to the state district court.

37. KSA 19-101. While most of the exemptions written into county home rule have a rational basis, as for example with respect to changing county boundaries or legislating on state services, more recent exclusions appear contrary to the intent of home rule. For instance, a number of exemptions preclude the exercise of home rule on state laws that are clearly nonuniform such as laws concerning hospitals, civic centers, community college tuition, library boards, sale of property, community mental health and retardation, zoning, domestic violence, and other such matters. Obviously state lawmakers may more easily intrude into county home rule than city home rule.

38. See H. Edward Flentje and Sammi Mangus, *Appointed County Administrators in Kansas*, Research Report of the Kansas Association of Counties (Topeka, March 2000). Since that report was completed, Ford, Seward, Cowley, Franklin, Leavenworth, and Harper counties have established the position of county administrator. The position in Dickinson County is inactive.

39. See H. Edward Flentje, "The Political Roots of City Managers in Kansas," *Kansas History* 7, no. 2 (Summer 1984).

CHAPTER EIGHT: TAXING, SPENDING, AND BORROWING

1. Unless otherwise noted, the primary source of current data on state revenues throughout this chapter is *Kansas Tax Facts: 2008 Supplement to the Seventh Edition* (Topeka: Kansas Legislative Research Department, 2008). For historic comparison, see *Summary History of Kansas Finance, 1861–1937* (Topeka: Research Department, Kansas Legislative Council, 1937), 26.

2. *Report of the Governor's Tax Equity Task Force*, Topeka, December 1995, 13.

3. This section draws upon the excellent history of the property tax by Glenn W. Fisher, *The Worst Tax? A History of the Property Tax in America* (Lawrence: University Press of Kansas, 1996).

4. Fisher, *Worst Tax*, 60.

5. James E. Boyle, *The Financial History of Kansas*, Bulletin of the University of Wisconsin no. 247 (Madison, August 1908), 35. While "uniform and equal" prescribed taxation of property in the broadest possible terms, additional provisions of the constitution's finance article challenged simplicity and equity in tax administration. Specifically, the article provided exemptions for property "used exclusively for State, county, municipal, literary, educational, scientific, religious, benevolent and charitable purposes," and pressures on state lawmakers to restrict or expand the definition of property used for "benevolent and charitable purposes" continue to the present day. The article also reflected Jacksonian suspicions with banking and called for taxation of various securities in order to assure "that all property employed in banking shall always bear a burden of taxation equal to that imposed upon the property of individuals." This provision constantly challenged those administering the property tax as well as state courts, and taxation of intangible properties would similarly haunt administration of the tax and eventually require change. Another exemption in the Wyandotte Constitution was the homestead exemption of personal property in the amount of "at least two hundred dollars for each family" that remained in place until all personal property not used in the production of income was exempted in 1974. An early attempt at repeal of this provision failed in 1879, according to Heller, *Kansas State Constitution*, 22.

6. Boyle, *Financial History of Kansas*, 50.

7. Paul Wallace Gates, *Fifty Million Acres: Conflicts over Kansas Land Policy, 1854–1890* (Norman: University of Oklahoma Press, 1997), 266–69, 268.

8. Boyle, *Financial History of Kansas*, 34.

9. Governor's Message, January 8, 1889, in *Kansas House Journal* (Topeka: State Printer, 1889), 44–45.

10. Boyle, *Financial History of Kansas*, 142; Fisher, *Worst Tax*, 145–47; Lawrence Leonard, "Property Taxation in Kansas: An Historical Analysis," *National Tax Journal* 11, no. 3 (September 1958), 231–33; Fisher, *Worst Tax*, 169.

11. Fisher, *Worst Tax*, 170–74.

12. Minor adjustments to the classification amendment were proposed by lawmakers and approved by voters in 1992. Assessed values were revised as follows: homeowners (12 to 11.5 percent), industrial and commercial real estate and agricultural improvements (30 to 25 percent), utility real estate and personal property (30 to 33 percent), and commercial and industrial machinery (20 to 25 percent). Property of nonprofit corporations was separately classified reducing their assessed value from 30 to 12 percent. For details, see *Kansas Tax Facts*, 7th ed. (Topeka: Kansas Legislative Research Department, 2000).

13. See Fisher, *Worst Tax*, 181–86.

14. Glenn W. Fisher, H. Edward Flentje, W. Bartley Hildreth, and John D. Wong, "Sizing Up Kansas Finance," *Kansas Policy Review* 29, no. 1 (Spring 2007): 15.

15. The graduated income tax may have first surfaced as an element of the populist cause in an early meeting of protesting farmers in the Jefferson County (Kansas) Alliance late in 1889; it was later endorsed in the Kansas Alliance convention of March 1890. See Elizabeth N. Barr, "The Populist Uprising," in *Kansas and Kansans*, ed. William E. Connelly (Chicago: Lewis Publishing, 1918), 1143–46. From that point on the graduated income tax became an integral element of most state and national populist gatherings. Other endorsements followed. The Platform of Northern Alliance in December 1889 stated that its members "favor a graded income tax"; the Ocala Demands in December 1890 and the Cincinnati Platform in May 1891 put forth that they demanded "a just and equitable system of graduated tax on incomes"; the St. Louis Platform in February 1892 and the Omaha Platform in July 1892 said that they demanded "a graduated income tax," with the Omaha Platform adding "that the revenue derived from a graduated income tax should be applied to the reduction of the burden of taxation now resting upon the domestic industries of this country." See Hicks, *Populist Revolt*, 427–44.

16. A congressional coalition of Democrats and Populists enacted a national income tax in 1894 that was declared unconstitutional by the U.S. Supreme Court a year later. After the court ruling sentiment began to build for a con-

stitutional amendment. In his annual message to congress in 1906 President Roosevelt called for graduated taxes on income and inheritances, and in 1909, during President Taft's first year in office, a Republican-controlled Congress approved a constitutional amendment authorizing taxation of incomes for submission to the states. Although bitterly divided into progressive and standpat Republican camps, the Kansas legislature easily approved the amendment in 1911, making Kansas the twenty-sixth state to do so. The required thirty-six states approved by 1913, and Congress with President Wilson's endorsement enacted a national income tax later that same year.

17. For background on state politics in the period 1900–1936, see La Forte, *Leaders of Reform*; Schruben, *Kansas in Turmoil*; Keith D. McFarland, *Harry H. Woodring: A Political Biography of FDR's Controversial Secretary of War* (Lawrence: University Press of Kansas, 1975); McCoy, *Landon of Kansas*.

18. Governor's Message, January 15, 1919, in *Kansas House Journal* (Topeka: State Printer, 1919), 14.

19. Sageser, "Political Patterns," 79–81.

20. Thomas D. Van Sant, *Improving Rural Lives: A History of the Farm Bureau in Kansas, 1912–1992* (Manhattan KS: Sunflower University Press, 1993), 73–74.

21. Farm land and improvements paid forty-six percent of the property tax burden in 1928, according to the Kansas Tax Code Commission, *Report of the Kansas Tax Code Commission* (Topeka: State Printer, 1929), 170.

22. McCoy, *Landon of Kansas*, 37, 44, 51, 55, 57. Also see Sageser, "Political Patterns," 84–86.

23. Schruben, *Kansas in Turmoil*, 62–65. For a sketch of the American Taxpayers' League, see George Wolfskill, *The Revolt of the Conservatives: A History of the American Liberty League, 1934–1940* (Boston: Houghton Mifflin, 1962), 234–36.

24. McFarland, *Harry H. Woodring*, 41.

25. Schruben, *Kansas in Turmoil*, 62.

26. McCoy, *Landon of Kansas*, 95. During the 1931 legislative session Woodring had issued a special message on taxation calling for resubmission and for a tax limitation amendment and campaigned for both in his reelection bid of 1932. In that campaign Landon endorsed the income tax amendment and opposed the tax limitation amendment. Surprisingly, Brinkley also on the ballot for governor in 1932 opposed the income tax proposition. See McFarland, *Harry H. Woodring*, 39, and McCoy, *Landon of Kansas*, 106.

27. Fisher, *Worst Tax*, 148.

28. While there is little evidence that Bennett's action contributed directly to his defeat, the income tax bill did put him in a political bind. First, his critics would use any opportunity to cast him as a Johnson County elitist, protector

of the rich, and opponent of progressive taxation, in other words, antiegalitarian. Second, by allowing the bill to become law without his signature, he was effectively precluded from using the issue against his eventual opponent in his reelection bid. That opponent was John Carlin, speaker of the house in 1977, who was instrumental in putting the bill on Bennett's desk.

Hayden faced a different dilemma. Kansas had adopted prospective conformity with federal income tax laws in the mid-1960s, and therefore, the national tax changes of 1986 generated an estimated one-hundred-and-forty-million-dollar windfall to the state treasury from taxpayers who itemized deductions. More specifically, lower national taxes created automatic increases in state taxes because of reduced deductions on state tax returns. The deduction of federal income taxes on state returns was permanently abandoned in 1992.

29. Clark, *Rise of Federalism*, 209. For purposes of brevity, the term "sales tax" in this discussion applies to both the state retail sales tax and its companion, the state compensating use tax.

30. Kansas Tax Code Commission, *Report*, 55–75. In 1934 the newly formed Research Department of the Kansas Legislative Council sponsored a careful sales tax study by Professor Jens P. Jenson of the University of Kansas; see *The Sales Tax: Analysis of Existing Laws and of the Experience of Other States with Special Application to Kansas* (Topeka: Research Department, Kansas Legislative Council, 1934). The retail sales tax was also among twenty-one possible revenue sources presented to the legislature in January 1937; see Research Department, Kansas Legislative Council, *Potential Sources of Additional Revenue from Taxation* (Topeka: State Printer, 1937).

31. Fisher, *Worst Tax*, 156–57; Schruben, *Kansas in Turmoil*, 159; Shane N. Galentine, "Huxman versus West: The Gubernatorial Race of 1936," *Kansas History* 11 (Summer 1988) 2, 108–22.

32. *Kansas House Journal* (Topeka: State Printer, 1937), 791.

33. Research Department, *Potential Sources of Additional Revenue*, 8.

34. Research Department, *Potential Sources of Additional Revenue*, 10.

35. Fisher, Flentje, Hildreth, and John D. Wong, "Sizing Up Kansas Finance," 18.

36. A more detailed discussion of the internal improvements prohibition may be found in Flentje, "Capital Finance and Public Infrastructure."

37. A starting place in tracking these constitution amendments is *Kansas Constitution/United States Constitution* (Topeka: Secretary of State, 1995), 29–34. See also Heller *Kansas State Constitution*.

38. H. Edward Flentje and W. Bartley Hildreth, "Fiscal Trends in Kansas: Taxing, Spending, and Borrowing," *Kansas Policy Review* 28 (Spring 2006): 24.

39. The Wyandotte Constitution did provide for the proceeds from public lands to be used for "the support of common schools" and charged lawmakers to

establish "a uniform system of common schools." Also, state aid to poor and sparsely settled districts was enacted prior to 1937. For details, see Charles Berger, "Equity Without Adjudication," *Journal of Law & Education* 27, no. 1 (January 1998).

40. Adel F. Throckmorton, *Kansas Educational Progress, 1858–1967* (Topeka: State Department of Public Instruction, 1967), 81.

41. *Kansas Tax Facts*, 2nd ed. (Topeka: Research Department, Kansas Legislative Council, 1965), 46.

42. *Mock, Robert, et al. v. State of Kansas et al.* (October 1991).

43. In 1992, for example, state aid was increased by a statutory weighting for vocational education, bilingual education, transportation, low enrollment, at-risk students, and new facilities.

44. *Montoy, Ryan, et al. v. State of Kansas et al.* (January 2005; supplemental opinion, June 2005).

45. Bruce D. Baker and Preston C. Green III, "History of School Finance Reform and Litigation in Kansas," *Kansas Policy Review* 27, no. 2 (Fall 2005): 2.

46. An additional seven million dollars for veterans benefits was authorized without a popular vote by action of the Kansas Supreme Court and a special session of the Kansas legislature in 1923; see *Kansas Session Laws, Special Session, 1923* (Topeka: Kansas State Printer, 1923) 6–8. See also in session laws a proclamation of Governor Jonathon Davis issued on July 28, 1923, calling the special session.

47. This review of debt history in Kansas is taken from Flentje, "Capital Finance and Public Infrastructure," particularly 114–19. For documentation, see this citation.

48. See W. Bartley Hildreth and H. Edward Flentje, "State Initiatives in Transportation Investment: The Evolution from Anti-debt to Debt-financed Programs in Kansas," in *Proceedings of the 92nd Annual Conference on Taxation*, ed. Daphne A. Kenyon (Washington DC: National Tax Association, 2000), 148–54.

49. In 1983 Kansas abandoned its fifty-year practice of relying on user fees for highway purposes during the administration of Governor John Carlin. Carlin secured approval of his proposal that a portion of sales tax revenues attributable to sales of vehicles be transferred to the state highway fund.

50. See W. Bartley Hildreth et al., *State of Kansas 2005 Debt Affordability Report* (Wichita: Kansas Public Finance Center, Hugo Wall School of Urban and Public Affairs, Wichita State University, 2005), 12–13.

51. The comprehensive annual financial reports of the Kansas Public Employees Retirement System stated that unfunded actuarial liability jumped from $968 million (June 6, 1993) to $4,026 million (December 31, 1993) without the issuance of bonds. The issuance of bonds reduced the unfunded actuarial

liability to $3,586 million in 2003. The unfunded liability as of December 31, 2004, was $4,743 million.

52. Hildreth et al., *State of Kansas 2005 Debt*, 14.
53. Moody's Investor's Services, State Debt Median Reports, 1989 and 2005.
54. Hildreth and Flentje, "State Initiatives in Transportation Investment," 30.
55. Kansas Legislative Research Department, "State General Fund Receipts, Expenditures and Balances, FY 2008–FY 2012," (presentation, Policy Summit of Regional Economic Area Partnership, Wichita KS, November 21, 2008).

APPENDIXES

1. For a complete description of the Kansas court system see Drury, *Government of Kansas*, chap. 11. The following description is based on this chapter.
2. Drury, *Government of Kansas*, 195.
3. The supreme court maintains two calendars, a summary and a general calendar. If a case is assigned to the summary calendar, each side is given fifteen minutes for oral arguments. If a case is assigned to the general calendar, each side is granted thirty minutes for oral arguments. Drury, *Government of Kansas*, 187, 191.

Suggestions for Further Reading

Two general volumes provide starting points for further study of Kansas politics and government. The first is James Drury's *The Government of Kansas*, first published in 1961 by the University of Kansas Press and most recently updated in its sixth edition (Drury and Stottlemire, 2001). As the title suggests, this volume covers the structure and functions of state government. State politics, political history and culture, local government, and the federal environment, among other topics, are addressed only lightly or not at all. Another single source was assembled by the late Professor Mike Harder of the University of Kansas in *Politics and Government in Kansas* (1989). The twenty-one essays by ten authors are rich in content and relevant to the topic, but the volume as a whole falls short of complete coverage and is now dated.

Numerous sources for further study of Kansas government and politics may be found in the endnotes of this volume. This bibliographic essay with its appended bibliography is intended to highlight and summarize those sources and is organized by subject area.

POLITICAL HISTORY AND CULTURE

Historian Craig Miner of Wichita State University has written an excellent, up-to-date and upbeat general history of Kansas (2002) that covers the period 1854–2000. Miner's volume draws primarily on contemporary newspaper sources and offers an excellent starting point as well as superb documentation for a more in-depth study into the politics of most any segment of state history. For a more pessimistic interpretation of Kansas history, Kenneth Davis's lightly documented bicentennial volume (1976) offers another view of major political developments in the state. A two-volume centennial history edited by John Bright (1956) offers more detailed but somewhat uneven coverage into pieces of the state's first one hundred years, with moderate documentation of sources.

Specific periods or topics in Kansas political history are covered in selected vol-

umes. Excellent histories of major political periods include for the populist movement John Hicks (1961) and Gene Clanton (1969), for the progressive era Robert
LaForte (1974) and William Allen White (1946); and for the 1930s Francis Schruben (1969). Robert Bader (1986) provides a well-researched volume on the history of prohibition in Kansas, and geographer James Shortridge of the University of
Kansas has two superb volumes on early migration patterns into Kansas (1995) and
municipal evolution in Kansas (2004). In addition, biographies of Kansas governors
provide another perspective on political history during their terms of office and are
listed below.

CONSTITUTION AND COURTS

The Wyandotte Constitution of 1859 has met the test of time in Kansas, providing
basic structure yet adapting through amendments over time into a modern framework that has precluded the necessity of a single constitution convention in the
state's 149-year history. The single best starting point for further study of the constitution is Francis Heller's excellent reference volume (1992), which provides a
comprehensive review of constitutional structure and evolution and a limited interpretations of the political climate leading to constitutional change. For study into
the Wyandotte Convention that produced the constitution, the state has published
the *Kansas Constitutional Convention* (1920), which includes the proceedings and
debates of the convention, historical sketches on the convention, descriptions of
convention participants, origins of constitutional provisions, and a bibliography,
among other material. While no single source of proposed and adopted constitutional amendments is available, the Kansas Secretary of State published the *Kansas Constitution* (1995) that contains a listing of all amendments adopted through
1995 with citations to legislative resolutions proposing amendments and the election outcome on each amendment.

Literature on the politics of Kansas courts is sparse. Disparate articles on the
separation of powers, judicial discretion, and the bill of rights may be found in
Harder (1989).

GOVERNORS

A starting point for further study of Kansas governors is the invaluable volume written by the late Professor Homer Socolofsky (1990), who through 1990 covers the
backgrounds and provides biographical sketches of the state's forty-one governors,
including the ten territorial governors. Socolofsky's excellent introductory chapter
summarizes in tabular and other forms an array of useful information on the governors, including birthplaces, families, occupations, elective experiences, religious af-
filiations, and electoral competitions and results, among other material. In addition,
four volumes of gubernatorial papers compiled at Wichita State University provide

documentary histories of the more recent governorships of Robert Bennett (Flentje, 1979), John Carlin (Pisciotte, 1993), Joan Finney (Armstrong and Harris, 1998), and Mike Hayden (Flentje, 2002). Four biographies of Kansas governors include Samuel Crawford (Plummer, 1971), Arthur Capper (Socolofsky, 1962), Harry Woodring (McFarland, 1975), and Alf Landon (McCoy, 1966).

THE LEGISLATURE

The *Kansas Legislative Handbook* (2008) prepared by Lynn and Kristen Hellebust is an excellent and periodically updated reference book on the legislature. It includes legislative organization, process, staffing, advice on monitoring and influencing legislation, useful and detailed appendices, and profiles of legislators and elected executive officials. The profiles of individual legislators offer contact information, election results, committee assignments, prior experience, business and financial interests, ratings of interest groups, summaries of campaign contributions and expenditures, and demographic and party registration data on the legislative district.

Further study of the Kansas legislature might begin with Harder and Rampey's good, although now dated, institutional analysis (1972), a volume that contains a reform agenda leading to the legislature's recognition in 1974 as the "most improved" state legislature in the United States. Burdett Loomis (1994) provides a more recent and comprehensive snapshot of state legislative process by focusing on key agenda items in the highly productive 1989 legislative session. There are also a series of topical monographs on the legislature that include reflections of seasoned legislators (Harder, 1982), legislative press relations (Kautsch, 1982), the appropriations process (Rein and Brown, 1982), and an introductory overview (Harder, 1986).

ELECTIONS, POLITICAL PARTIES, AND INTEREST GROUPS

Several titles offer starting points for studying the politics of elections, parties, and interest groups in Kansas. Harder (1981) assesses the history of Republican party factionalism through an examination of gubernatorial elections covering the period from the 1880s through the 1950s. Allan Cigler and Burdett Loomis (1991) assess party competition from the mid-1950s through the 1980s by looking at voter registration, survey data, election results, and party success in state legislative races. Aistrup and Bannister (1995) review the history and development of state party organizations. Cigler and Kiel (1989) analyze characteristics of interest groups in Kansas and their growing influence. Insights into electoral, party, and interest group politics in Kansas may also be gained through the gubernatorial biographies listed above and through a number of excellent books on selected topics, specifically Glenn Fisher (1996) on the history of the property tax, Bader (1986) on prohibition, Loomis (1994) on the 1989 legislative session, and Thomas Frank (2004) on Republican party politics.

Official state documents useful in the study of Kansas government and politics are available in printed form, and many are accessible electronically at the websites of executive and legislative agencies. Selected listings of these documents and their accessibility are as follows:

LEGISLATIVE DOCUMENTS. Legislative bills, resolutions, executive reorganization orders, journals, and calendars are available from the documents room
of the state capitol and may be obtained online at www.kslegislature.org.

KANSAS LAWS. All enactments of each legislative session are compiled and
published annually in the *Session Laws of Kansas* by the secretary of
state. The revisor of statutes codifies statutory enactments periodically in a
multivolume series, *Kansas Statutes Annotated* (KSA), and annually in *KSA*
Supplements; these volumes are available through the secretary of state. KSA
may be accessed at http://www.kslegislature.org/legsrv-statutes/index.do.

LEGISLATIVE RESEARCH PUBLICATIONS. A variety of timely and useful
reports are published by the Kansas Legislative Research Department,
and most are accessible at http://skyways.lib.ks.us/ksleg/KLRD/klrd.html.
These reports include *Summary of Legislation,* an annual summary of
enacted bills; *Kansas Tax Facts: A Reference Booklet on State and Local
Taxes,* an excellent reference that is revised periodically and that also has
an annual supplement); and *Legislative Procedure in Kansas.*

LEGISLATIVE POST AUDIT REPORTS. The Legislative Division of Post
Audit conducts performance and financial audits of executive agencies and
prepares audit reports, which are accessible at http://www.kslegislature
.org/postaudit/.

EXECUTIVE BUDGET DOCUMENTS. Detailed information on the executive budget as well as on economic and demographic data supporting the
executive budget may be found in *the Governor's Budget Report* and the
Governor's Economic and Demographic Report, which are available at the
website of the Kansas Division of the Budget: http://budget.ks.gov/.

SELECTED BIBLIOGRAPHY

Aistrup, Joseph A., and Mark Bannister. "Kansas." In *State Party Profiles*, ed. An-
drew M. Appleton and Daniel S. Ward, 110–19. Washington DC: Congressional
Quarterly, 1997.
Armstrong, Warren B., and Dee A. Harris, eds. *Populism Revived: The Selected
Records of Governor Joan Finney*. Wichita: Hugo Wall School of Urban and
Public Affairs, Wichita State University, 1998.

Bader, Robert Smith. *Prohibition in Kansas*. Lawrence: University Press of Kansas, 1986.

Bright, John D., ed. *Kansas: The First Century*. Vols. I and II. New York: Lewis Historical Publishing, 1956.

Cigler, Allan, and Burdett Loomis, "Kansas: Two Party Competition in a One-Party State." In *Party Realignment and State Politics*, ed. Maureen Moakley, 163–78. Columbus: Ohio State University Press, 1991.

Cigler, Allan J., and Dwight C. Kiel. "The Changing Nature of Interest Group Politics in Kansas." In *Politics and Government in Kansas: Selected Essays*, ed. Marvin A.Harder, 151–68. Topeka: Capitol Complex Center, University of Kansas, 1989.

Clanton, O. Gene. *Kansas Populism: Ideas and Men*. Lawrence: University Press of Kansas, 1969.

Davis, Kenneth S. *Kansas: A Bicentennial History*. New York: Norton, 1976.

Drury, James W. *The Government of Kansas*, with Marvin G. Stottlemire. 6th ed. Topeka, Public Management Center, University of Kansas, 2001.

Fisher, Glenn W. *The Worst Tax? A History of the Property Tax in America*. Lawrence: University Press of Kansas, 1996.

Flentje, H. Edward, ed. *Selected Papers of Governor Mike Hayden: Advancing a Progressive Agenda*. Wichita: Hugo Wall School of Urban and Public Affairs, Wichita State University, 2002.

———, ed. *Selected Papers of Governor Robert F. Bennett: A Study in Good Government and "Civics Book" Politics*. Wichita: Center for Urban Studies, Wichita State University, 1979.

Frank, Thomas. *What's the Matter with Kansas? How Conservatives Won the Heart of America*. New York: Metropolitan Books, 2004.

Harder, Marvin A. *Electoral Politics in Kansas: A Historical Perspective*. Topeka: Capitol Complex Center, University of Kansas, 1981.

———. *Introducing the Kansas Legislature*. Topeka: Capitol Complex Center, University of Kansas, 1986.

———, ed. *Politics and Government in Kansas: Selected Essays*. Topeka: Capitol Complex Center, University of Kansas, 1989.

———. *Reflection on Being a Kansas Legislator*. Vol. I. Topeka: Capitol Complex Center, University of Kansas, 1982.

Harder, Marvin, and Carolyn Rampey. *The Kansas Legislature: Procedures, Personalities, and Problems*. Lawrence: University Press of Kansas, 1972.

Hellebust, Lynn, and Kristen Hellebust. *Kansas Legislative Handbook*. Topeka: Government Research Service, 2008.

Heller, Francis H. *The Kansas Constitution: A Reference Guide*. Westport CT: Greenwood Press, 1992.

Hicks, John D. *The Populist Revolt: A History of the Farmers' Alliance and the People's Party.* 1931. Reprint. Lincoln: University of Nebraska Press, 1961.

Kansas Constitutional Convention, compiled under the direction of state librarians James L. King and Winfield Freeman by Harry G. Larimer. Topeka: State Printer, 1920.

Kansas Constitution/United States Constitution. Topeka: Secretary of State, 1995.

Kautsch, Mike. *Kansas Legislators and the Kansas Capitol Press Corps: Good News and Bad.* Topeka: Capitol Complex Center, University of Kansas, 1982.

La Forte, Robert Sherman. *Leaders of Reform: Progressive Republicans in Kansas, 1900–1916.* Lawrence: University Press of Kansas, 1974.

Loomis, Burdett A. *Time, Politics, and Policies: A Legislative Year.* Lawrence: University Press of Kansas, 1994.

McCoy, Donald R. *Landon of Kansas.* Lincoln: University of Nebraska Press, 1966.

McFarland, Keith D. *Harry H. Woodring: A Political Biography of FDR's Controversial Secretary of War.* Lawrence: University Press of Kansas, 1975.

Miner, Craig. *Kansas: The History of the Sunflower State, 1854–2000.* Lawrence: University Press of Kansas, 2002.

Pisciotte, Joe P., ed. *Selected Papers of Governor John Carlin: An Index of Social and Political Change.* Wichita: Hugo Wall School of Urban and Public Affairs, Wichita State University, 1993.

Plummer, Mark A. *Frontier Governor: Samuel J. Crawford of Kansas.* Lawrence: University Press of Kansas, 1971.

Rein, Marlin, and Sherry Brown. *The Appropriating Process in the Kansas Legislature.* Topeka: Capitol Complex Center, University of Kansas, 1982.

Schruben, Francis W. *Kansas in Turmoil, 1930–1936.* Columbia: University of Missouri Press, 1969.

Shortridge, James R. *Cities on the Plains: The Evolution of Urban Kansas.* Lawrence: University Press of Kansas, 2004.

———. *Peopling the Plains: Who Settled Where in Frontier Kansas.* Lawrence: University Press of Kansas, 1995.

Socolofsky, Homer E. *Arthur Capper: Publisher, Politician, and Philanthropist.* Lawrence: University of Kansas Press, 1962.

———. *Kansas Governors.* Lawrence: University Press of Kansas, 1990.

White, William Allen. *The Autobiography of William Allen White.* New York: Mcmillian, 1946.

Index

In the Politics and Governments of the American States series

Alabama Government and Politics
By James D. Thomas and William H. Stewart

Alaska Politics and Government
By Gerald A. McBeath and Thomas A. Morehouse

Arizona Politics and Government: The Quest for Autonomy,
Democracy, and Development
By David R. Berman

Arkansas Politics and Government, second edition
By Diane D. Blair and Jay Barth

Colorado Politics and Government: Governing the Centennial State
By Thomas E. Cronin and Robert D. Loevy

Delaware Politics and Government
By William W. Boyer and Edward C. Ratledge

Hawai'i Politics and Government: An American State in a Pacific World
By Richard C. Pratt with Zachary Smith

Illinois Politics and Government: The Expanding Metropolitan Frontier
By Samuel K. Gove and James D. Nowlan

Kansas Politics and Government: The Clash of Political Cultures
By H. Edward Flentje and Joseph A. Aistrup

Kentucky Politics and Government: Do We Stand United?
By Penny M. Miller

Maine Politics and Government, second edition
By Kenneth T. Palmer, G. Thomas Taylor, Marcus A. LiBrizzi, and Jean E. Lavigne

Michigan Politics and Government: Facing Change in a Complex State
By William P. Browne and Kenneth VerBurg

Minnesota Politics and Government
By Daniel J. Elazar, Virginia Gray, and Wyman Spano

Mississippi Government and Politics: Modernizers versus Traditionalists
By Dale Krane and Stephen D. Shaffer

Nebraska Government and Politics
Edited by Robert D. Miewald

Nevada Politics and Government: Conservatism in an Open Society
By Don W. Driggs and Leonard E. Goodall

New Jersey Politics and Government: Suburban Politics Comes of Age, second edition
By Barbara G. Salmore and Stephen A. Salmore

New York Politics and Government: Competition and Compassion
By Sarah F. Liebschutz, with Robert W. Bailey, Jeffrey M. Stonecash,
Jane Shapiro Zacek, and Joseph F. Zimmerman

North Carolina Government and Politics
By Jack D. Fleer

Oklahoma Politics and Policies: Governing the Sooner State
By David R. Morgan, Robert E. England, and George G. Humphreys

Oregon Politics and Government: Progressives versus Conservative Populists
By Richard A. Clucas, Mark Henkels, and Brent S. Steel

Rhode Island Politics and Government
By Maureen Moakley and Elmer Cornwell

South Carolina Politics and Government
By Cole Blease Graham Jr. and William V. Moore

West Virginia Politics and Government
By Richard A. Brisbin Jr., Robert Jay Dilger, Allan S. Hammock, and
Christopher Z. Mooney

West Virginia Politics and Government, second edition
By Richard A. Brisbin Jr., Robert Jay Dilger, Allan S. Hammock,
and L. Christopher Plein

Wisconsin Politics and Government: America's Laboratory of Democracy
By James K. Conant

To order or obtain more information on these or other University of Nebraska Press
titles, visit www.nebraskapress.unl.edu.